2000

LIVING ABOARD

LIVING ABOARD

The Cruising Sailboat as a Home

JAN and BILL MOELLER

International Marine Publishing Company
Camden, Maine

Photographs and illustrations by the authors.

© 1977 by International Marine Publishing Company
International Standard Book Number 0-87742-079-3
Library of Congress Catalog Card Number 76-8790
Printed and bound by The Alpine Press, Stoughton, Massachusetts

Sixth printing, 1983

Published by International Marine Publishing Company
Camden, Maine 04843
(207) 236-4342

CONTENTS

ACKNOWLEDGMENTS

Many of our friends unwittingly, and unbeknownst to them, contributed to this book. We profited by their experiences, good and bad, and we have drawn on them for compiling the material for the book. Some of them are: Paul McSorley and Eddie Fairclough, who gave us invaluable advice and assistance when we first moved aboard; Marian, Bill, and Tom Rumsey, who know so much about living aboard and have generously shared their knowledge with us; Marty and Ed Willis, for their practical solutions to many boating problems; Ed Lowe, who owns the best live-aboard do-it-yourself boatyard anywhere; Mary Jo and Dick Bennett, who can see the humor in all situations on land or sea; and Betty and Jimmy Balcarras, Tex Downs, Dave Hanks, Sandy and Don Mackenzie, Betty and Dale Nordlund, and Berta and Garry Saxon; Al Muss, who sold us our first cruising sailboat and got us "hooked"; Pete Smyth, who encouraged us in the early stages of writing the book; Ernie Barta of the Annapolis Sailing School, for the use of their darkroom; and, of course, Sparkman and Stephens, who did such a superb job of designing the Crusader that became *Whiffle*.

PREFACE

This book is written for those who want to live, or who now live, on a cruising sailboat. It will tell you how to live aboard at dockside, at anchor, or underway.

It will tell you how to make a boat into a comfortable home. "Comfort" is the key word. If you aren't reasonably comfortable, the "novelty" of living aboard soon wears thin.

We will not tell you how to sail. If you are thinking about living on a boat, you should already know how to sail, and you should not only know how, you should be proficient at it, because you should have done it for many years. Your boat-home should not be the first boat you have owned, and probably not the second. You should be conversant with nautical life in general before you move aboard, so you will have a good idea of what life afloat will be like.

We hope this book will help you to live aboard a boat successfully and with great satisfaction.

Jan and Bill Moeller
Aboard the yacht *Whiffle*

I. SHOULD YOU MAKE
A BOAT YOUR HOME?

If we were asked why we like living on a boat, we might not be able to give one good, solid reason for wanting to do so. We like the water and we like to sail. We enjoy the mobility of a boat-home. Water people seem to be friendlier than shore people. We like being able to travel in our home without packing for each trip. We seem to be healthier, physically and mentally, since we moved aboard (although many new live-aboards experience exactly the opposite reaction, as far as their mental condition is concerned).

Perhaps what it all boils down to is freedom — escapism, if you will. Living aboard boats is still one of the less restricted, easier ways of life, yet every year more rules, laws, and regulations encroach upon that freedom. We know that the specter of so many restrictions looming in the future prompted us to move to a boat at the time we did, but that was not our prime motivation. We felt it was time for a change in our lives, so we changed — drastically, and for the better — by moving to a boat-home.

For many people, cruising and living aboard boats offer challenges. You can arrange for as much of a challenge as you want, through the selection of areas in which you will cruise (or tie up, if that is all the stimulation you seek).

Perhaps your métier will be an ocean passage with its attendant hazards. Maybe navigating safely and successfully from one point to another on a protected waterway will satisfy you. Having a boat as your home enables you to set up your life as you wish it set up, more than is possible with any other type of home. Living aboard a boat can be exciting, peaceful, exhilarating, or sedate. You can surround yourself with people or be completely alone. If your neighborhood changes in a frustrating way, it is easy to leave and go to a new community.

Becoming a successful live-aboard depends on having the right mental attitude for it beforehand. Long before buying a boat-home, you should analyze your reasons for wanting to live aboard and what you expect to get out of it. Then, perhaps with the help of this book, you will be able to decide whether you are being realistic about what to expect from a home afloat.

We feel it is the best way of life we have experienced, yet many other live-aboards we have met have been very disillusioned by boat living. For the most part, the people who weren't satisfied had only recently moved aboard their boats. Most of the others we have encountered, who have been living on their boats for a year or more, seem to feel as we do: it is the only kind of home to have.

The first year we lived aboard, we made the popular migration south from New York to Florida. As is typical, we met people in other boats doing the same thing. We were amazed at how many others were intending to make their boats their homes and were not just seasonal travelers. Some of the people became good friends and others were only casual acquaintances. All of us shared the common enthusiasm of the new live-aboard.

In the spring, as we came north, we met many of the same people going "home." We were still happy with our boating life, but many (and again we were amazed at how many) were giving it up. Some of the reasons why they didn't make it are mentioned in this chapter, and if any of them ring true to you, you should think twice about trying to live on a boat. Most of those we mention had comfortable live-aboard boats. The problems they had stemmed mainly from the personalities of the people involved.

When you begin thinking about living on a boat, you will realize eventually that some of the things that represent safety and security to most of us (because we have been brought up that way) may have to be dispensed with. If you are going to be living on your savings or a reduced income, you may not be able to afford as much medical and life insurance coverage as you have now. Boat insurance, because of its incredibly high cost, may have to be reduced or eliminated. Doctors, dentists, electricians, or mechanics may not be readily available in the area in which you are cruising. If they are, these professionals will be strangers, and you will not have the secure feeling that comes from dealing with people you know.

If you are without a car, as you certainly will be sometimes if you cruise at all, you will have to discover other methods for obtaining the supplies and groceries you need. The lack of a telephone is a traumatic experience for many. There is no question about it — you will have to relinquish many things that represent security to most of us. The older you get, the harder it is to do this, which is as good a reason as any for beginning *now*.

When you are cruising, it is difficult to keep up subscriptions to periodicals, and maintain memberships in the many organizations that are important, and often necessary, to a landlubber's life. Because it is so difficult, and often costly as well, some or all of these may have to be eliminated.

Some sacrifices will have to be made if you are ever to depart from the security-conscious land world, but whatever you give up is replaced by enjoyment and adventures you cannot get any other way. Any sacrifices we thought we were making did not look like sacrifices after a while. We merely traded some things we found we didn't need for something much better.

If you are not cut out for the live-aboard's life, it will become evident very quickly, once you have moved aboard, but that is too late to discover that you don't want to live on a boat.

Jim and Susan's destination was the Caribbean when they left New Jersey in the trimaran they had built themselves. We first met them in North Carolina and traveled with them for a few days, until we reached the marina where we planned to stay over for a week and they went ahead. Their boat was 36 feet long and quite roomy. She was nicely decorated and had a feeling of airiness below. They had done a good job of building her, and she did not look like the work of amateurs. She was well outfitted for living aboard and cruising, and her owners seemed to be very happy and excited about their new way of life.

The next spring, when we were on our way north on the Intracoastal Waterway, we met Jim and Susan again in North Carolina. This surprised us, since they had planned to cruise the Caribbean extensively and live there permanently on their boat, if they liked it. Instead, they were on their way back to New Jersey.

Jim told us that originally he had wanted to live on a boat because of the freedom that that way of life offered. As it turned out, there was no freedom for him. He decided that cruising was worse than the job he had left. When cruising, he got up early every morning, sailed or motored steadily all day, and stopped only at dark. He carried out this routine every day of the week. He said when he was working at a regular job he got the weekends off, at least.

Jim wasn't able to regulate his cruising to get any pleasure out of it; it was only drudgery for him. He was bent on doing a minimum of 50 miles a day no matter what. He had set such a stringent routine for himself he couldn't relax and enjoy the pleasures cruising has to offer. He took no time off for sightseeing or pulling into a nice anchorage and just goofing off once in awhile. Jim is only one of many people we have met who feel they have to keep pushing on, even with no schedule to meet. There is usually just as much of interest close at hand as there is 50 miles over the horizon.

Our shortest day's run has been 1½ miles. Often we do only eight to 15 miles a day, simply because we do not want to go any farther. Some days, if we like the spot we are in, we stay put, even if the weather is good and there is a fair wind.

It is hard to learn to take it easy and set a new pace, especially when you have just left a regular job. When dawn comes and you reluctantly tumble out of your bunk thinking, "I've got to get to Muckabout Bay by tonight," ask yourself, "Why do I have to get there tonight?" Why not tomorrow or even next week? Relax. Slow down. This is why you wanted to live on a boat in the first place, isn't it?

If you are a couple and only one of you has the live-on-a-boat bug, you had better forget the whole idea, or else find another partner who feels as strongly about boating as you do. It will not work unless *both* of you *really* want to do it. If one person is lukewarm about the idea, but willing to give it a try anyway, it might work — but the odds are very much against it. If both of you want to live aboard but have widely divergent ideas about the size or type of boat you need, you will have to make compromises. If there is any compromising to be done, however, it will have to be done ashore, before you move to the boat that will become your home. Otherwise, you will never be able to achieve a satisfactory arrangement later. One of you will always feel slighted.

Too many times one partner will humor the other when he or she has had a long-standing desire to live on a boat. They will look at boats and plans together and talk about where they will cruise. The one who does not actually want that way of life thinks, perhaps: "This all will blow over eventually. I'll go along with the idea because it keeps peace in the family, but it will never really happen."

It is better to be honest about your feelings from the outset, because those who want something badly enough usually will find some way of getting what they want. Participating in a way of life you don't particularly like on weekends or vacations is bearable, but the total commitment of living on a boat full time is quite another thing.

We met Allan and Ruth in Florida. They had come down the Intracoastal Waterway and were going to the Keys and then, perhaps, the Bahamas. They were a middle-aged couple who had been married only four years. Allan retired from his job just before they left on their trip. He had been sailing since childhood, and he and his first wife had cruised extensively, but Ruth had done little sailing of any kind. During the four years of his marriage to Ruth, Allan had turned an empty, 40-foot, fiberglass hull into a beautiful floating home. Ruth had been accustomed to nice things, and Allan wanted her to be happy living on the boat, so the accommodations were quite luxurious. They planned to stay in Florida for a month or so, over Christmas, as we did. We got to know them rather well during this time.

All seemed to be going well at first, but then, little by little, it became evident that Ruth was only living on the boat for awhile, so that Allan could "get it out of his system." Allan, however, had hoped to make it a lifetime arrangement, and it was sad to see his enthusiasm dwindle as he came to realize that Ruth was longing to get back to their house (which they were renting to earn extra income). Shortly after we met them, Allan said to us, "For the first time in my life I'm really living!" He was so exuberant then. It was a very different person who headed "home" in April. By then, Ruth was quite open about the fact that she wanted to get off the boat, and the sooner the better. We know they made it back "home" safely, but we don't know what has happened to their relationship. We can safely assume it hasn't improved.

Jeff and Laura had a good-sized 30-footer to live in, and they intended to do just that, spending a lot of time in the Virgin Islands, an area they both loved. Jeff had done most of the outfitting on the boat. He designed ingenious holders and racks for all his tools. He arranged them so he could get at any tool almost instantly. Jeff was also very interested in survival, and he had put together kits that he and Laura had to wear whenever they were away from land. He had other survival kits for the life raft and all kinds of gadgets to help them out of any conceivable difficult situation. The boat was crowded with survival gear.

The last time we saw Jeff, Laura was not with him. He told us that she was due to join him later. As we talked, we found out that "later" was an indefinite date far in the future. We learned that Laura had been with him only a few times over the years, for two weeks or a month at a time. She seemed to prefer living with her mother, ashore, most of the time. Jeff couldn't understand why. As a mutual friend of ours remarked, "Jeff has it arranged so Laura can survive anything, but she can't be comfortable in that boat, for even a day." Jeff was ready for any emergency, but he forgot that emergencies usually are infrequent, whereas three meals a day must be cooked, and bunks are slept in once a day with regularity. It was no fun at all for Laura to stumble around and through so many tools and so much survival paraphernalia in order to do the simplest housekeeping tasks. Jeff's tools were handy, but hers were not, and he liked it his way. Since Jeff wouldn't give it up, she had to give up Jeff, at least on a full-time basis. Several people tried to tell him what was wrong, since it was obvious to nearly everyone who saw the boat; but he didn't, or didn't want to, believe them. We don't know whether Laura has ever told him why she doesn't like living on the boat, or whether it would do any good if she did. Jeff seems to be concerned only with his own interests, and his way is the way it must be done. One of these times when Laura is due to join him, she won't show up — ever.

When you meet a couple living aboard a boat, you probably are witnessing a better relationship than most couples have ashore. The boat couple must enjoy each other's company simply because any size boat is too small a place to harbor any kind of enmity. They must work well together and respect each other's opinions. They must trust one another, because they know a time may come when their very lives may be dependent on one another. Rarely, if ever, do you see couples living on a boat who are not well adjusted to each other. If they don't get along well together, they don't live on a boat together. Unfortunately, the business of living in such close quarters with another person has been instrumental in the separation of many couples. On land, where emotions and temperament have more room to dissipate, separation might not have occurred. Only you can judge, or make an educated guess, as to whether your particular relationship will benefit or suffer from living on a boat.

There are very few disorders that would actually prevent anyone from living on a boat. Sometimes, though, one partner will develop a physical infirmity before moving onto the boat or shortly thereafter. It may be an old ailment that suddenly worsens, or it may be something entirely new. If this happens, it is frequently an indication that the "ailing" person wants to get out of the situation. When someone complains at length about aches and pains or disabilities, it usually means he or she wants "off."

One woman had moved aboard in June and found that by August her knee was acting up from an old injury. It was hard for her to get on and off the boat to help with the docking. She had a valid complaint, and was not faking, but she didn't like living aboard, so she was not interested in working around her difficulty. She was using it as the excuse to go back to a house.

Another woman has a deformity in her left leg as well as a foot problem. She is always at the helm when they dock so she can stand in one spot. Her husband handles the lines and does all the dock work.

In another case, a woman had polio 20 years ago, long before she moved aboard. It left her with a useless leg; there is feeling in it, but she cannot move it, because all the muscles were destroyed. She literally drags it along with her. When she crosses her legs, she has to lift the useless leg over the other one. About all the leg is good for is to support her, to some degree, when she is standing. She lives on a fairly small boat and manages quite nicely. She decided a long time ago that her disability was not going to stop her from doing what she wanted.

One of the most determined people we ever met was a young man who had both legs amputated at the knees. Among other things, he drove a car, surfed, and owned and operated a 30-foot power boat. When we met him, he was thinking of getting a sail-boat to live on!

For some people, the prospect of moving to a boat-home opens up all sorts of opportunities for making excuses about why they "can't" live on a boat. If they feel they can't, they shouldn't. They never will be happy, and they eventually will blame their partner for making their situation worse than they think it might have been, had they stayed ashore.

You will have to give up a few, or several, conveniences that you once took for granted, and you must be willing to give them up. We are still amazed at one fellow we met who was so totally unprepared, in this respect, for living on a boat.

Dave and his wife, Sylvia, had sold all their worldly goods and moved aboard a very spacious 35-foot ketch. It was a brand-new stock boat ordered from the manufacturer. There were many items of optional equipment that could have been ordered with their particular boat, any of which could have been installed easily at the factory. One of these options was a shower, but they did not have one installed. For their shakedown trip, they planned a cruise through the Out Islands of the Bahamas.

We met them after they had made the trip. Dave was very disillusioned, because the islands were not the paradise he had expected them to be. There were hardly any marinas to put into, and what few there were, were many miles apart. If they were lucky enough to find a place to dock, they were disappointed because there were no showers. Dave told us that in hot weather he needed *two* showers a day to be comfortable.

The sad part of Dave's story is that his boat was extremely well suited for a roomy shower installation, and we cannot imagine why he didn't have one put in, since showers were so important to him. If there are things you feel you cannot do without, look for a boat that will allow you to incorporate them somehow, or be realistic about what facilities to expect in the cruising areas you choose. If frequent showers are necessary to your well-being, don't go where they are not available. There are plenty of books about cruising in all areas of the world, and most of them tell you what you can expect to find.

We found out later that Dave had never read anything about others who had cruised the Out Islands. He just knew he liked warm weather, and he had heard that the islands were beautiful. He bought the necessary charts and one guidebook, and left. He now goes from marina to marina (and, presumably, from shower to shower) in Florida, and he is rather disenchanted with the boating life.

Consideration for, and sensitivity to, the feelings of others who live with you is very necessary. Cigar or cigarette smoke in the living quarters may be intolerable for some, as may be certain cooking odors from foods one person prefers but the other dislikes. Personal possessions, including clothes, cannot be strewn about. If neatness is not one of your virtues, you will have to develop it to some degree, or be content to live in a floating pigsty.

Lack of consideration, on a much greater scale, was the primary reason for another couple's failure as live-aboards. Spence had grown up around boats and had many years of sailing behind him, but nearly all of his experience was in racing. His wife, Louise, had accompanied him on a few of the races, but generally he raced with a group of other men. The boat this couple selected as a home was capable of a good turn of speed as well as being very comfortable. Louise was excited about living on a boat and seemed to want it as much as Spence. Once they got going, though, the racing skipper could not stop racing. When the winds came up, he always carried too much sail, and it was uncomfortable going.

Spence consistently sailed, even when conditions warranted staying put. He seemed to think it was unseamanlike to stay over somewhere because the weather was bad. He felt he had to battle the elements to get to his destination, as fast as possible, under sail. Given the right amount of wind, his boat was always on her ear and going like a shot.

We especially remember one day when the winds were a steady 50 miles an hour with gusts up to 60 miles an hour. Both of us were staying at the same marina. We were pinned against the pilings and couldn't have gotten away without difficulty, even if we had wanted to. There was no question about our leaving. We were staying put. Spence could see no reason for staying over, however, even though Louise did not want to leave — but leave they did. Even before Spence was into the main channel, his jib was up and he was barreling down the Intracoastal Waterway. Boats can be sailed so that they are comfortable and still get where they are going. Naturally, a little speed must be sacrificed in the process — a thing unheard of as far as a confirmed racing man is concerned. Spence could never settle down and stop racing, and Louise found she could not live heeled over all the time. They live ashore now, but if Spence had shown more consideration for Louise, they might still be living aboard. He chose to ignore her feelings. He cannot understand why she was so excited about living aboard when they set out, and why she became so unhappy in such a short time.

Consideration for people in other boats is important, too. In a marina, or even at an anchorage with others, noises of any kind will carry across the water farther than they do on land. When you are alone, you can make all the noise you want, but when other boats are around, even at quite a distance, you will have to remember to tone down everything.

If you are not in the habit of tying off your halyards when anchored or docked, you may find that someone will request that you tie them off. Whether you are asked nicely will depend on how much you are disturbing the person making the request. If you don't, or won't, tie them off yourself, someone may do it for you.

Carelessness and consideration go hand in hand. If you are careless, your inconsideration will certainly affect the people around you. Nearly everyone is guilty of carelessness at one time or another, but if your life is composed of a series of mishaps that could have been avoided by being more careful, perhaps a boat-home is not for you.

Small mistakes are magnified on a boat and they usually affect more people. If a house ashore burns down because of someone's carelessness, usually only one house will be lost. However, if a boat burns in a marina, chances are that many boats and, perhaps, the marina itself, will be lost.

It is the careless, inconsiderate person who leaves hoses, electric cables, and other gear strewn about the dock for others to trip over. His boat often bangs against pilings, or against the boat next to him, because she is not tied up properly. He is the one who does not take the time to anchor properly and drags into other boats in the anchorage. He is the "klutz" who does not use the shut-off valve on his propane tank after he has finished cooking. He releases the brake on a wire-reel winch without removing the winch handle. He has a habit of heaving a dock line that is not cleated to his boat. If he is lucky enough to get into the dock, when he is ready to leave, he will pull away with one line still tied. He is the one everyone wishes had stayed ashore.

Procrastinators are the type of people who are better suited to life ashore. On boats, things have to be repaired when they break, or, ideally, replaced or repaired *before* they break.

The small things that can be put off for another day ashore cannot be put off afloat. Chafe, vibrations, leaks, etc., must be remedied before they are allowed to do any real damage. Unseen forces are constantly gnawing away at your boat and creating problems that must be attended to. If the stuffing box is not taken up today, tomorrow there will be a bilge, or more, full of water. Tomorrow the unwhipped end of that dock line will unlay unless it is taken care of today. The chafed, broken threads on the seam on the sail will rip in the first strong wind unless it is sewn up while the tear is small.

The opposite of the procrastinator is the planner. If you plan out your living/cruising life to the last item, you won't have much fun, and overplanning may contribute to your unhappiness with this kind of life. Nearly everyone who sets out on a cruise has a tendency to overestimate where he will go in a given period of time; everyone, that is, who hasn't done much cruising. The first few days of any cruise will demonstrate the futility of a strict itinerary. Very few schedules allow for the inevitable bad weather, or breakdown delays, which everyone experiences.

The usual first-time cruise-planner may plan a cruise such as this: leave New York in September and be in the Bahamas by December. The first thing wrong with this plan is that he probably won't leave by September. He will be late getting started, as nearly everyone is. It wouldn't have mattered if he planned to leave in October or November; chances are, he still would not have left on time. We know of very few people who have gotten away when they had hoped to. But, let us assume that our first-time cruiser does leave in September, as scheduled. He will be knocking his brains out to reach the Bahamas by December. Then what? He will be impatient to get going again, to be where he planned to be by June.

The real fun of cruising and living aboard comes from the ability to relax. If you don't get to the Bahamas by December, you can arrive in January or February. If you don't get there at all this year, you can go next year, or the year after. In fact, one dictionary reads: "cruise, v., 1. to sail about without proceeding directly from one point to another, as a yacht on a pleasure trip...."

We have learned not to make plans that are too definite. They always seem to get changed. We have also learned to be happy wherever we happen to be. We know that sooner or later we will cruise to all the places we want to see.

A tough schedule is tiring for the crew. They need a day or so of layover every once in a while, just to catch up on laundry, shopping, and rest. Unless you are crossing an ocean, it isn't necessary, or wise, to keep going every day. If you should have the unheard-of cruise with no layovers for bad weather and no breakdowns, take a day off anyway, now and then, just to change the tempo. Don't turn your cruising into the same kind of rat race you left behind.

We have heard of itineraries written out on a week-to-week or

day-to-day basis, but the most impractical one we heard of was one
that read something like this:

> 7:00 A.M. — breakfast
> 8:00 A.M. — underway
> 12:00 noon — anchor for lunch in Whatsitsname Creek
> 1:00 P.M. — underway
> 2:30 P.M. — stop for fuel at Noville
> 4:30 P.M. — anchor in Whatchamacallit Bay
> 6:00 P.M. — cocktails
> 7:00 P.M. — dinner
> 8:00 P.M. — bedtime

Every day was outlined the same way. The schedule was completely unworkable, but if it had worked, it would have taken the
elements of chance and surprise out of the cruise — the elements
that make cruising interesting, at least for most people. If the
weather is rainy and you are snug in an anchorage, why bother
going anywhere that day? Or, if you have been sailing all day
with beautiful winds and weather, it might be more fun to go far
into the night, or all night. The sailor who made up the detailed
schedule above probably had a lot of fun working it out, but we
hope he wasn't too upset when he found out that he had wasted
his time.

If you are extremely lazy and accustomed to having everything
done for you, you simply will have to be wealthy in order to live
on a boat and be happy. Even then, you might have plenty of your
own kinds of problems. We will not go into this aspect of life afloat.
Never having been wealthy, we know nothing about the subject.

After you have been living aboard and/or cruising for awhile,
your personality may undergo drastic changes. As the old saying
goes about military service: it will either make or break you. When
you have navigated your boat from Point A to Point B and arrived
safely, or when you have had a bout with some rotten weather and
come through it unscathed, your self-confidence will increase, and
you will be a better person for it. On the other hand, you may
have found out that you cannot, or do not want to, cope with the
problems that cruising presents.

One man we knew had an excellent sailing boat well suited for
living and cruising. He tried living aboard her for awhile, encountering the ordinary amount of cruising problems, none of
which was too serious. He was a stubborn and rather short-
tempered man, and too impatient to take the time to learn how
to cope with the problems as they occurred. After he had lived
aboard awhile, he realized that there would always be problems of
one kind or another. In that respect, life afloat is different from
life ashore. He began to spend more and more time at dockside,

hoping to avoid the problems he could not seem to handle. As so many others have, he expected smooth sailing all the time. His boat is now for sale, and he is living far from the water.

It took only three months of living aboard to turn another man from a jovial person into a grouchy one. It was a case of bad planning combined with an unrealistic approach to his own particular situation. He and his family had the typical suburban home, two cars, and a decent income. Jerry, who was just 30, saw the years stretching ahead in the same rut — coming home to the same house from the same dull job day after day, weekend sailing, a cruise every year or so. What was he working for? A fancier house? A bigger boat? His life was shaping up to be the humdrum existence that he didn't want. He decided to do something about it, without thinking it through as thoroughly as he should have.

Jerry found a beamy, old, 35-foot ketch and moved aboard with his wife, Sally, and their three children, ages five, six, and nine. After they had moved aboard, Jerry kept his job for a month, until school was out. Then they set off on their new way of life. For a month everything was fine, because there was something new every day. But when they began doing more living than traveling, the problems began.

The boat was almost, but not quite, big enough for the five of them — on sunny days. When the weather was bad and they were all below deck, she was very crowded. Jerry didn't have the control over the children that he should have had, and they were usually noisy, rowdy, and obeyed only at the brief moment when they were told to be quiet. Instead of taking correspondence courses, the children were enrolled in a local school, so any traveling was out of the question during the school year.

Jerry had given up a spacious permanent home for a cramped permanent home. His boat was no better than a house ashore because they didn't take her anywhere. Even on weekends, when the children were free, it became too much work to go sailing. They had done more sailing when they were land-bound. Jerry and Sally's venture into boat-living lasted only six months. They sold the boat and are now living in a house again. If Jerry could have waited a little longer to get a slightly larger boat, and arranged for the children's schooling to be done by mail, they would have been able to cruise and not have the penned-up feeling Jerry complained of. Jerry had only substituted living on a boat for living in a house. He hadn't changed his way of living at all. He was still as land-bound as ever.

If you cannot change your own way of life, for the better, by living on a boat, it would be more prudent to remain ashore until you can improve it. The only way to figure this out is to think through your own situation thoroughly in all respects, and do it carefully and objectively. Nobody ever moved onto a boat and sailed blissfully off to the island of his dreams without any problems. Some do it with fewer problems than others, because they are realistic about what they will encounter.

By moving onto a boat, you will have a different — maybe better, maybe worse — lifestyle than you had ashore. What you get depends on your planning and your outlook.

If you have children, you will have to think hard and long about moving onto a boat. Their education is the least of your worries, since many children have been schooled completely by the excellent correspondence courses available today, and often they have a better education this way. The problem, bluntly stated, is: can you stand living with your children in the relatively small confines of any boat? And, while we are on the subject, can you put up with your spouse in the same situation? If you are having any family problems ashore, they will be intensified in a boat. If you don't have the proper authority over your children ashore, you won't develop it in a boat. If you and your spouse are constantly at odds, you will find even more things to disagree about if you move onto a boat.

If you think you would really like to live on a boat, but don't really want to change your way of life, stay where you are. One couple we knew enjoyed entertaining their friends in the grand manner. They often had formal sit-down dinners in their home. We could never figure out why they decided to move onto a boat in the first place, but it didn't last long. Within a year, they were back in a house in their previous social routine.

Another fellow did a lot of woodworking in his well-equipped shop, before he moved aboard the boat that was to be his home. After a few months, he found he missed all his equipment and the many hours spent working with it. Now he is leading the same kind of life ashore that he led before he moved onto the boat, but he is content with it. When the equipment for a hobby, vocation, or avocation that is important to you won't "fit" into your boat-home, it might be better to live ashore, although space has been found on some very small boats for decent workshops, darkrooms, etc. Again, if you want something badly enough, a way will be found to make it possible.

If you plan to live aboard someday, but at present you can only afford a small boat for weekending, try to get a boat you can cruise in, instead of an out-and-out daysailer. On your cruises, and weekending too, you learn how to live aboard, in a sense, because that is actually what you are doing for a short period. Our first boat was a 20-footer that had four bunks; a head; a galley with a sink, a two-burner gimballed stove, and a removable dining table; life lines; and a ventilator on the forward hatch. Even on such a small scale, you can begin to formulate ideas about how things can be improved and made more workable on your next boat, which may be the one you will live aboard.

When we owned our small boat, we weren't thinking about living aboard, but we found several things we decided we must have in any other boat. The stove must be gimballed. There would have to be some sort of ventilation other than the main hatch. Some means of providing heat was necessary for cold days. There must be proper stowage for the anchor and rode on or near the foredeck, so it could be dropped quickly, if necessary. We wanted enough tools for repairs and a place to keep them. Life lines. Curtains and carpeting. (Yes, we had "wall-to-wall" carpeting in our 20-foot boat.)

We also learned that there were certain things the 20-footer didn't have that we wanted on any larger boat, such as two sinks — one exclusively for the galley and one for the head. When we were looking for a boat to live aboard, it was not uncommon to find some older boats with only a galley sink.

While we were cruising and weekending in our second and third boats, we were mentally making notes of the things we would like to have in a boat to make her more comfortable, even though, as yet, we weren't planning consciously to become live-aboards. When we made the decision to move onto a boat, our mental note-taking paid off.

Don't make the mistake of buying too big a boat for weekending, even if you can afford a big boat. You can learn just as much about living afloat in a 23- or 26-footer as you can from anything larger. You will have more fun in a smaller boat, and you will be inclined to take her out more often than you would a big one.

If you can tolerate the inconveniences and make-do situations that always are present when cruising with a small boat, and not become disgusted about the whole business, moving up to a larger boat-home will be an easy, pleasant transition. If you have never experienced small-boat living, you will have no experience to draw on to help you in your decision about what kind of boat will be best for your particular boat-home. The right choice can be made, but it is easier if you have done some boat living before.

One of the best ways to find out about living aboard is to talk to those who have done it, or those who are doing it. Even people who have tried living aboard and didn't like it, or were forced to give it up for some reason, will have valuable advice.

It is easy to talk to most boat people. One of the best gambits for getting a conversation going is to hang around the boat you are interested in. Sooner or later, if anyone is aboard, they will come out and you can say, "I've been admiring your boat for some time. She's a Tahiti ketch, isn't she?" Or, "Isn't she an Alden design?" Hardly any boat owner can resist telling you about his particular boat and how he had her outfitted. Questions about living aboard just follow naturally.

If you are in an area where there are no people to talk with, do some reading. Most books written by people who have boat-homes are heavily slanted toward the ocean-cruising aspect, but nearly all of them have some useful information.

Nearly all the boating magazines from time to time carry articles dealing with living on boats. If you have a specific question about the subject, you can try writing to your favorite magazine for help. It will have to be a very specific question. Don't ask, "Will I be able to live aboard a boat for $2,000 a year?" Or, "Can I buy a 40-foot live-aboard boat for $8,000?" (The answers to both are a very qualified "yes," but the questions are too ambiguous to be answered briefly.)

You might want to know if there are any regulations about living aboard in localities where your job might take you, or where you can find work. Perhaps you want to know how much you can expect to pay for dockage in certain areas. Some magazines have special question-and-answer columns dealing with specific subjects, or you might get an answer if you write to the Letters to the Editor section.

If you want to live aboard, try to get your boat-home as soon as possible. When you set long-range goals for yourself, they usually don't work out as you had hoped — if at all. How often have you heard: "We'll do it when the house is paid for." "When the children are out of school, we can consider it." "When I retire in four years, I'm going to take off in a boat." Most people who think this way will stay where they are forever.

Obviously, not everyone who wants to live on a boat can do so just when he or she decides to, but more people can do it than not. A mortgage does not have to be paid off before you can sell a house. If you can't get enough money from the sale of the house to buy the boat you want, finance the boat and pay off the mortgage on the boat. At least then you will be working constructively toward your goal. If your children are in grade school or high school, they can complete their education by correspondence. If they are in college, they can visit you on a boat on their holidays just as easily as they could in a house. Maintaining a house "so the children will have a place to come home to" is only a handy excuse for someone who does not want to move to a boat.

Since you probably won't need as much money to live on a boat as you might on land, consider an early retirement. You will have less to live on than you might if you retired at 65, but it may be more than enough for comfortable boat living. Consider it. It's worth some serious thought.

II. HOW MUCH WILL IT COST?

The expense of living aboard probably will be less than what you are living on now — but more than you might figure it would. At this writing, with prices going up all the time, two people can live afloat, rather comfortably, for $5,000 a year. We are talking, of course, about living, as opposed to simply existing. Naturally, you can spend much more than $5,000, if you have it to spend, and you can exist on much less than $5,000. It all depends on how lavishly you have to live to be happy. At the bottom end of the scale is one man whose total expenditures for one year were $800. He lived mostly on rice, in the islands, and his boat was in a terrible state of disrepair. The next year, needless to say, he spent considerably more.

The figures mentioned in this chapter apply to persons who own their boats free and clear. If you are still financing your boat, you will have to allow for the payments in your yearly budget.

Boat living is less expensive than land living only because some of the big land expenses can be eliminated, such as real estate taxes or high rent, purchases of furniture and major appliances, monthly utility bills, the upkeep of a car or two, and dressy and winter clothing. Many of the other expenses will remain the same or be replaced by similar but boat-oriented expenses. The basic things you definitely will have to spend money on are food, supplies for the galley and head (such as soap and toilet paper), fuel for cooking and fuel for the engine, supplies and parts for necessary maintenance and repairs, and charts and other navigation aids. These are only the basics, and they represent items that money will *have* to be spent on, even for the barest of bare-bones living aboard.

In articles you may have read about how much it costs to live on a boat, three major items often are omitted: stores on hand, charts and other necessary navigation publications, and major repairs. If someone takes a year off to cruise and keeps accurate records, he can very well say, at the end of the year, "I spent exactly such and such," and it may be a very low figure. The sailor on sabbatical probably has done the normal annual painting and any repairs, major and minor, before he sets off; therefore, these maintenance costs are not included in the expenditures for his year of cruising. The year-round live-aboard will have to include these costs, and you can usually count on having a major (and costly) repair job every now and then, even if you do it yourself.

If our temporary live-aboard bought charts covering the places he would need to know about for a cruise from New York to the Bahamas, as well as the other publications necessary, such as *Tide and Current Tables*, the *Nautical Almanac*, *Light List*, and *Sailing Directions*, it could easily cost at least $400. These publications usually are purchased well in advance of the trip, and they are not included in the yearly costs. However, they must be included in your annual expenses if you live aboard full-time, unless you always cruise the same areas.

The take-a-year-off sailor probably would include the canned food he takes aboard on his list of yearly expenditures, but the regular live-aboard might not. In our own case, we bought nearly two months' worth of canned goods, as a reserve, before we moved aboard. If we made a long passage where these stores were used up and others were not bought to replace them right away, two months' worth of groceries might not appear for that year's expenditures.

It is every live-aboard's tendency to talk about how little he can live on. In order to get an accurate picture, several live-aboard years must be averaged out. Five thousand dollars averaged out this way is a comfortable income, but reasonable boat living also can be done for $3,000 to $4,000 annually.

The $5,000 includes luxuries such as liquor, cigarettes, restaurant meals, film, sightseeing, books, magazines, movies, taxis or car rentals, and even some yard-done maintenance. Three thousand dollars is a skimpy income for two middle-aged adults who are used to even an ordinary standard of living ashore, and every penny will have to be counted carefully.

When a live-aboard tells you he spent $3,500 last year, ask him whether that is his average yearly expenditure. If it is only the figure for what he spent last year, and not an average, it will not give you a true picture of what boat living really costs.

The amount spent for food when you live aboard will be basically the same as when you lived ashore. Most live-aboards find that they cook the same way and eat the same things they did ashore, as long as they aren't making long offshore passages, where more canned goods than usual are consumed. Perhaps if a little more is spent for food afloat, it is because many times we do not have access to large supermarkets, where prices are usually lower. Sometimes we must shop in small grocery stores in some of the ports we put into. The extra amount spent on these now-and-then shopping trips is negligible, unless you have to do a lot of shopping in market places in the islands. In the islands, food costs much much more than food on the mainland — even the "native" foods — so you should carry as much as you will need if your stowage space allows it. Even if you can't stow it all properly, the way you would like to, get it aboard somehow. You will be eating it up gradually, and the crowded conditions will be alleviated a little more every day.

The idea of living off the sea is not practical. Some days you are lucky, but on the whole, it is not wise to count on Neptune's bounty to feed you on a regular basis. You can sustain life by eating nothing but your gleanings from the sea, but it will not provide you with three squares a day without a lot of hard work and more good fortune than most of us have.

Electrical appliances, televisions, clocks, watches, and the like, will need repairs just as often as they did ashore, and cost just as much. However, there probably won't be as many appliances to break down in a boat.

Keeping up memberships in yacht clubs and paying dues to various organizations you belong to can cost as much or as little as you decide it will, depending on the number of organizations to which you feel you must belong.

The amount of your actual or estimated yearly income determines how much insurance you can afford. Most of the people we have encountered with a $5,000 income have no medical insurance at all. If they have life insurance, it is usually a paid-up policy that was taken care of before they entered the boating life full-time. Your own feelings toward insurance will have to be considered; if you are uncomfortable without it, you should make allowances for its purchase, but the premiums take a sizable chunk of money out of a budget.

Boat insurance is something all of us would like, but most of us can't afford. The rates, which already are high, increase rapidly when coverage is needed for 12 months of navigation, instead of the more usual six months navigation and six months lay-up.

Our insurance, when we had it, was over $600 a year, with a $750-deductible clause. With the standard policy, written for the East Coast of the United States, we were covered only when we were between Eastport, Maine, and Cedar Keys, Florida. We could not winter above Cape Henry, Virginia, and be covered. A rider for the Bahamas was not too costly at that time — about

$35 if you didn't go during the hurricane season, but the cost of coverage for any of the other Caribbean islands was unbelievably high. If you plan to cross an ocean, forget about insurance. If any company will insure you, which is highly unlikely, you couldn't begin to afford it.

We wanted insurance only for a total loss of the boat, hoping that anything short of total loss could be taken care of by us, eventually. But insurance companies do not make enough money on that kind of policy, so they will not consider writing one. Evidently there have been many boats deliberately wrecked or sunk by the hand-to-mouth chartering companies, and the insurance people have had enough of paying off total-loss claims. We would feel a lot better if we had insurance, but without it, we consider each situation a little more carefully, and don't take chances that might endanger our boat.   As for circumstances beyond your control — you just worry a little more.

Dockage can be either a big item or a negligible one, depending on the area you are in and how often you want to anchor out. For an average-size boat in an average marina, an average cost would be about $50 to $60 a month. We have spent time in places that cost half that amount, and have heard about marinas where the charges are more than double that amount. If you keep a boat in one area, year after year, you might be able to get an attractive yearly rate.

If you plan to stay a couple of weeks in the same place, inquire about a monthly rate; it might be cheaper than two weeks at the regular daily rate. The same applies to three or four days; there may be a weekly rate that could save a few dollars. Besides saving money, you also have the option of staying over for as long as you have paid for — if there is bad weather or the parts you have ordered haven't arrived.

As for marina costs, you will have some, no matter how determined you are to anchor out all the time. Once you have made the break and have gotten away from it all for awhile, you may, eventually, want to get back to at least a part of it all.

We don't know of any real live-aboards who *always* anchor. Sooner or later, the "fun" of taking the laundry ashore in the dinghy wears off, as does the carrying of groceries and ice by the same method. When rough weather arrives, who wants a sloppy row ashore to get bread, milk, Scotch, or other necessities? On those hot days when the sun is beating down, it is pleasant to be able to use a fan that won't run down your batteries, or even plug in an air conditioner to cool off (more about this later). Sometimes it is convenient to use electric appliances for cooking in the cockpit, so the cabin won't heat up too much. If you have to do a repair job, it's handy having electricity for your power tools and a dock to work on, especially if you are doing a big job and need to spread out. And an honest-to-goodness shower now and then is especially welcome.

Barring unforeseen illnesses, your medical expenses will be about what they were ashore, or a little less. Most of us, having broken away from the shoreside routine, unfortunately do not have regular medical and dental checkups. We tend to put them off until a problem arises. By neglecting them, then, whether on purpose or not, medical expenses for these examinations may be less. Of course, if you let a problem go too long, the expenses may be considerably more.

For those who had visited a doctor frequently because it was convenient and comforting, rather than because of an actual illness that required medical attention, the doctor will not be so accessible. You will find, perhaps, that you can live with, and get over, your "illness" on your own — and at no cost. We have not met any live-aboards, nor have we heard of any, who have to spend any of their funds for psychiatric help on a day-to-day or week-to-week basis, as is so common ashore. Again, it may be because the psychiatrist is not convenient to visit on a continuing basis, but we think boat people are just generally better adjusted to the ups and downs of daily living — or they wouldn't be boat people.

Sometimes, getting away from smog-bound cities will clear up problems that needed regular medical attention when you were in a polluted area. We both had minor problems with our eyes, as well as persistent headaches and coughs, and everything cleared up after we got out of the dirty city.

An important part of living inexpensively is becoming a do-it-yourselfer for maintenance and repairs. If you cruise at all and want any degree of peace of mind, you will have to be able to do it yourself when there is no one else around. And if you have an income like most of the live-aboards we are writing about, you cannot afford to pay to have very many things done for you. Even if you can afford boatyard prices, knowing how to do maintenance and repairs will give you the knowledge to keep from being "taken" — which, unfortunately, is just as prevalent in boatyards as it is wherever you have anything repaired these days.

How do you learn? By picking the brains of anyone connected with boats and by reading, reading, reading, and then practicing what you have learned. If you are one of those unhandy bumblers who can't do anything, don't even think about a boat-home unless you have lots of money to spend to have work done for you.

Nearly every boat is different from the next one, even two boats built by the same manufacturer in the same year. One might have a diesel engine and the next, a gasoline engine. One could have a factory-installed, 110-volt system and another might not. After living with your boat for a few months, you will know more about her than any mechanic in any boatyard anywhere — whether you want to or not. You will also know the best way to get at any equipment that needs fixing, so you might just as well learn how to fix it.

Most boats have some kind of electronic equipment, such as depth sounders and radiotelephones; these are the items that need the most specialized training to repair. But there are books that will give you as much information as you want to know about electronics if you will study them. The major drawback for a do-it-yourselfer in this field is that specialized equipment is often needed for some repairs. Still, even a little knowledge will enable you to tell what is wrong and decide whether it is something that needs the attention of a bona fide repairman, or whether it is a loose-wire/blown-fuse sort of thing you can fix yourself. Most electronics repairmen charge $15 an hour or more for their services (and it always takes longer than an hour to repair anything).

Engines may seem formidable at first, but they can be conquered by amateurs. We knew next to nothing when we started out, but recently we did a valve job on our engine.

Any painting is done easily. If you have never held a paint brush before, just read and follow the instructions on the paint can. By the time you are halfway through the job, you will be astounded at how easy it is and how much you have already learned about painting.

Of course, maintenance and repair go far beyond painting and a little engine work. You may need to repair sails, or even make a new one from scratch. When a rope-to-wire splice (or any other splice) is needed, do it yourself. Learn to sew anything that might need repairing or replacing in your boat, including awnings and dodgers. Relatively complicated carpentry is easy if you have patience, can measure accurately, and have the right tools. Learn how to use them. Learn basic electricity and wiring.

Doing most or all of the maintenance and repair yourself can reduce the costs of these jobs tremendously. The lowest price we have ever heard that a yard has charged for labor per hour is $6, and the rate can go as high as $30 an hour for specialized work. The money you save by doing it yourself can be applied to buying the supplies and parts for doing the work — smaller expenses in the long run than paying for labor.

Hauling out, for various reasons, is a job that most of us have to pay for now and then; but if you need to be hauled and happen to be in a tidal area, you can beach the boat or moor it to a non-floating dock. When the tide goes out, you can do your work, and it costs nothing.

If you have repairs that you can't or won't do yourself, shop around for the yard where you can get the best deal and an estimate for the job — just as you would do if you were having a car fixed.

One of the best ways to save money is to try to avoid buying supplies and equipment in marine stores. There is much you can't get anywhere else, but there is more that you can. Stove alcohol is a good example. When we were new live-aboards, we asked the price of a gallon in a general hardware store that also handled a few marine supplies. The clerk consulted a list and said, "Marine alcohol is $4 a gallon." We asked him if he had any alcohol that was not designated "marine." He said he had several brands. We chose the least expensive of all, which was then $2 a gallon. The label listed its many uses, one of which was stove fuel. In all the years we had an alcohol stove, we never used "marine" alcohol, and we never had any problems. Neither will you, if the label on the alcohol you buy lists stove fuel as one of its uses.

Marine clothing is lovely to look at but expensive to own. An ordinary ski parka is water repellent, warm, has many more pockets, is more comfortable to wear, and costs half the price of a flotation jacket. The ski parka will not support you in the water, but how often do you fall overboard when you have on a flotation jacket? Wear a life jacket over the parka when conditions warrant. Shoes with good deck soles can be purchased in discount stores for $5 and in regular shoe stores for $10 to $15. You don't have to spend $25 or more to have safe, sure footing on slippery decks.

One-hundred-percent-wool sweaters can be purchased in nearly every department store for a fraction of the cost of those in marine stores. Sometimes you can even get them in navy blue with a turtleneck. Satisfactory, although ugly, foul-weather gear, as well as other clothing with a nautical flavor, is available at low cost in Army-Navy outlet stores. Those expensive vinyl sailing gloves with rough gripping surfaces on the palms are nothing more than the gardening gloves we buy for a dollar a pair — $4 less than the sailing variety. So what if ours are blue with a green thumb instead of all white? They are great for hauling in the anchor. They keep mud off your hands and provide a secure grip on the line. Other than rubber sea boots with a good tread, you won't really need any other "marine" clothing. Everything but the boots can be purchased in department stores or specialty shops. It is not difficult to find clothing with a nautical motif, if that is what you want.

If you still have a job ashore after you move aboard, you might have to keep up appearances and have a larger and fancier wardrobe than if you were cruising full-time; but the boatyard/cruising/social life among live-aboards is very casual, and no one ever dresses for anything if they can avoid it.

One new live-aboard asked Jan how many dresses she had aboard. She said she had none. The woman said, "What will you do if you have to go somewhere where everyone is dressed up?"

"I simply won't go," Jan answered.

A woman we know of had to go to a rather fancy dinner one night. She didn't have a dress either, and she wasn't about to buy one. She ended up borrowing a dress and the necessary accessories (shoes, handbag) from no fewer than six other women who lived in the marina, and she managed to turn up at the dinner looking presentable, even by landlubbers' standards.

Trailer supply stores are an excellent source for many items that can be used in boats, especially those items, such as light fixtures, that use 12-volt power. We had a good little wall-mounted, stainless-steel reading lamp in one of our boats. It cost $15. We found the very same light for $3 in a trailer supply store. The light was aluminum, with a cheap-looking brass finish. For our live-aboard boat, we bought three of these lamps, and we spray-painted them white to match the bulkheads on which they are mounted. After three years, there is not a sign of rust on them anywhere.

Many trailer stores have scaled-down items, such as refrigerators (110 volt and 12 volt), that are useful on boats. These stores carry propane accessories and appliances, as well as 12-volt electric fans and air conditioners. They also have plumbing supplies, sinks, and pressure water systems that are as good as or better than the marine types.

Compact electric heaters, which can be bought in appliance and discount stores, will do the same job as "marine" heaters. They usually cost less, yet they deliver the same wattage as those sold as "marine" heaters.

Automotive stores are an especially good source for 12-volt lights. Our spreader lights actually are tractor lights purchased for $3.50 each. We painted them white to match the spreaders, since they originally had a black finish. Even though they seemed to be relatively watertight, we put a strip of white waterproof tape around the light where the lens cover joined the body. In the marine catalogs, the same style of spreader light costs $20 a pair.

Stainless steel is attractive to the eye and sometimes necessary to use, but it is not the ultimate marine metal. Galvanized metal, which can be painted or not, is perfectly satisfactory for most marine applications above the waterline. Americans seem to be especially addicted to shiny chrome and stainless steel. Europeans find galvanized metal satisfactory for most purposes for which we normally would use stainless steel, including the rigging.

We needed a metal strip just aft of the bow, along the wooden cap rail, to protect the bow from dents and gouges during docking. Instead of the traditional, expensive bronze normally used for this purpose, we used aluminum strips purchased at a building supply company and protected both sides of the bow for $2. We painted the aluminum the same color as the cap rail, and no one is the wiser.

Nonsparking, nonmagnetic, and nonrusting tools are the ultimate; they are sold in some marine stores, but they are a waste of money. Any tool, including the cheapest you can buy, will not rust if it is stored properly. And what good is a nonmagnetic tool anyway, unless you can use it to adjust the compass? These fancy tools come in little kits that contain only a fraction of the tools you will need, yet the smallest kit, containing three tools, costs $42!

Most of our tools are Sears Craftsman brand, because Sears will replace any of their tools that break. The stores are located all over the country, and many of them are accessible to boaters.

Paint is another item that doesn't necessarily have to be "marine." We had a faded yellow horseshoe life ring that was faded and not very visible. We could have recovered it with bright yellow plastic, but instead we painted it with a small can of "lemon accent color" — *interior* latex. We painted a couple of small spots, then exposed them to the sun and submerged them in salt water. The paint stayed on and did not fade, so we painted the whole ring. It has lasted, so far, more than two years. None of the paint has rubbed off, and it is just as brilliant as when it was first applied. If it ever fades, we will just repaint it with the paint left in the can, which cost a dollar.

All our bulkheads are painted with interior latex, which not only is much cheaper than marine paint but also will not harbor mildew, since latex paint "breathes." It also dries in an hour, which is one of our main reasons for using it. Living aboard in a small area is no place to apply paint that takes many hours to dry, unless you can go off and live somewhere else while it is drying.

Naturally it is in the paint manufacturers' best interest to recommend painting every year for decks, masts, hulls, and bottoms. Sometimes that is too soon to repaint. There is no need for painting over a surface that is not cracked or crazed. If the paint is dirty after a year, consider washing it instead of repainting. Washing saves lots of time and money. All bottoms don't have to be painted every year, especially on fiberglass boats, if there is no growth on them. Paint everything when it needs to be painted, not when the manufacturers say it should be done.

III. SELECTING

THE LIVE-ABOARD BOAT

When you finally, definitely, and irrevocably decide to become a live-aboard, the first thing you have to have (besides the money) is the boat. Chances are, if you already own a boat, she won't be suitable as a home, even if she is a cruising boat. You will probably have to buy a larger or at least roomier vessel. If you are like most of us, you will begin by looking at boats that are too big.

When you tell yacht brokers what you are going to do, they will try to convince you that no boat under 40 feet would be adequate for living aboard. They never seem to pay attention to the amount of money you have to spend. When we were looking for our boat-home, one broker insisted we take a look at a 50-footer. We didn't want a boat that big, and we firmly told him so. He said, "If you are going to live in a boat, you've got to have room to live." It might have been interesting to find out what kind of living he had in mind, but we left him and his grandiose ideas and went to see other brokers. We had decided that 35 to 40 feet was the size range we wanted, and we refused to look at anything over 40 feet, so we wouldn't be tempted.

The day we saw the boat we eventually bought, the broker was bent on selling us a 37-footer we already had seen once and had rejected for a number of reasons, the major one being that we couldn't afford her. The broker also thought that we would be interested in seeing the quality of workmanship on a 32-foot Dutch-built boat, in the same yard, that had been listed with him just the day before.

We took a quick look at the Dutch boat and knew instantly we wanted her; however, the broker was determined to get us back to the 37-footer. We humored him and took another look at her, but we insisted on taking a longer look at the smaller boat again, and she was the one we bought. Only *you* can make the final decision as to which is the best boat for you.

In spite of their shortcomings, yacht brokers can be more helpful than anyone in locating a boat for you. When you are ready to buy, let several brokers know what you want. But wait until you really are ready; don't waste their time. You can get a reputation among the brokers as a perpetual looker, and they will not take you seriously when you finally are ready to lay out your cash.

Be specific about what you want as to size and price. If you want to spend as little as you possibly can on an older, neglected boat to fix up, let him know. This is a perfectly reasonable request, and there are all kinds of boats for sale for all kinds of buyers at all kinds of prices. Do not, however, come up with a pie-in-the-sky idea and tell a broker that you have never owned a boat before, but you and your family of six want a 70-foot boat for $10,000 so you can sail around the world — and you want to leave next month. No reputable broker with a conscience would sell you a boat for a venture like that, even if he had it to sell and you had $10,000 cash in your hot little hand.

The ads in magazines' brokerage sections will give you an idea of the size and kind of boat you can get for a given amount of money. Although most of the boats pictured on these pages are the larger, more expensive ones, there usually is a brief listing elsewhere in their advertisement of other boats that the brokerages have for sale. If any of these appeals to you and you want more information, write to the broker for details. Most brokers have specification sheets, and sometimes photos, on all boats listed with them, and they usually will send this information to you. In your inquiry, let them know what you are looking for and how much you can spend, and they may be able to send you the specifications on several boats. If you live near a yacht broker, by all means visit him in person to see what he has to offer.

Many boats are listed with several brokers, but many are not, so list your requests with more than one broker. There is no charge to you, as a buyer, for a broker's services. He makes his money on the commission he gets from selling the boat.

For all practical purposes, a 30-foot sailboat is the minimum size two adults can live on year-round in any decent degree of comfort. There are many people who are living on smaller boats and making do, simply because they want to live on a boat and it is all they have and all they can afford. There are people who are taking a year or so off to go cruising and will return to a land home eventually. There are those who spend half of the year on their boat and the other half in a house, apartment, trailer, or camper. This is not considered living aboard permanently, so some things we advocate will not seem necessary to such persons. They can always look ahead and say to themselves, "I can put up with this because I'll soon be ashore."

We knew a young couple whose only home for 18 months was a decked-over 17-foot Folkboat that they lived in while anchored in a river in England. After that time, they sailed the same boat across the Atlantic, sold it, and went to work and live in Boston. Another couple, with four sons between the ages of five and 10, cruised for a year on their 32-foot sloop. They had a good time, but they all were anxious to get back to their spacious home in a New York suburb.

If there is a failure in living aboard, chances are that it is because the boat selected is too big. We have no figures to prove it, but from what we have seen ourselves and what we have read, it seems that 80 percent of the failures happen because people have a boat that is too big, hence too expensive to keep up and too large for the crew to handle with ease. Don't be gulled into buying a boat you can afford simply because you *can* afford her. Ask yourself if you can afford to *maintain* her. We could have purchased the above-mentioned 50-footer and had money left over. She was a bargain for the size, but we would never have been able to keep her in decent condition and still have money left for living expenses.

Nearly everything you have to pay for in maintenance and dockage goes by the foot, so it is sensible to keep the boat length as short as possible. A simple haul-out for a 50-footer can cost as much as $40 more than it would for a 30-footer. And it takes more of that expensive marine paint to cover a big boat. In marinas where the charge is 20 cents a foot for overnight tie-ups, you will pay $4 more a night if you have a 50-footer rather than a 30-footer.

If you have a 30-foot fiberglass boat, with an aluminum mast, in reasonably good condition, you will have to spend a minimum of $600 a year just for basic maintenance, if boatyards do the work. That figure includes hauling and bottom-painting (which is the biggest expense), basic engine maintenance (such as oil changes), other minor maintenance (such as a leaking faucet or a small electrical problem), and sail-cleaning with minor repairs by a sail-maker. If you did all your own work, the figure could be lowered to about $200.

These figures are for a fiberglass boat that is new enough not to need the topsides painted. The sums include no topside paint except the boottop. We figured the labor at $10 an hour, but it also could be as low as $8 or as high as $12. These are, at best, very rough figures. There is always something that needs to be done that boosts the yearly maintenance costs. You might have to unstep the mast — about $50 to unstep and another $50 to step it again. Your depth sounder or radio may have to be fixed. You might have to replace rigging (stainless-steel cable, depending on its size, is at least a dollar a foot) or sails. The possibilities are endless, and sooner or later you will encounter most of these problems with your boat. If you have a big boat and are not going to do your own maintenance, you had better have a sizable income with which to pay the bills.

All the equipment for a big boat has to be proportionately larger.   The anchor, which is hard enough to handle in the smaller sizes, becomes more unwieldy as it gets larger. The hardware, especially winches and turnbuckles, must be bigger, and there must be more of it. Dock lines must have a larger diameter and be longer. Heavier rigging and sheets are needed. When and if you need a new sail, the cost is calculated by the number of square feet, and bigger boats naturally need bigger sails. On a large boat, the mast will be taller and the draft will be deeper, which will severely limit the areas where you can cruise.

We met Gary and Wanda in Florida one winter; they had owned their beautiful 65-foot ketch since the previous September. The only other boat they had ever owned was a 25-foot cabin cruiser. They had purchased the boat in Fort Lauderdale and sailed half-way up the coast of Florida so they could use the boat as their home while Gary finished up his job assignment there.   At the same time, they planned to outfit it for the cruising they intended to do.

Their boat was purchased for one-fifth of the asking price because the owner was becoming desperate. She was definitely a bargain at the price, but she consumed more than half the money Gary and Wanda had planned to spend on cruising. Gary would be leaving his job in a few months, and neither of them had any other income to fall back on.   The boat was in good condition, so on the surface it seemed as if she would need little in the way of repairs. Soon, though, the planked pitch-pine decks developed some minor leaks, so Gary and Wanda decided to recaulk them entirely.   They bought a few tubes of caulking, which covered only a fraction of the deck. Then they began buying caulking by the case.   Even so, they were unable to get any price reduction, and that particular caulking was very expensive.

The starter on their boat needed rewinding, and since the engine was one of 300 that the manufacturers had converted from truck engines in Europe, the starter had to be sent there to be repaired. The job took five months and cost $600. Of course, all this time they were paying dockage for 65 feet of boat.

Before Gary and Wanda could leave and begin cruising, the bottom of their boat needed painting. Only a commercial yard was capable of handling the boat because of her size, and the lowest quote they received for bottom painting was $1,500.

Only $4,000 of their once-sizable nest egg remained when we last saw them. They could not sail the boat themselves, and the only crew they could count on was a young man whom Gary had been working with who knew relatively nothing about sailboats.

Up to this point, they were still quite happy with the boat, but they were becoming increasingly concerned about the money required to maintain her. We have no way of knowing, but we suspect they will sell their beautiful boat soon and get a smaller and more practical craft. We feel that if a boat cannot be handled with relative ease by one person, should the need arise, it is too big a boat.

Another couple, who had owned five boats during their 20 years of boating, dreamed of living aboard. Finally they acquired a semicustom 40-foot motorsailer and lived on the boat for eight years in Norfolk, Virginia. During this time, they both worked in Norfolk and had a sizable income. When they stopped working and started cruising, the two decided to try to live on the income they were receiving from investments made over the years.

Their shakedown cruise was a trip to Bermuda. After that, they planned a circumnavigation after a cruise down the east coast of the United States to the Panama Canal. While going through the Canal, however, their boat suffered a good deal of damage in one of the locks, and they then realized what they had been suspecting for some time — they could not afford to maintain a boat of that size. Aside from the money that must be allowed for general repairs and maintenance, this particular boat had too many systems (autopilot, deep freeze, refrigeration, hot-water heater, etc.) that could not be kept in top-notch shape by the owners alone, although they always tried to do their own work. It would have been out of the question for them to pay for outside help to maintain the systems, because they simply did not have the money.

This couple found out that for any long passage they really needed an extra hand. They could handle the boat themselves, but it was very tiring for them to do so for an extended period of time.

Their misadventures in Panama made them decide that they needed a smaller boat. They are still living on a boat and cruising within their small income, but their new boat is a 32-foot stock fiberglass sloop that was nine years old when they bought her. They have made a few minor modifications to make her comfortable for living aboard. They realize that she is not the boat for a round-the-world cruise, but they discovered that they weren't too keen on long ocean passages anyway.

Then there is another example. Harry and Evelyn have lived on one boat or another for 24 years. Their two sons grew up on a boat and never knew another home. Their older son is now living ashore and going to college, but their younger son, Mike, who is six-feet-two-inches tall and 16 years old, lives with them on their present boat — a stock fiberglass boat only 34 feet long. They have found this size adequate for three adults.

Their first boat was a 55-foot wooden schooner, which they had had for several years. They were living in Hawaii when they acquired the boat, and they eventually sailed her to California, where they lived for some time. Harry and Evelyn were working ashore at that time and not sailing very often, so the maintenance, while time-consuming, was not making too big a dent in their budget.

When they started cruising in earnest, they discovered that the roominess was convenient, but maintenance costs were prohibitive, and the boat was too much for them to handle. Realizing their boat was too big, Harry and Evelyn started their search for the right size boat. They tried a 25-foot sloop, which definitely was too small for them and their two growing children. They finally settled on a roomy 34-foot sloop that had been known more for the races she had won than for being a live-aboard boat. She was well constructed and fast, but fortunately not at the expense of the living accommodations, as so many racing boats are. They bought a new boat, since they couldn't find a used one of the type they had settled on, and they have been living aboard happily for four years.

There are some things, such as more books, they would like to add, but cruising is more important to them now, and their present boat is just the right size to live aboard in relative comfort and maintain adequately on their income. She is also a boat that can be handled easily by one person.

The amount of money you can pay for your boat determines whether you will be able to purchase a new or a used boat. After outfitting three new boats, we decided we didn't want to do *that* again, so a used boat was the only kind we considered. No matter what you pay, we feel that a used boat of recent vintage is a better bargain than a new one. Usually the bugs have been taken out of her, and her shortcomings have been rectified. Used boats always have more equipment included in the price. You will have to buy all that same equipment and more for a new boat before you can even think of living aboard, and most boat equipment is bought with fifty- and hundred-dollar bills — lots of them. A used boat should be in reasonably good shape, however, unless you can do most of the repairs yourself or can spend a fortune to have them done at a boatyard. There are many excellent designs among older boats. Some of these designs have been around for 50 years or more; they have lasted because they were good designs and have proved themselves in all kinds of conditions.

Most boat manufacturers today are building a variety of cruising sailboats, so if you can afford a new boat, you have a wide choice. The cost varies with the boats' size and equipment. The minimum price of a new stock fiberglass boat, large enough for two people to live aboard comfortably, is $25,000. For this amount of money, you can get something in the 30- to 33-foot class equipped with the minimum in sails, engine, and below-decks equipment. For another $5,000 or so, you probably will be able to equip her with most of the things you need and some of the things you want. You may or may not get quality, depending on the manufacturer you choose.

Expensive? You bet. And the price skyrockets as the size increases, until you get the ultimate sailboat home — 50 to 60 feet long, and equipped with air conditioning, microwave oven, radar, automatic pilot, and tile tubs and showers. This home would cost in the neighborhood of $350,000.

If you want a new boat with a wooden hull, she will almost certainly have to be custom built; consequently, she will be much more expensive than any stock fiberglass boat of the same size. Today, wood for boats is difficult to obtain, and it is extremely expensive when it is available. Wooden boats also need the attention of highly skilled labor, such as cabinetmakers and shipwrights, who will have to be paid a higher wage than less skilled workers who turn out fiberglass boats on an assembly-line basis.

The same general rule of thumb applies to new boats with hulls of steel, aluminum, and ferrocement. There are very few stock boats being turned out in any of these hull materials. If you want a boat made from one of them, she will probably have to be custom built, and each of these materials calls for that expensive skilled labor to handle them.

A used fiberglass boat 30 to 33 feet long can be obtained for $12,000 and up, depending on age, condition, and equipment. A used wooden boat is one of the best bargains to be had today. If you look long enough and hard enough, you might be able to come up with something for as little as $5,000. There is a bigger selection of used wooden boats for sale than any other kind.

A used boat in reasonably good condition has the advantage of being ready for moving aboard and sailing almost immediately. There are no months of waiting for your new home — while you remain in limbo between what you moved out of and what you are moving onto.

After raising your hopes about finding an inexpensive boat, we must now dash those hopes. Chances are, you will pay more than any of the low figures given here for either new or old boats. The bargains are rare and hard to find, and it could take months or even years to locate a suitable boat for a relatively small amount of money. The figures given are what you might pay if you were lucky enough to be in the right place at the right time when an owner was desperate to sell his boat.

Any used boat, especially a wooden one, should be surveyed. The surveyor's fee is a small one, and it is worth every dollar. Get the best surveyor you can find; prices are about the same no matter who surveys the boat. If he has a reputation for noting every little thing that is wrong with a boat, so much the better. Nit-picking and ruthlessness are desirable traits in a surveyor. Don't make the mistake of being so anxious to get a boat that you will take the word of any survey that happens to be available, even if it is a recent one. Have the boat surveyed again by the surveyor of your choice.

We saw a boat we liked well enough to consider buying even though she seemed slightly overpriced. We wanted a busy, well-known naval architect/surveyor to look at her for us. Two weeks hence was as soon as his schedule would allow him to do it. That was fine with us, but the owner of the boat wanted the boat surveyed within three days. Another person was interested in the same boat, and he wanted her badly enough to comply with the owner's survey requirement. The yard where the boat was kept was acting as the broker in this case. The other interested buyer arranged for the yard's surveyor to look at the boat. Of course, since the yard was the broker as well as the surveyor, this boat passed with flying colors, and she was purchased by the other party. After that bit of business, we had no regrets about losing the boat.

If an owner is unwilling to allow the kind of survey you want, you can be sure there is something he does not want you to know about. He may even offer the boat at a lower price if you do not have her surveyed. Don't buy her at any price. Insist on a survey by a disinterested independent surveyor. Don't worry if the surveyor finds many things wrong with the boat. She still may be worth the asking price. The faults may be minor, or so major it may not be feasible to correct them, but you will be aware of them and can decide, intelligently, whether the boat is what you want for the money. With a survey, you at least will know what *is* wrong without having to worry about what *might* be wrong.

Many people who have bought new boats have had them surveyed before the final payment is made. Unfortunately, quality is not automatically included in a product that is so costly. Some manufacturers still have high standards of workmanship, but too many of them have shoddy manufacturing procedures. A survey won't guarantee a quality boat if you don't choose a quality manufacturer, but it will bring to light things that might have been overlooked by the builder and, in the case of bad workmanship, force the builder to make good under the warranty.

An acquaintance of ours purchased a new fiberglass boat, and shortly after she was launched, the bilge began filling slowly with water.   At first it appeared to be rainwater, and the bilge was pumped out — only to fill up slowly again. After the boat was hauled out, a pinhole was found at the junction of the hull and the keel.   A good surveyor might have found the hole before the boat was launched.

Another couple bought a new fiberglass boat and found out, a year later, that one of the chainplates had never been glassed in. It was fortunate that this defect was found when they were cleaning out the locker, instead of in a gale at sea. The owner had to pay for the repair himself. The manufacturer would not absorb the cost, because the warranty had expired. That is the sort of thing a surveyor will look for on a new boat, and it is worthwhile to discover any defects early.

If you buy an old boat with an excellent survey and want to insure her, insurance companies will not rush to sign you up. You probably will be able to get insurance, but it will be expensive. All boat insurance is costly, and the older the boat, the more expensive the insurance.

If you want to document your boat, the older she is and the more owners she has had, the harder she will be to document. You will have to obtain a bill of sale from every previous owner, as well as a certificate signed by the master carpenter in the shipyard where the boat was built. The older the boat, the harder this is to do, but it usually can be accomplished.

There seem to be two distinct types of boat people, or potential boat people. There are those who are happier building a boat, and those who want to get going and cruise in a boat that is already built. There is, of course, some overlapping of these groups, but most people who have the patience to build their own boat derive more pleasure from the actual building than the cruising. Many times they will finish one boat and then start immediately on another. The other group wants to have a boat ready for cruising as soon as possible, and does not want to spend the two years or more it takes to build one. You have to have a certain mental attitude for building a boat and be realistic, before starting to build, about how long it will take (and it always takes longer than that).

Contrary to popular opinion, you won't save a lot of money by building your own boat, no matter what material you use. The hull represents only about 10 percent of the total cost of the boat. You still will have to purchase all the rigging, sails, engine, and other equipment needed to outfit the boat at their retail prices.

One noted designer thinks you might save only five percent by building a boat yourself, as opposed to purchasing a comparable new boat from a manufacturer. Obviously, if this figure is correct, it will cost you *more* to build your own boat than to buy a similar used boat.

In the money department, then, the advantage of building a boat yourself is that you can spend the money over a period of time, instead of paying a large amount all at once. For some people, this is the only way they can obtain a boat. The amateur builder also has the advantage of being able to choose from the many designs that are available. He can adjust the accommodations to suit his own needs and wants.

Above all else, the amateur builder must be a skilled carpenter, no matter what hull material he is using. If the boat is not finished in a professional way, he is going to have spent a lot of money for a boat that looks just like what she is — an amateur, backyard-built boat. Should he ever want to sell her, he will never come close to being reimbursed for what he has put into her. It doesn't cost any more to build a professional-looking boat than to build an amateur-looking one; it just takes more talent. If you can't finish a boat the way she should be finished, don't consider building in the first place.

One couple who did a passable job on the hull of the boat they were building ran short of money, and they did the interior in plywood. They weren't careful about the joiner work because they were in a hurry to get her ready to live aboard. The end result is that below decks she is very crude. Although she is "finished" now, the builders are not happy with the boat, and they are trying to sell her, but they are having little luck doing so.

Aside from the woodworking, you will have to know how to install the engine and the electrical system in your boat. You could hire electricians and mechanics to do these jobs, but every cent spent for outside help cuts down on the amount you "save" by building your own boat.

We have seen beautiful boats built by their owners with nearly every hull material; it can be done. But you should weigh carefully all the pros and cons as they apply to your particular situation. If you won't have the money to complete the boat, don't start the project. If you have any doubts about your skill as a builder, don't build a big boat; first try a dinghy or something very small to see if you can build. If you are anxious to get cruising, don't build a boat yourself. Your impatience will be your undoing.

Documenting a boat you have built will be fairly easy, because you are the first owner as well as the master carpenter. Insurance, though, will be difficult or impossible to obtain. Insurance companies seem to feel that an amateur builder cannot build a boat that won't fall apart in the first high wind. They tend to generalize and cannot, or will not, take the time to analyze each individual situation.

We are of the buy-it-and-sail-it school, but we must admit that building a boat would include a tremendous amount of satisfaction, as well as intimate knowledge of what went into the boat.

In January 1971, when we began looking in earnest for our boat-home, there were few used boats in any size that were suitable for cruising and living aboard. There seem to be even fewer today, so it will probably take you some looking to come up with the right boat. We looked from Maine to Maryland in the dead of winter. We even considered flying to Florida to look at one boat that sounded very promising in the broker's listing. As it turned out, though, we found our boat in a yard less than 10 miles from our home.

Unless you are buying a new boat, don't have too many "wants" and "don't wants" when you set out to look for your boat, or you will never find the right one. It is no different than looking for the perfect dream house — it doesn't exist.

The important thing is to find the boat in the size you can live with at a price you can afford to pay. Keep an open mind about everything else and your search will be that much easier. Also, if you are going to live aboard but not cruise much (which many people do), your first consideration should be the accommodations. If you intend to do as much cruising as living, the first consideration must be the seaworthiness of the boat. The second is her draft, which will be determined by your cruising plans. The third is the living accommodations.

It is amazing to us that scores of people who are shopping for a boat to live on give so much thought to the looks of the boat; looks, that is, as far as design is concerned. No one, certainly, wants a clumsily built boat, but we have seen people reject boats simply because they did not like a reverse sheer or a reverse transom or a flush deck. If this sounds familiar, remember that you will be living *inside* the boat, and for a good part of the time you won't be able to see the offending bit of architecture. And don't concern yourself about whether other people like the looks of your boat. Lots of others must have liked the things that are offensive to you, or they would never have been designed and built in the first place.

An even more serious mistake is to buy a boat simply because you *do* like her looks. This should never be the prime consideration. We met a cruising couple who seem to have been influenced in this direction when they purchased their modern fiberglass version of the Chesapeake Bay skipjack. While the boat is well constructed, she is more a conversation piece than a good live-aboard cruising boat. The helmsman's chair on this 35-footer is as far aft as it can be. It offers no protection from any kind of weather, and it is impossible to add a dodger or awning to get any protection. This couple never ventures out when it is raining or when it is even threatening to rain. The only relief they can get from the hot sun is a big hat. The decks are flat, with no cockpit; consequently, there is no bridge deck of any kind to keep water from entering the cabin should they be pooped. The cabin below is not as large as most cabins on boats of this length, and it is chopped up in a most inconvenient way. However, she is an interesting boat to look at and always draws a lot of attention.

One of the things we wanted very much was a diesel engine, but we looked at more boats that had gasoline engines than diesels, simply because there were more boats available with gasoline engines. We figured that if the basic boat suited our needs and she came with a gasoline engine, we could possibly change it for a diesel engine later.

Since we thought we might want sometime to make offshore passages, we did not want a boat with a large cockpit. We rejected two boats for this reason alone, although they were suitable in most other respects. Most people look at a cockpit and visualize it filled with all their friends; we visualize it filled with water. A large cockpit can be a definite hazard at sea, and it is something that cannot be altered very easily. So, for us, those boats with cockpits that were too large were ruled out, for safety's sake. Our cockpit is not as small as we would like, but on an offshore passage, we would fill up the excess space with styrofoam or other flotation material, or the life raft.

Needless to say, the cockpit should be self-bailing. Fortunately, most boats nowadays have self-bailing cockpits, but unfortunately, most of them do not have drains large enough to get rid of the water quickly enough.

We set a limit of five feet as the maximum draft we wanted, because of the areas we planned to cruise: the Atlantic coast, the Chesapeake Bay, the Bahamas, and other Caribbean islands. Our boat draws 4½ feet, according to her plans, but with everything aboard for our way of living, it is closer to five feet. We have raised the waterline once. Keep this in mind when considering draft. Tools, books, a good supply of canned goods, and the other living accoutrements will bring any boat down on her lines — some a little, some a lot. This is a critical factor with catamarans and trimarans, since their buoyancy and seaworthiness depend on their light displacement. If, however, you prefer ocean sailing and plan to do little else, the draft does not need to be considered so carefully.

Another thing we felt we needed in order to be content with a boat-home was plenty of convenient, accessible storage space for our books.   Without our books, we couldn't be happy in any kind of home.

Our mental "shopping list" for buying a boat, therefore, had five things on it: the amount of money we could spend, the length of the boat, her draft, a boat designed to make ocean passages, and stowage space for the things we had to have to make her "home."   We felt that any other things we wanted could be added or modified in any suitable boat we might find, or we could adapt to whatever she did have.   We had no firm preferences as to hull material, or even a monohull as opposed to a multihull.   For awhile we seriously considered a trimaran, even though we had had no previous experience with multihulls.

There is something to be said for every kind of boat.   Whenever we encountered something new or unfamiliar, we read everything about it we could get our hands on, and we talked to people who had had experience with whatever we wanted to know about. There are many excellent books on hull design and rigs, as well as books written by people about their voyages and the performances of the boats they sailed in.   If you are to make a wise decision about buying a boat, it is absolutely necessary to research the subject thoroughly.

Many types of sailboats are available.   The list includes shoal-draft cruising auxiliaries; deep-draft ocean cruisers; motorsailers that can do a good turn of speed under power and, in the better designs, perform just as well under sail; catamarans, trimarans, Bermuda rigs, gaff rigs, square-sail rigs, ketches, yawls, sloops, cutters, and schooners.   If you have your heart set on a gaff-rigged schooner, read accounts about those who have sailed boats of that type.   Get to know the good and bad points about them and make up your own mind as to their suitability for your own particular situation.

It is always difficult to find just the right boat, but researching the subject will make it easier. You will be able to reject unsuitable boats more easily. The chances of making a bad choice are lessened when you know as much as you can about what you are looking for.   It is a lot of work to find the boat you want and need, and it is not something you will want to do often, so try to get the right boat the first time.

If you see a nearly perfect boat, but she is a ketch and you loathe the ketch rig, don't count on changing her to a sloop or something else.   There are many people who wouldn't have anything but a ketch.   If you cannot bring yourself to buy a rig you don't like, look for another boat.

Sometimes the rigging can be modified on a boat, but you should seek the designer's advice if you are contemplating any changes.   If the designer is not available, consult a naval architect.

We successfully changed our original sloop rig to a cutter, but not before checking with both the designer and a naval architect. If the conversion would have been complicated, we would have kept the original sloop rig. We only added another forestay and running backstays, leaving the existing rigging unaltered.

A diesel engine is preferable to a gasoline engine because of the safety factor, the lower cost of the fuel, and the extended cruising mileage it offers. If the boat you want has a gasoline engine, it will cost a minimum of $2,000 to convert it to a diesel. Sometimes this can be done easily, but it might require major alterations. You might have to replace the fuel tanks, since some tank materials are not compatible with both fuels. A diesel engine of a given horsepower will probably be larger and certainly weigh more than a gasoline engine of the same horsepower. A diesel develops its full horsepower rating at fewer revolutions per minute, but with more torque, than a gasoline engine provides. Therefore, a boat will get the same performance from a low-horsepower diesel as from a higher-horsepower gasoline engine. The space available for an engine, its accessibility for repairs, and the engine's weight must all be considered carefully.

The general consensus is that while a diesel is desirable, it will take years of operation to break even with the cost of replacing a gasoline engine with a diesel one. Economy should not be the prime reason for replacement, because the lower cost of diesel operation will not manifest itself for some time. Your personal preferences and what you can afford should be the deciding factors.

On the following pages are descriptions of several boats that are well suited for living aboard and cruising. The manufacturers of the new boats we have shown generally have a good reputation as far as construction is concerned, but this aspect cannot be guaranteed. Quality has to be checked at the time of purchase. We had originally planned to include a description of an especially spacious, presumably seaworthy boat built by a major manufacturer, but the quality of her construction has gone down so much in the last few years we felt we had to omit her. The boats shown represent only a few we think are particularly suited for our way of life, but there are many others that are equally suitable. We have not listed any prices, because they are subject to change.

Because we are dealing with live-aboard boats in the range of 30 to 40 feet, we have shown mostly boats in the 30- to 35-foot size. It takes a good designer to get so much livability into a small hull. If a designer cannot make a good, spacious live-aboard boat out of a 40-foot hull, he should be in another business.

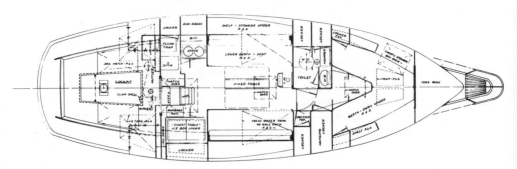

CRUSADER

L.O.A.—32'6½"   Hull material—steel
L.W.L.—26'3"   Power—Mercedes Benz OM
Beam—10'10"   636 diesel
Draft—4'6"   Fuel capacity—60 gals.
Displacement—19,200 lbs.   Water capacity—80 gals.
Ballast—3,450 lbs.   Designer—Sparkman & Stephens
Sail area—563 sq. ft.   79 Madison Avenue
                            New York, N.Y. 10016

Since this is our own boat, we are especially partial to her. Since we bought her, we have never found one we like better. She has proved to be the ideal cruising, live-aboard boat for two people. After having hit all kinds of debris floating in the water, we are convinced a steel hull is the only hull to have. Crusaders were built in the Netherlands, and nothing was spared to make them quality boats. Of the eight ports, six of them can be opened, and these are all screened. All the ventilators are screened, as are all the hatches. There is more stowage space than we have been able to fill. The Delft tile fireplace has kept us warm on many cold nights. The Mercedes diesel engine is one of the best on land or sea, and it has never failed us. Our boat is especially seakindly. Occasionally we have seen ads for used Crusaders (only six of them were built). They are referred to as motorsailers, which is something of a misnomer, because they perform very well under sail alone.

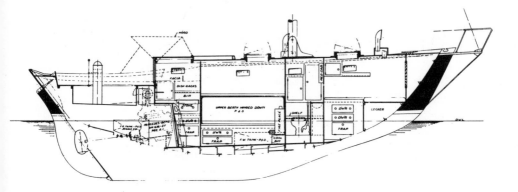

CAL-CRUISING 35

L.O.A.—35'1"
L.W.L.—28'9"
Beam—11'
Draft—4'8"
Displacement—15,000 lbs.
Ballast—5,000 lbs.
Sail area—546 sq. ft.

Hull material—fiberglass
Power—Perkins 50 hp 4-107 diesel
Fuel capacity—170 gals.
Water capacity—110 gals.
Builder—Cal-Boats
    235 Fischer Street
    Costa Mesa, California
    92626

Over the years, several good cruising boats, such as the Cal 34 and the Cal-Cruising 36, have come from the drawing board of William Lapworth. The most recent, introduced in 1973, is the Cal-Cruising 35, which should perform just as well as her predecessors. She has a fairly conventional layout and is very spacious, with lots of storage space and many drawers. By using a vee drive, the engine is located under the cockpit, which allows for more cabin space than in most boats of this size. The main cabin has a high doghouse, which provides good light below. The Cal-Cruising 35 is available as a ketch or double-head sail sloop.

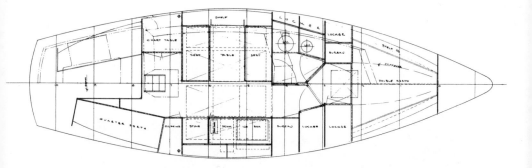

DICKERSON 36

L.O.A.—36'
L.W.L.—26'10"
Beam—10'5"
Draft—4'
Displacement—12,000 lbs.
Ballast—4,000 lbs.
Sail area—500 sq. ft.

Hull material—fiberglass
Power—Universal Atomic 4
Fuel capacity—20 gals.
Water capacity—20 gals.
Builder—Dickerson Boatbuilders, Inc.
Trappe, Maryland 21673

These well-known boats should need no introduction, since they can be found sailing all over the world. Up until the late 1960s, the Dickerson was wooden and 35 feet long. Now she is 36 feet in length and built of fiberglass. Many of the wooden boats can still be found for sale at reasonable prices. Used fiberglass versions can also be found, but there seem to be fewer of them available. The boats are a good, proven-seaworthy design with a lot of livability built into them. The shoal draft of four feet makes her a good gunkholer anywhere you might take her. Dickersons have always had a reputation for being well-built quality boats, and you get a lot of boat for the money.

Both the wooden and fiberglass models may be had with either a single cabin or an aft cabin arrangement.

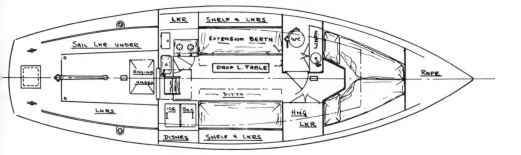

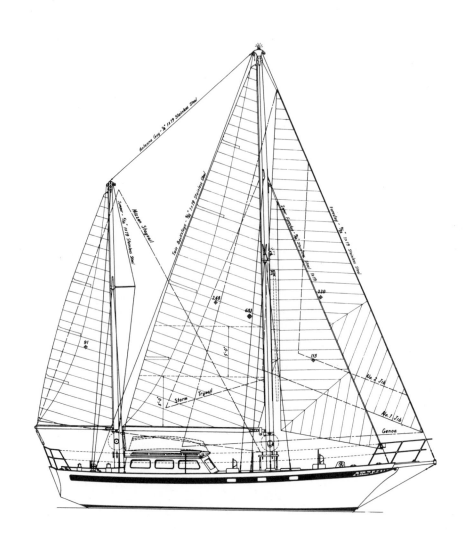

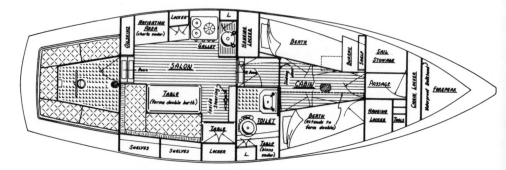

ENDURANCE 35

L.O.A.—35'3"
L.W.L.—26'8"
Beam—11'
Draft—5'
Displacement—18,550 lbs.
Ballast—ferrocement, 2 tons
    wood or fiberglass,
    3½ tons
Sail area—683 sq. ft.

Hull material—wood, fiberglass,
    ferrocement, or steel
Power—Perkins 4-108 diesel or
    Volvo Penta MD3B diesel
Fuel capacity—100 gals.
Water capacity—100 gals.
Builder—Ferro Boat Builders, Inc.
    2 Binnacle Lane
    Owings, Md. 20836;
    or Windboats Ltd.
    Wroxam, Norwich
    Norfolk, England NOR 037

The Endurance 35 is an extremely well-thought-out design and an excellent boat for living aboard. How many designers actually include dinghy stowage in their plans, as has been done here? Other evidence of designer Peter Ibold's thoroughness is the design of the forepeak. Skillful partitioning makes this a very useful area. Though originally designed for ferrocement and wood strip planking, plans now are available for construction in fiberglass and steel. This boat is popular with amateur builders. The high salon provides a roomy, light area for navigating, cooking, and dining. The sleeping area is private and separate from the salon, and it is far enough aft to be comfortable in a seaway. There is both cockpit and inside steering. She is available as a well-balanced ketch or an efficient cutter. Further information and plans can be obtained from the designer: Peter A. Ibold, 69 rue Galande, 75005 Paris, France. Windboats Ltd. is producing the Endurance 35 in ferrocement in any stage from a bare hull to a completely finished boat.

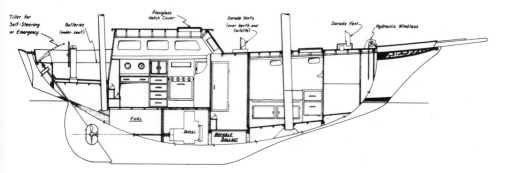

GH31

GOLDEN HIND 31

L.O.A.—31'6"
L.W.L.—29'9"
Beam—9'
Draft—3'7½"
Displacement—11,600 lbs.
Ballast—4,100 lbs.
Sail area—370 sq. ft.

Hull material—wood sheathed with
            fiberglass
Power—15 hp Lister diesel
Fuel capacity—20 gals.
Water capacity—20 gals.
Builder—Terry Erskine Yachts
            Newport Street, Stonehouse
            Plymouth, Devon, England

The Golden Hind 31, designed by Maurice Griffiths, is a wooden boat of double-chine construction covered with fiberglass. The underbody is a unique design. She has a long, full center keel plus two steel bilge keels. She will always remain upright if the water goes out from under her, and, more important, the bilge keels act as stabilizers in heavy quartering seas or when running downwind. Bilge keel designs always result in a very shallow draft boat, yet they aid in the windward performance. This is a very well-balanced boat. We were impressed by the performance of one sailing up the Elizabeth River in Norfolk, Virginia, dead downwind, with the genoa out on a whisker pole and being steered by a Quartermaster wind vane, while her owner was standing nonchalantly on the foredeck enjoying the scenery. Many of these boats have made successful Atlantic and Pacific crossings. The Golden Hind is an English boat, but used ones can be found in the United States. New boats can be ordered from Terry Erskine Yachts, the exclusive agent for the boats. The Golden Hind is available rigged as a sloop or a ketch.

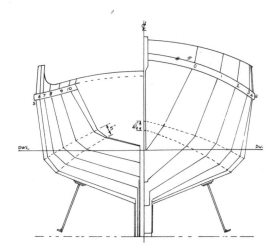

BOMBAY CLIPPER

L.O.A.—31'   Hull material—fiberglass
L.W.L.—25'7"   Power—Yanmar 12 hp diesel
Beam—11'   Fuel capacity—30 gals.
Draft—3'5"   Water capacity—60 gals.
Displacement—10,000 lbs.   Builder—New Bombay Trading Co.
Ballast—3,400 lbs.   4655 118th Ave. N.
Sail area—419 sq. ft.   Clearwater, Florida 33520

The Bombay Clipper incorporates many unusual features into
its 31 feet. The forward cabin not only has a double berth (with
a six-inch-thick mattress) but also space for an optional wash
basin (which would be in addition to the one in the head). Because
the head is sensibly located aft next to the companionway ladder, it
is exceptionally roomy, and the shower can be used conveniently.
Both head and galley sinks use foot pumps to draw water. There
are eight opening, screened ports. The steering pedestal has, in
addition to the wheel, a permanent cockpit table with two fold-up
leaves.   The base of the table is an inverted Y and provides a
footrest when heeling.   The inside of the base is a stowage area.
The forepeak is divided to accommodate rope and chain in
separate compartments.

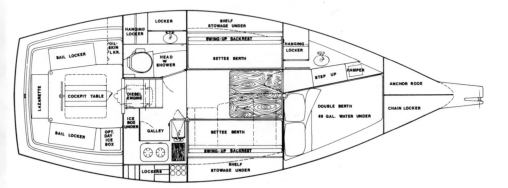

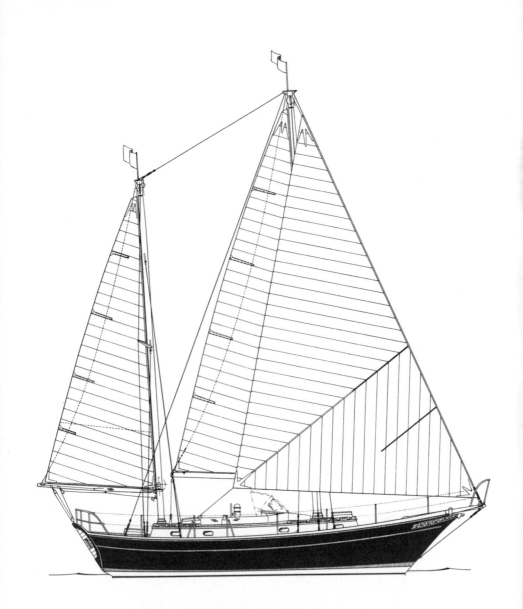

MASON 37 STERN CABIN KETCH

L.O.A.—37'9"
L.W.L.—29'7"
Beam—12'4"
Draft—5'7"
Displacement—11.6 tons
Ballast—4 tons
Sail area—710 sq. ft.

Hull material—wood
Power—Westerbeke 37 hp 4-107
    diesel or Perkins 85 hp
    4-236 diesel
Fuel capacity—60 gals.
Water capacity—120 gals.
Designer—A. Mason
    P.O. Box 5177
    Virginia Beach, Virginia
    23455

One of the most appealing aspects of this boat is a great cabin, but this is only one of her many unique features. She also has a walk-in engine room with full headroom and space left over for a generator, batteries, and a water heater, plus a spacious galley with plenty of room for a stove with an oven and large ice box and/or refrigerator. The dinette in the great cabin will seat seven easily. It would take some doing to fill up all the storage space this boat provides. The decks are spacious, and you are never cramped when working on deck. The boat handles magnificently under sail; under power she can do seven knots with the Westerbeke and eight knots with the Perkins. Although designed for strip-planked wood construction, Mr. Mason says she could be built in steel if desired. She is available only as a custom boat, in any case. This happens to be our favorite of the many excellent cruising live-aboard boats that Mr. Mason has designed in sizes ranging from 33 to 40 feet.

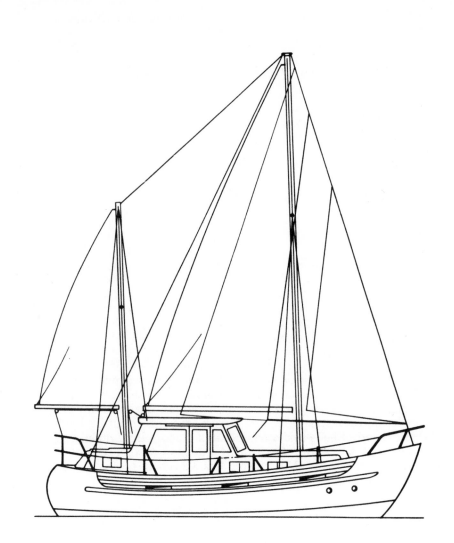

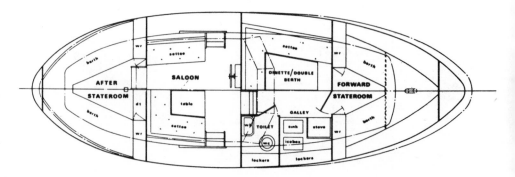

berth				
	settee		wc	berth
AFTER STATEROOM	SALOON	DINETTE/DOUBLE BERTH	FORWARD STATEROOM	
d1	table			
berth		GALLEY		berth
wc	settee	wc TOILET	sink	stove wc
		wc	icebox	
		lockers	lockers	

NORTHEASTER 30

L.O.A.—30' (approx.)
L.W.L.—25'
Beam—10'6"
Draft—4'3"
Displacement—6.5 tons
Ballast—3¼ tons
Sail area—330 sq. ft.

Hull material—fiberglass
Power—Volvo MD3B 36 hp diesel
Fuel capacity—50 gals.
Water capacity—50 gals.
Builder—Fairways Marine
    Rope Walk, Hamble
    Southampton
    S03 5HB England

   This boat is unusual because she is a motorsailer only 30 feet long with plenty of livable space. The Northeaster 30 is one of three designs utilizing the same hull. The rig choice can be either a ketch or a sloop. They are under-rigged by U. S. standards, putting them into a definite motorsailer class, but, as a result, they are good heavy-weather boats capable of long, comfortable offshore passages. The hull is based on a Baltic fisherman double-ender that has a reputation for seaworthiness. High bulwarks make for a safe, dry deck. The wheelhouse and aft cabin, in place of a conventional cockpit, provides an unusually large living area in a 30-foot hull. The boat can be ordered with the mast in a tabernacle for easy raising and lowering. She can also be equipped with twin engines. There are two United States dealers: Sumner B. Ladd, Ladd Marine, 5933 Naples Plaza, Long Beach, California 90803; and Paul W. Larson, Larson Yacht Sales Inc., 4th and Severn Avenues, Annapolis, Maryland 21403.

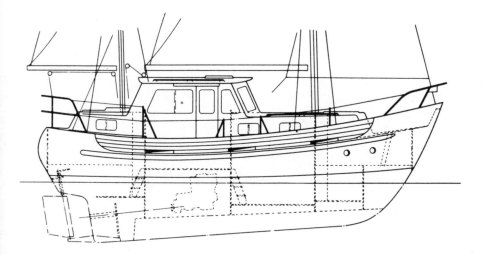

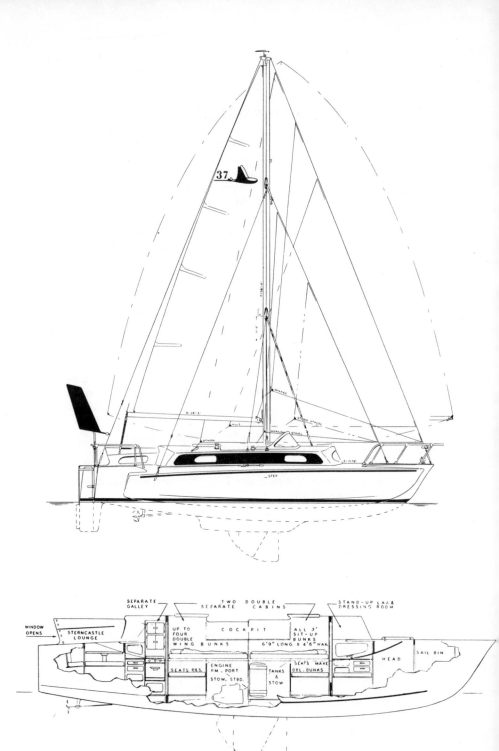

SEARUNNER 37

L.O.A.—37'4"   Hull material—plywood
Float length—33'2"   Power—30 hp maximum, 300 lbs.
Beam—main hull, 5'10"   maximum weight
    overall, 22'3"   Fuel capacity—30 gals.
Draft—3'1" centerboard up   Water capacity—45 gals.
    6'4" down two-thirds   Designer—Jim Brown Trimarans
Displacement—9,200 lbs.   P.O. Box 14
Sail area—681 sq. ft.   North, Virginia
                                          23128

Since many people prefer a multihull boat-home, we include this especially seaworthy and livable one. The Searunner makes use of a deep centerboard and cutter rig to give her very good performance to windward, which has never been a multihull's best point of sailing. The midship cockpit, located over the centerboard trunk, adds strength to the design and eliminates the trunk from the cabin. The mast is stepped in the cockpit, so sail handling is convenient and safe. Even though the cockpit separates the forward and aft cabins, we feel, as Mr. Brown does, that in a multihull a cockpit amidships is the best location. This location is especially effective on the Searunner, because Mr. Brown has designed the boat so that all the heavy weight of the engine and tanks is concentrated amidships, where it should be, since weight distribution is so critical on multihulls. Four very private double berths can be achieved with this design, or some of the berth areas can be turned into lockers, navigation area, etc.

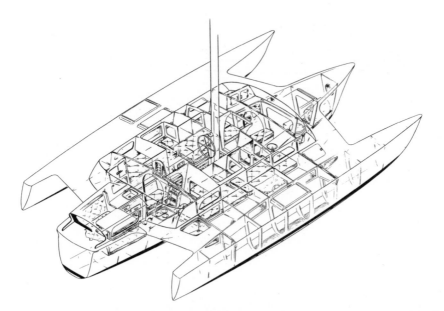

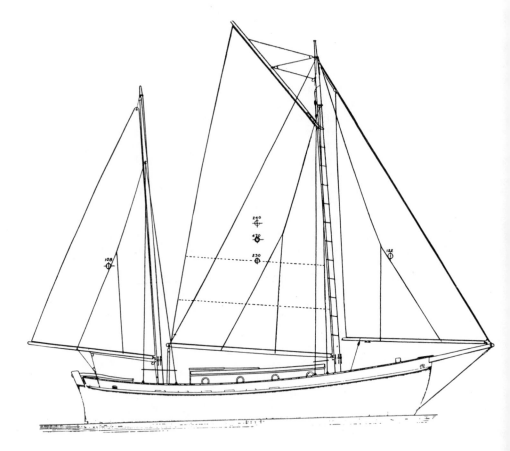

TAHITI KETCH

L.O.A.—30'   Hull material—wood
L.W.L.—26'   Power—optional
Beam—10'   Fuel capacity—optional
Draft—4'   Water capacity—optional
Displacement—18,100 lbs.
Sail area—422 to 540 sq. ft.

No collection of cruising live-aboard boats would be complete without including a design by John Hanna. His 30-foot Tahiti ketch is perhaps the most famous, although he has designed many others that would make good boat-homes. Ever since the Tahitis were designed in the 1920s, they have been steadily slogging their way around the world and putting up with anything the seas could throw at them. They are short-rigged but very husky, dependable boats for long-distance cruising. Many Tahitis have been built by both amateurs and professionals, so used models are fairly easy to find. Because they were built individually, their construction, cabin accommodations, and engine may vary considerably from the layout illustrated. If you want to build your own, plans are available from Mrs. Dorothy T. Hanna, 6647 El Collegio Road, #302A, Goleta, California 93117. An enlarged fiberglass version, the Dreadnought 32, is available as a finished boat or bare hull from Dreadnought Boatworks, P.O. Box 221, Carpinteria, California 93013.

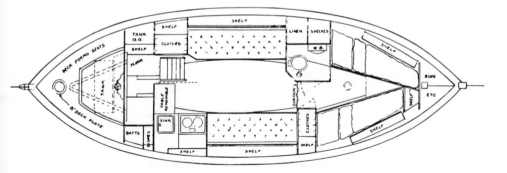

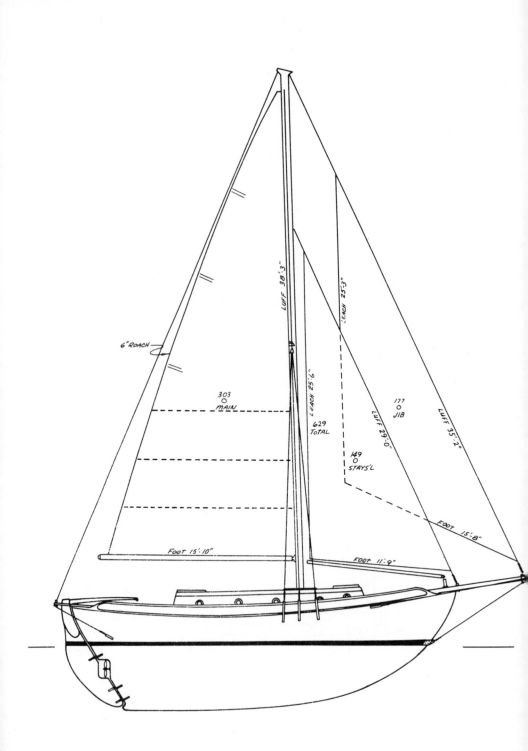

WESTSAIL 32

L.O.A.—32'
L.W.L.—27'6"
Beam—11'
Draft—5'
Displacement—19,500 lbs.
Ballast—6,600 lbs.
Sail area—629 sq. ft.

Hull material—fiberglass
Power—Volvo Penta MD2B 25 hp
    diesel
Fuel capacity—40 gals.
Water capacity—50 gals.
Builder—Westsail Corporation
    1626 Placentia Avenue
    Costa Mesa, California
    92627

The Westsail is a modified Colin Archer double-ender designed by William Atkin and once known as the Eric. W. I. B. Crealock brought the design up to date for fiberglass construction. Of the current boats being built in the United States, the Westsail is one of the best suited for living aboard and serious cruising. She is such a popular boat that there is a long wait if you want one, but she is worth waiting for. The interiors are well thought out, with every nook and cranny used for stowage of some kind. There are 14 drawers, 22 cabinets, two hanging lockers, and 13 other lockers. For ventilation, there are 10 opening ports. You can get a finished boat, either cutter or ketch, or buy the hull in various stages of completion to finish yourself.

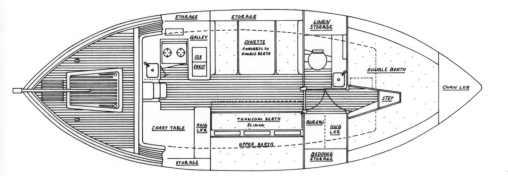

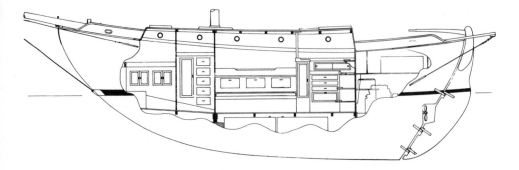

Westsail 32 starboard interior profile.

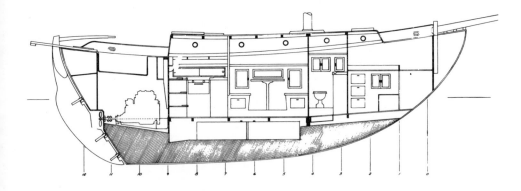

Westsail 32 port interior profile.

IV. BOAT DESIGN FEATURES

APPLIED TO A BOAT-HOME

The purpose of this chapter is not to go deeply or at length into a discussion of boat designs and the features that make up those designs. It is a brief compilation of facts we have learned about boats we have sailed, and things we have learned from other sailors' experiences. As we have said before, the perfect boat does not exist; and if one sailor says he has the perfect boat, others will consider her far less than perfect. The design features discussed below are only generalizations, and they should be read as such.

MONOHULLS

A narrow, deep hull will go to weather better than a shallow, beamy hull; but the narrow hull will have a quicker motion in a seaway. On a long passage, the quicker motion would be very tiring to the people on board. Obviously, the beamier boat will have more living space in a given length. The deep, narrow hull will stand up to her canvas in a blow better than the other type, but the passage will be wetter and rougher. Good initial stability is a feature of the beamy boat, as is her dryness with easier motion.

For the amateur who builds his own boat, a hard-chine or vee-bottomed hull would be the easiest to build, because neither has compound curves. But if the design is not extremely good and well thought out, the boat may be tender and tend to pound in a head sea. A round-bottomed boat is a stiff boat, but she has more of a rolling motion in certain sea conditions.

The fast, light-displacement designs are very popular today, but a heavier-displacement boat of the same waterline length as a light-displacement hull will usually be roomier below. More gear and provisions can be stowed aboard the heavier-displacement boat without bringing her much below the designed waterline. The performance of a lighter-displacement boat is hampered when she is heavily loaded for cruising, and if a very long voyage is planned, with all stores aboard, the freeboard might be reduced so much as to be unsafe. Boats of heavier displacement are known for their ability to punch through heavy seas. Their speed, though, is considerably slower than the lighter boats.

Hull form is one of the more hotly debated subjects in the boating world, and there are too many pros and cons about the different forms to touch on them any more than briefly. If the boat you select is what you want except for the design of the hull, buy her, unless she is a one-of-a-kind radical shape. In that case, don't even consider buying her.

The racing sailor is the only one who needs to be vitally concerned with hull design. Nothing should deter the cruising sailor from buying a boat with any of the normal, proven hull shapes, because all of them have their good and bad points. The perfect hull has not been designed yet, and when some designer thinks he finally has got it, you can be sure hordes of sailors will come rushing to tell him what is wrong with it.

MULTIHULLS

The arguments about hull shapes are petty compared to a multihull enthusiast's debate with a confirmed monohullist. The dispute as to which is best will go on for years, and it probably will never be resolved. We do not wish to add fuel to the arguments on either side, but you should be aware of some facts that have proved to be true over the years.

Catamarans and trimarans are the easiest type of boat for the novice to build and the hardest to sell. There probably are more multihulls being built by amateurs than any other kind of boat in a cruising size. You must be just as skilled to build a multihull as you have to be for building any other type of boat, or you will end up with a crude product. Whether the multihull boats are crude, beautifully finished, or factory-built, they still are harder to sell than monohulls. A well-designed tri or cat, however, has more living area and stowage space than a monohull of the same size.

Multihulls are the fastest of sailboats, but the hulls must be narrow and light to realize their fantastic speed potential. Narrow hulls do not offer much in the way of livability, and when the hulls are widened to increase the living area, and all the gear and provisions for living and cruising are stowed, the maximum speed of a multihull is little better than a monohull.

For those who don't like tippy boats, trimarans, especially, sail on an almost even keel, with none of the heeling that all mono-hulls experience at some time or other. Catamarans will capsize readily if they are not sailed properly. It is harder to capsize a tri, but it can be done. Once capsized, a multihull will not sink unless the hulls have been severely damaged and fill with water. This gives you something to hang onto while waiting to be rescued, but this may be little solace in midocean.

Multihulls perform well when they have a large body of water for maneuvering. In confined, narrow channels, they are hard to handle, because they have little lateral stability and are not as lively in response to the helm as monohulls are.

Getting into a marina with trimarans or catamarans can be a problem, because they usually are wider than a normal slip. Un-less there is a space where you can lay alongside, you may be out of luck.

HULL MATERIALS — WOOD

In these days of plastics and synthetics, there still is much to be said in favor of wooden boats. Though no one yet knows how long a well-constructed fiberglass boat will last, she probably will not be in as good shape in her old age as a well-built and well-maintained wooden boat. There are wooden boats being sailed today that are well over 50 years old, and only their "old-fashioned" designs give away their ages.

One man's argument for never owning anything but a wooden boat is: no matter where you are in the world, wood is available for repairs, and most people are familiar with it. This is a valid argument.

A wooden boat, new or old, requires more maintenance than any other kind of hull. She must be sanded, caulked, painted, and usually refastened at some time or other. But repairing a wooden hull is easy, compared with repairs on other hull materials. Wood is easy to work with, and if you ruin the job, you can rip it out and try again. Worms and rot are always threats. Taking care of either of these problems may require more haul-outs than might be needed for boats built of other hull materials. If you have to haul out to fix a leak, you never are sure it is really stopped until you are back in the water again. If a wooden boat is left out of the water for any length of time, she will dry out and the seams will open up. When she is launched, pumps will be needed to prevent her from sinking until the wood swells again. In hot weather, boats can dry out very quickly, and this is something to consider when hauling.

An exception to almost all of the above is a wooden boat built by the strip-plank method, which is the way most wooden boats are built today by both amateurs and professionals (unless plywood is used). Thin, easily bent strips of wood are attached to the ribs. All the strips are glued to each other as they are put on, and sometimes they are edge-nailed as well. Boats constructed this way do not need caulking, and they will not develop leaks as readily as a carvel-planked boat. But because of the method of construction, the strip-planked boat is more difficult to repair. Strip-planked boats sometimes are covered with fiberglass, which reduces maintenance somewhat and protects boats from worms.

When buying an older wooden boat that is not strip planked, pay particular attention to the fastenings. They will be of galvanized metal, Monel, or bronze. Monel is the best fastening material and galvanized is the least desirable. Many old galvanized fastenings will weep rust and can disintegrate eventually. It is possible to refasten a wooden boat completely if the hull is in a condition good enough to warrant the considerable expense.

On wooden boats some interior space is sacrificed, because wood gets its strength from its thickness. Therefore, the knees, ribs, carlins, and other structural members in wooden boats take up more space then they do in boats made of other materials. Fiberglass and ferrocement boats don't have or need knees, ribs, and carlins. The ribs on metal hulls are small compared to those on wooden boats because of the metal's greater tensile strength.

Plywood is easy to work with, so it is popular with amateur builders. Many boats have been designed purposely to use this material for home building. Nearly all amateur-built trimarans and catamarans are constructed of plywood, as are most of the multihulls built commercially. Powerboats and small stock sailboats are often constructed of plywood. Some larger sailboats also are built of plywood, but the wood usually is covered with fiberglass.

Plywood is less expensive than regular wood: it is easy to bend, and large sections of a boat can be completed quickly with it. If a given boat could be built in either regular wood or plywood, the plywood one undoubtedly would be cheaper to build. But we don't know of any one design that could be built interchangeably of either material, so it is not fair to say a boat constructed of plywood will cost less than a planked one.

Both plank and plywood construction can be strong; the strength depends entirely upon the design. Successful seaworthy boats have been built both ways. Maintenance on a plywood boat is about the same as for other wooden boats, except that caulking usually is not necessary. Plywood can delaminate if water gets to it, so leaks cannot be ignored for long.

HULL MATERIALS — FIBERGLASS

For many sailors there will never be anything but a wooden boat, and these same people decry the plasticity of the fiberglass boat. But the development of mass-produced fiberglass boats has made boat-owning possible for more people than ever before. If you asked them, these new boat owners would probably say, "I'd rather have a fiberglass boat than no boat at all."

The widest selection of boats, both new and used, can be found in fiberglass. For a few years after they are built, the low-maintenance aspect (one of a fiberglass boat's best selling points) holds true. Eventually, though, the topsides will have to be painted just as on any other boat. Waxing and polishing the hull may postpone temporarily the need for painting, but we have seen people spend as much time waxing their boat as they would have spent if they had painted her. If you feel that waxing is necessary to preserve the finish on a fiberglass hull, then there really isn't less maintenance; it is just maintenance of another kind.

Fiberglass will not rot, nor is it included in the diet of the teredo worm; but it can leak. The junction of the deck and the hull is the most common source of leaks. We have personally seen water enter in sheets at the deck joint. This usually happens under sail when the rail is well down. We met a professional captain who was delivering a new, stock fiberglass boat to Florida for the owners, and he told us that that boat leaked at the deck joint in a driving rainstorm whether she was sailing or docked. He was thoroughly disgusted with the boat and wanted only to be rid of her. Ports, whether fixed or opening, are another common source of leaks, and so are hatches. Porthole leaks are easy to fix, but leaking hull/deck joints on most fiberglass boats are almost impossible to get at and repair. Hatches are part of the deck mold, so their structure cannot be altered very easily to stop them from leaking.

Friends of ours have a fiberglass boat that was built when the industry was just getting started. Their boat is now 13 years old, and she shows no signs of structural weakness. There are virtually no cracks in the gel coat. Their boat was built before the real strength and longevity of fiberglass was known, so manufacturers were building their boats much stronger than necessary. This may account for her good condition. When you step onto the deck, it does not "give" under your weight, as do many of the decks on newer boats. She looks and "feels" like a ruggedly built boat. Few stock boats are built as well today. It is easy to hide cheap, flimsy hull construction under fiberglass, and too many builders take advantage of this.

Learn how a fiberglass boat is constructed before you buy one.

The experts say the best way is to build up the hull to the desired thickness with alternate layers of mat and roving. (Mat is a rather stiff material made of bits of fiberglass. Roving is a silky-looking "cloth" woven of fiberglass strands.) This method is the most time-consuming. Some builders of lesser-quality boats use a chop gun to build up the hull: chopped-up bits of fiberglass are sprayed onto a thin surface of mat and roving until the desired thickness is obtained. Then other layers of mat and roving are applied. In structural strength, this system falls far short of the first method. The strength of a fiberglass hull depends upon the different directions in which the roving is applied, much as the grain of wood is utilized for strength.

The method of using a balsa or plastic foam core between two layers of fiberglass is being employed frequently. It saves much time over the laying-up of several layers of mat and roving. The process still is too new for anyone to know whether these hulls will stand up to the same punishment as those with the mat and roving system.

In the past, if you wanted a fiberglass boat, you had to be happy with the stock boats made from the molds of the various manufacturers. Today it is even possible to build a one-of-a-kind boat in fiberglass. It is expensive now, but the cost will come down as better methods are developed. All things considered, it is no more expensive than having a new wooden boat built.

In a given size, fiberglass construction provides the most interior space. Repairs or modifications are much more complicated than on a wooden hull. Used fiberglass boats hold their dollar value well as long as they still look new, and most of them do for several years after they have been built, if they have been cared for.

HULL MATERIALS — METAL

The two materials used for metal hulls are steel and aluminum. We know of only four builders in this country who build only boats with metal hulls. They are: Burger, Manitowoc, Wisconsin; Palmer Johnson, Sturgeon Bay, Wisconsin; Gilbert Klingel, Gwynn Island, Virginia; and Striker Aluminum Yachts, Fort Lauderdale, Florida. Several yards have the equipment to build custom metal boats, but they concentrate more on building with other materials.

Metal hulls, or more specifically, steel hulls, are more commonly built in Europe, where the Dutch and Germans have made this form of boatbuilding a fine art. Our steel boat was built in the Netherlands, and the workmanship is so good that we are always plagued by hull-thumpers trying to find out whether she is wood or fiberglass. Their knuckles find out quickly that the hull is steel. Even when the sun shines on the hull at a low angle, there is no evidence of where the plates are joined. It is as smooth as any fiberglass hull. Most steel hulls are faired with troweling plaster, which gives them their smoothness.

Steel is the strongest and heaviest boatbuilding material. Steel will last as long as, or longer than, any other material. We saw a steel boat that was built in the Netherlands in 1898. The family that lives aboard her sailed her across the Atlantic when she was 68 years old. She is now cruising in Florida and the Bahamas.

Aluminum is not as strong as steel, but it has the lightest weight of any hull material. Its longevity is unknown.

Rust seems to make steel an unpopular material, but this is certainly due to a lack of knowledge about steel. Anyone who lives near the water has seen rusting hulks left to decay on the beach, or commercial ships covered with rust. Steel boats will rust, but not if certain precautions are taken when they are built, and not if they always are maintained properly.

Some builders spray molten zinc over the outside of the entire hull to prevent rust, before any painting is done. Another method is to sandblast the hull and apply several layers of various paints and coatings to build up a thick, protective surface. We recently saw a 32-year-old steel boat without a bit of rust on her.

To the uninformed, rust seems to be the worst drawback to owning a metal hull, but electrolysis and galvanic corrosion can cause more damage to a metal hull than anything else. If proper procedures are followed, however, even these problems become nonexistent.

When two different metals that are in contact with one another are immersed in water (either fresh or salt), the least noble metal will be eaten away by an electric current that is generated in the water and passes between the two metals. This is known as galvanic corrosion. Steel and aluminum hulls would not corrode if they had no bronze seacocks, Monel shafts, or stainless-steel fittings in contact with the hull. In water, however, the hull, being a less noble metal than the metals in the fittings, would be the metal that is eaten away, unless some even less noble metal is provided for the galvanic corrosion to attack. Zinc, one of the least noble of all metals, is used for sacrificial plates or anodes that are attached to various underwater parts of the hull.

Isolating all dissimilar metals from one another by rubber or plastic gaskets or washers is another way to prevent galvanic corrosion. Yet another type of corrosion preventive is the impressed current corrosion control system, which is installed on many metal boats and ships. This is a system that uses anodes, usually made of platinum, to emit a small amount of electric current into the water to reverse the normal galvanic current flow. Aluminum, also being

one of the least noble metals, is more susceptible to galvanic corrosion, and so requires more intensive protection than does steel.

Metal hull repairs can be done only by welding, and either you
or the yard must have access to welding equipment in order to
accomplish these repairs. Although welding equipment is not
readily available in some places, this fact should not deter you
from buying a boat with a metal hull; she will rarely, if ever, need
repairs that require welding. If a steel boat were rammed by a
ship or lay stranded and pounding on rocks or reefs for days, the
hull certainly would be damaged seriously, but it takes abuse such
as this to damage a steel hull enough to require welding repairs.

At seven knots, under power, we have hit both a submerged
12-foot rowboat and a two-foot-diameter by 20-foot-long log
floating in the water. We have gone into harbors and crashed
through cypress stumps that set the rigging twanging. The previous
owner of our boat confessed he had hit nearly every rock in the
Connecticut harbor where he kept her, yet there is no hull damage
whatsoever from any of these collisions.

Aluminum gains its strength, which can be considerable, from
the way it is structured. Large powerboats and several large,
custom racing sailboats have been built with this material, but the
chances of your obtaining an aluminum hull are slim unless you
have it built for you.

Some builders seem to feel that the welds are a weak point in
aluminum construction, but this point is debatable. Perhaps they
aren't as good or as strong as steel welds, but there are aluminum
boats that were built many years ago that are perfectly sound today.

A rounded bilge on a steel hull requires expensive specialized
equipment. This is the reason for so many hard-chine steel boats.
On the other hand, since aluminum is so much more flexible than
steel, it is easier to form into rounded and other complex shapes.

If you set out to buy a boat with a steel hull, you may have to
wait a long time before one comes on the market. It is difficult
to design a steel boat in a small size and still have the proper
weight distribution because of the weight of the steel itself. This
is the reason that more small boats haven't been designed or built
in steel.

HULL MATERIALS — FERROCEMENT

Ferrocement is the newest and most controversial material for boat
construction. It is reputed to be a simple, inexpensive material
for the backyard builder. True, cement is relatively cheap, but to
get a good-looking ferrocement hull, you must hire professional
plasterers to apply the cement. Welding is required too, and

unless you can weld, you will have to hire someone who can. The cost of these skilled workmen can wipe out anything you might have saved on the cost of the cement itself.

Contrary to advertising, you can't whip out a ferrocement hull in a short time. In reality, the actual hull construction, done properly, takes longer than building in *any other material.*

After steel, cement is the heaviest construction material, and too many designers, eager to climb on the ferrocement bandwagon, haven't taken this into consideration. The result has been many lumbering vessels that will not perform in light airs and will not go to windward well.

Though ferrocement is heavy, it is not as strong as some "experts" would have you believe. In fact, with the most common method of construction, ferrocement is one of the weaker hull materials. The hull strength can be increased by the use of different and much more expensive types of reinforcing rods and mesh, and using more of them than are normally used.

Rust and leaks are problems in sloppily built ferrocement boats. The rust can come from moisture getting to the steel rods and the wire mesh used in construction and then weeping through the cement. The metal in the rods and mesh is also subject to electrolysis if the mortar is not applied properly. Water seepage, through the cement itself, occurs on some of the boats. Most repairs, however, can be done easily by the owner if he has built the boat himself.

It is unfortunate that ferrocement, which showed so much promise, is getting such a bad reputation from home builders. Most of them didn't realize what they were getting into and became discouraged before they had completed enough of the boat to sell it and recover their material costs.

When looking for a secondhand ferrocement boat or a partially completed one, you might find a large boat at a very small price. Be sure she is really the bargain she seems before you hand over your money. Many sensible amateurs, who realized no boat of any material can be built in a few weeks for only a few dollars, have produced excellent ferrocement boats.

RIGS AND SAILS

Sloops, ketches, yawls, schooners, and cutters are the five most common rigs to be found today. The most popular of these are sloops and ketches. Over the years, certain generalizations have evolved about each of these rigs.

A sloop is the most efficient of all rigs, and it is the fastest; witness the America's Cup contenders, which are all sloops. A sloop goes to weather better than other rigs. Since a sloop has only one mast, it is easy to stay, and it requires less maintenance than two-masted boats, especially if the masts are wooden. There are fewer sails to maintain and repair than on other rigs. A sloop is one of the easiest boats to handle as far as normal sailing is concerned, but when it comes time to reef or reduce sail, a larger sail area will have to be handled at one time than on the divided rigs. A sloop 40 feet or more has only two sails, but they are very large and difficult for one person to change. A 600-square-foot sail area is about the maximum that can be handled easily by one person, and even that is an armful in any but the mildest breeze.

A cutter is a variation of the sloop rig, the main difference being that a cutter's mast is located amidships, while the sloop's mast is more forward. (Many of the newer sloops have their masts stepped farther aft to allow larger headsails to be set.) A cutter has two headsails, and these can be used to good advantage when running downwind. The use of the forestaysail with a reefed main makes the boat better balanced than if a smaller jib were used. A big genoa is not necessary for a cutter, since the two overlapping headsails have the same effect as one large sail.

Ketches, yawls, and most schooners have two masts, at least three working sails, and much more rigging than sloops and cutters. These facts affect the time it takes to maintain the boat, and also will raise the maintenance costs.

When the wind pipes up, ketches and yawls are the most convenient rigs for reducing sail quickly. Either the mizzen or the main may be dropped, and the boat still will be reasonably balanced. Schooners usually need a reef in the main for balance.

Ketches are notorious for not going to weather well, and, when sailing downwind, the mizzen tends to blanket the main, thus destroying much of its efficiency. The yawl, however, with a much smaller mizzen, performs nicely to weather and downwind. A yawl does not sail as well under mizzen and jib as does a ketch, so in heavy weather, it usually is best to take down the mizzen and sail her as a sloop, with the mainsail reefed as necessary.

One of the drawbacks of most ketches is the fact that the mizzenmast cannot be stayed independently of the mainmast. For some of its support, the mizzenmast relies on a stay, the triatic, from the top of the main to the top of the mizzen. The triatic acts as a forestay for the mizzen. Should anything happen to the mainmast, the mizzen certainly will be affected. This is always a potential trouble spot.

A schooner rig offers the greatest number of sail combinations and is fairly efficient on all points of sailing. Most schooners have a bowsprit, usually a long one, in order to balance the large sail aft. A schooner usually has two jibs. The rigging, of course, becomes quite complicated, and there is a lot of it to maintain. With a schooner or a ketch, there always will be a mast in front of the steering station, which may or may not affect your visibility, depending on the layout of the particular boat.

Unless you do a lot of offshore sailing, the process of heaving to probably will not present itself. Just for the record, though, and in a very general sense, sloops are the hardest to heave to successfully under reduced sail, and ketches are the easiest.

Ketches can fly a very useful sail in the triangular area formed by the front of the mizzenmast, the triatic, and the backstay of the mainmast. This sail is called a mule, and it is very efficient, because it is high and thus catches more of the wind than the lower sails do. We owned a ketch at one time, and the mule was our favorite sail. It can be set flying or the luff can be hanked to the main backstay. Another useful sail for yawls and ketches is a mizzen staysail. This sail is always set flying. The head is at the top of the mizzenmast, the tack is in the vicinity of the lower main shrouds, and the clew is at the end of the mizzen boom.

Schooners can set so many sails in so many different combinations that we can mention only a few of them here, but one of the most common and useful sails is a fisherman staysail, which is similar to the mule on a ketch and serves the same purpose — to catch the wind aloft. It is trapezoidal rather than triangular, and it flies from the mainmast and the foremast above the foresail. Yankees, topsails, gollywobblers, and main staysails are a few of the other sails on some schooners.

KEELS AND RUDDERS

There are modern fin-keel boats and those with the more traditional long, full keels. A boat with a fin keel will theoretically go faster, because there is less wetted surface to cause friction as the keel passes through the water. A boat with a fin keel will not be as easy to steer in a seaway as a boat with a full keel. The full keel gives more structural stability to a boat. Boats with fin keels are almost impossible to heave to.

A plus for a full keel presents itself when the boat must be hauled. In a travel lift, it doesn't make much difference what kind of keel a boat has; but if you want to be hauled on a railway, many yard managers will flatly refuse to haul a fin-keel boat. They have had too many bad experiences trying to get the keel positioned just right on the cross beams of the railway, and they have found it is not profitable to spend so much time hauling a boat.

When you find a boat with a fin keel, you usually will find she also has a spade rudder. This type of rudder is very vulnerable, because it hangs from under the transom with nothing to protect it fore or aft. Some of the newer designs have a skeg in front of the rudder, and this offers some measure of protection. A skeg of some kind also will virtually eliminate the tendency to stall that develops when most spade rudders are turned to too great an angle in relation to the hull. Spade rudders do not offer much control under power at low speeds, and they offer less in reverse. When running before the wind, a boat with a fin keel, coupled with a spade rudder, tends to make the boat hard to steer, and, in certain sea conditions, may cause it to broach.

On long-keeled boats, both outboard and inboard rudders are, in effect, flexible extensions of the keel, and the keel itself offers protection to both types of rudders. An outboard rudder is more vulnerable, but it also is repaired more easily than an inboard one.

AFT CABINS AND CENTER COCKPITS

The main drawback of an aft cabin, as we see it, has been its greatest selling point — the complete privacy it offers. This cabin usually becomes the master stateroom. Normally one of the occupants of the aft cabin cooks breakfast, so he or she must scamper across the open deck to get to the galley. Usually this isn't a great problem, but it's uncomfortable and inconvenient in a bad rainstorm or cold weather. Lots of breakfast cooks don't want to have to get dressed to prepare the meal. They cook in whatever they sleep in — night clothes or nothing. In a crowded marina, the dash across the deck in sleeping attire might not appeal to some. Most new boats with aft cabins have a head in them, but this is not so common in older designs. How would you like to go out on deck in the middle of a cold or rainy night to get to the one head forward? Some boats have elaborate zippered and windowed enclosures for the part of the deck that serves as access to the forward and aft cabins, and these provide some privacy and protection from the weather.

We feel that an aft cabin is not worthwhile unless there is an inside passageway that provides access to the main cabin. Until recently, this feature was found only in boats over 40 feet in length. Now several boats under 35 feet have this feature. An inside passageway is so much more convenient, even if you have to stoop a bit to go through, as you must do in some of the smaller boats. If you are still worried about privacy, hang doors on the passageway (if they aren't there already), and you will have just as much privacy as with a completely isolated aft cabin.

Aft cabin/inside passageway designs usually have the cockpit in the center of the boat, and it is elevated enough so that your field of vision is better than on any other kind of sailboat. Since it is in the center, this cockpit is less likely to be pooped by a following sea, but you will get more of the spray from the bow unless you have a permanent steering enclosure or a dodger that can be raised or lowered as conditions warrant.

FLUSH DECKS AND TRUNK CABINS

Many boats today are built with trunk cabins because they are traditional, not because there is a valid reason for adherence to this type of design. A flush deck will increase the below-decks space tremendously, an important consideration for the potential live-aboard. A flush deck provides more space on deck for stowage and working, and it is less vulnerable in heavy weather; whole trunk cabins have been known to have been swept away in severe storms. Trunk cabins usually have larger ports, which are additional weak spots if a heavy sea comes aboard, but it is pleasant to sit below and be able to look out of the ports, and this cannot be done in most flush-deck models.

Although a flush-deck design is not as aesthetically pleasing as a trunk cabin, boat manufacturers are ignoring this fact and turning out more flush-deck boats. They have found that they are much less expensive to build than conventional trunk-cabin models.

Whiffle has the traditional flush deck but some center-cockpit boats can be considered to have a flush deck, too, such as the Morgan Out Island series.

WHEELS AND TILLERS

Wheels used to be a rarity on any boat under 35 feet. Today they are installed frequently on smaller boats. Are wheels better or worse than a tiller? A wheel inherently provides a mechanical advantage that could only be obtained by a long tiller. But a wheel does not provide the sensitive "feel" for the helm that exists with a tiller. Docking with a tiller is somewhat more difficult than with a wheel, but if you are used to docking with a tiller, it won't be a problem. Should you want to equip your boat with a self-steering wind vane for long-distance passages, it will be easier to arrange with a tiller. Both tiller and wheel can be lashed so that the boat, if she is well balanced, will steer herself. If a boat has a wheel, she also should have an emergency tiller.

A large boat with a tiller must be perfectly balanced if she is to be manageable. A bit of weather helm is desirable on any boat, but the pressure from the weather helm on the tiller of a large boat is much greater than that of a small boat. As a result, the larger boat is difficult — sometimes impossible — to handle.

Try out the steering arrangement on the boat you want to buy. Can you sit down and steer with ease? If you must stand to see and steer, a wheel will be easier to use than a tiller. Some of the arrangements for sitting at a wheel are rather awkward, so experiment to see what is comfortable for you. Keep in mind that sometimes you might have to be at the helm for many hours.

There is a popular boat being built today that is a wonderful cruising boat in most respects, but the only way to steer her and see where you are going is to stand on the helmsman's seat behind the wheel and steer with your foot. Most owners of this boat install an autopilot very soon after they take delivery. This seems to be the only solution for comfortable steering on this particular boat, but it still doesn't solve the difficulty-in-docking problem.

SPARS

Masts and booms on older boats are always wooden unless someone has replaced them recently with aluminum ones. Aluminum masts and booms are now used almost universally on new boats made of wood as well as fiberglass.

Aluminum is much lighter than wood, but it is just as strong. However, since all aluminum masts are hollow and rather thin walled, they are more likely to bend and break than a wooden mast if an unexpected sideways strain is put upon them, such as might occur if a stay or shroud parted.

After aluminum masts were developed about 15 years ago and installed on fiberglass boats, the combination of aluminum and fiberglass was said to reduce the maintenance to almost nothing. This turned out to be wishful thinking. Aluminum will pit and therefore must be treated to prevent pitting. Anodizing, which is a protective-coating method applied to the mast by a chemical or electrolytic means, will add years to the finish of a mast, but it is subject to scratching. Some owners clean and wax both anodized and unanodized masts each year. Such maintenance does help to preserve them, but this takes just as long as painting a wooden mast. If an aluminum mast has been neglected for so long that waxing will not restore it, a proper prime coat can be applied, followed by painting as if it were a wooden spar.

A wooden mast is easy to repair unless it has snapped in two. It is a simple task to add additional fittings to a wooden mast or boom, but fittings on aluminum must be fastened on either by sheet-metal screws or rivets. These methods of fastening are satisfactory only if enough of them are used and if they are properly applied. Fittings put on at the factory are sometimes bolted or welded on, which is the strongest way of attaching them.

MAST STEPS

There are two ways masts are stepped. Most older boats and most large boats have them stepped through the deck to the keel. Newer, smaller boats have masts stepped on deck in a socket or tabernacle. Masts stepped through the deck have the strongest support, since they are resting on the keel itself. In the event that a stay or shroud parts, a stepped-through mast is more likely to remain upright until repairs can be made.

A mast coat or collar must be fitted around the mast where it goes through the deck, to keep water from running down into the cabin. This coat is always a potential source of leaks, and it must be checked often to see that it still is in good shape. It must be removed and replaced every time the mast is stepped and unstepped. The older collars were made of canvas and painted. The newer types are made of any number of waterproof, synthetic materials. They can be whipped or taped on. Whenever a mast is stepped through the deck, the services of a crane usually are required to step it and unstep it.

Masts stepped on deck, and especially those in a tabernacle, can be managed by one or two people, if necessary, in boats of up to about 40 feet. Any mast stepped on deck will have to have extra and sufficient reinforcement of the deck under it. For a while, there were several stock boats built with the mast in a tabernacle, but this practice seems to be disappearing in favor of stepping it in a socket (probably because a socket costs much less to manufacture than a tabernacle). A mast in a socket is not as easy to raise and lower as one with a tabernacle arrangement, but this method of stepping a mast is satisfactory, provided that the socket is deep enough. On too many boats, the socket has a very low lip, and masts have been known to pop out of them.

A tabernacle is a two- or three-sided holder into which the mast fits. A bolt runs through the mast and the tabernacle, and this is the pivot on which the mast is raised or lowered. Aside from the convenience of maintenance of a tabernacle-stepped mast, it is a feature to be looked for if your cruising plans involve canals, either in the United States or Europe. Irving Johnson's famous ketch, *Yankee*, which is 50 feet long, was designed to have both masts in tabernacles, because he planned extensive cruising in European canals.

BOWSPRITS AND BOOMKINS

There is nothing quite so beautiful as a boat under sail with a long bowsprit set with her jibs and staysails. Bowsprits, however, can be a problem. Long bowsprits, five feet or longer, may be necessary for the successful sailing capabilities of a particular design; but on a cruising, live-aboard boat, a long bowsprit will present problems sooner or later. The boat must be rigged and outfitted in such a way that you can safely go out on the bowsprit when necessary. Sometimes a pulpit and lifelines can be added. If the bowsprit is narrow, a platform can be installed for its whole length; then, perhaps, a pulpit and lifelines can be added. If none of these safety features can be installed, then a net should be slung under the bowsprit to catch anything that might fall, such as people, sails, etc. It is no fun to have to venture out onto a plunging (or nonplunging, for that matter) bowsprit with nothing to hang onto. Chances are that you will not do as much sailing as you would have if you had had a safe area in which to handle the foresails.

If the bowsprit is a long one, it probably will be counted in the total footage of the boat, and dockage costs will go up accordingly. We have been charged only a few times for our three-foot bowsprit, but marinas generally charge for bowsprits that are longer than that. Most marinas don't want, or won't allow, a big bowsprit to stick out over the walkway on a dock, so a boat of this type will have to be stern-to in a slip. Some older designs have long boomkins as well as bowsprits. No matter which way a boat like this is put in a slip, she will be inconvenient and often difficult to get on and off.

Boomkins are less of a problem than bowsprits. They usually are short, and it is seldom necessary to walk out on them for sail tending. There is nothing much that can be done about eliminating a bowsprit or boomkin if either is on your boat. They were put there because the designer felt they were necessary. If you find a suitable live-aboard boat with extremes at either end, do not worry about changing the rig. Instead, consider whether it will be a problem for you, and whether you can live with it.

V. BELOW-DECKS
ACCOMMODATIONS

When you have found what appears to be a suitable boat outside, you will have to go below to see if you can live with her as she is or adapt her to your needs. Interiors can be adjusted somewhat, but it is best not to plan to move any supporting bulkheads, since they contribute to structural stability. If you plan to move anything heavy from one location in the boat to another, consider how the new location will affect the overall weight distribution. You may have to move something else to compensate for it. Aside from these two considerations, you can change anything you want below decks, but plan thoroughly before you begin rearranging.

Look at the below-deck accommodations with a critical eye; a carefully thought out list will be needed so you won't overlook anything. Is the interior light and airy? Are there ventilators and opening ports? (If you are going to live in a warm climate, the matter of ventilation is extremely important yet sadly lacking in many boats.) Is there adequate headroom below for the tallest member of the crew? Is there an airy berth long enough and wide enough for each crew member? Will the berths be comfortable? Is there a double berth or can one be made if desired? How about a proper sea berth? Can you find a comfortable place to sit below with plenty of sitting headroom? Can others find a comfortable place to sit too? Will there be enough room to stow all clothes, including foul-weather gear and other personal possessions? Will you be able to store sails somewhere other than on a bunk? Is there a locker where sleeping bags, bed linens, and towels can be stowed? Will the things you use every day be convenient? (We heard of one 36-foot boat in which access to the refrigerator/ice chest could be gained only by removing the companionway ladder.)

If you want to install a generator and/or refrigerator, is there room for them? Is there room to put in a stove with an oven if the boat is not equipped with one? Is the galley equipment easy and safe to use, or do you have to lean over the stove to use the sink, as was the arrangement in one boat we saw? Can you carry an adequate food supply for your needs?

Is there a sink and room for toiletries and medications in the head? Is there room for *you* in the head? Some heads obviously were not designed for human use. Try pulling your pants up and down in the head with the door closed. Sit down to find out if you can use the head normally. You will be surprised at how many heads require angled sitting. You should be able to perform all your normal daily functions (and this includes shaving and washing, too) comfortably in your own boat instead of having to make the trek to the marina's washrooms. If there is no shower, can one be installed?

Is there a place to stow charts and other navigation equipment? Where can you stow safety equipment, such as lifejackets, so that they will be easily accessible? Is there plenty of room for tools so that they can be reached easily? Will there be room for maintenance items, such as paints and varnish, as well as spares, such as rope and lumber? Are the engine and stuffing box accessible?

Make a detailed list of items geared to your own requirements and preferences. It will keep you from being overwhelmed by the general layout and appearance of any boat and from overlooking the things that are really important to you. This is especially true if you are buying a new boat. There she sits, in the full-color advertisement or on display, with the huge bouquet of plastic flowers cluttering up valuable work space. Dozens of colorful but useless cushions are scattered around. There are always a number of decorative objets d'art cunningly lined up on the shallow shelves above the settees and the port and starboard berths. Boats on display and in ads will never heel, so these items always will stay in place. Mentally remove all these trimmings and consider whether you can live with those same shelves full of binoculars, flares, horns, flashlights, charts, and the other necessary (but unattractive) paraphernalia you will have to put there.

If you have a special interest or hobby, look for a boat that has enough room to accommodate its equipment — within reason, of course. If your hobby is collecting antique pianos, you probably wouldn't want to live on a boat.

We gave up many things that would have been nice to have, but it was either give them up or give up the idea of living on a boat. Most of us are too tied down by possessions of one kind or another anyway. We heard of one lady who could not part with her large collection of china, so she took it with her when she and her husband moved to a boat-home. We wonder how much of it is left now, after they have lived aboard for several years. We had several model boats that we didn't want to part with, but we certainly didn't have room for them in our boat-home. We sold some of them and gave others to friends and relatives.

Since everyone needs a good night's sleep to function efficiently, the berths are of prime importance. Many berths in both old and new boats will not allow a tall person to stretch out full length. Be sure there is a berth of adequate length for each person who will be living aboard. Ideally, a berth should be used only as a berth. It should not have to be made up each night and dismantled each morning. In most small boats, the only berths that can be utilized in this manner are the forward ones.

No one should have to use a quarter berth as his permanent sleeping accommodation if it can be avoided. In warm climates, berths of this type are too enclosed to allow air to circulate and they are uncomfortably warm, if not so hot that they are unbearable. In colder climates, the condensation from body heat, especially in a fiberglass boat, makes a quarter berth most undesirable. One family of four had no choice but to use the two quarter berths for sleeping. To ventilate them and add a little more light, they installed an opening port under the seats on each side of the cockpit well. The ports were located at about the center of the quarter berths and improved the sleeping accommodations considerably.

Every berth that is used as a berth should at least have overhead ventilation. This can be a hatch, a Dorade, or another type of ventilator. The more air you can get below, the more comfortable will be the sleeping area. If there is no ventilation, install something that will provide it. Putting in a hatch is quite an undertaking, but this project might be worthwhile if it doesn't weaken the surrounding deck. There are many different types of ventilators, and usually something suitable can be installed without too much difficulty. If one ventilator isn't enough, put in as many as necessary. We have never seen any boat with *too* much ventilation. Air flow is good for both the boat and her inhabitants.

On many of the smaller-size cruising boats, the trunk cabin often stops so far short of the bow that the light and air a trunk cabin usually provides in the main cabin are virtually nonexistent in the forward cabin. This design feature turns the forward berths into something only slightly better than quarter berths. If the cabin extends far enough forward, you might be lucky enough to have a small port on each side. Chances are, however, that they won't be opening ports, so they should be converted to the opening type.

Most of the sleeping that is done in boats, singly or doubly, is done in the forward vee berths. Most people seem to sleep with their feet forward and their heads aft. This is probably a holdover from smaller boats in which this was the only possible way to sleep. If the bottom of the vee is wide enough and the overhead isn't too low, try reversing your position so your feet are aft and your head forward. Then, when you have to get up, you can swing down your legs in the normal manner, instead of having to turn around before being able to get out of the berth.

Try this method especially if you have turned the vee berth into a double with the addition of the triangular piece of wood and its corresponding cushion filling in the center of the vee (Fig. 5-1). If your legs are pointing forward, getting out of this arrangement is enough to try your patience. You have to sit up as high as you can in the limited headroom available, roll yourself up into a little ball, pivot completely around on your behind until your legs are where your head just was, and then you can begin your descent out of the bunk. These maneuvers will disturb the other person who is sharing the double with you, and you undoubtedly will crack your head as you get out.

If you have made the vee berths into a double, you will find it difficult to get out of the berth and even harder to get back in, because of the height of the berth from the cabin sole. In a 26-foot boat we once owned, it was barely possible for a person with

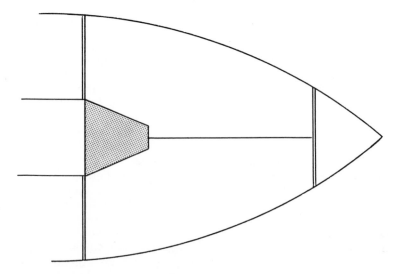

Figure 5-1. Typical vee-berth installation converted to double berth with filler piece. (Shaded area represents filler piece.)

long legs to clamber up onto the berth. In our present boat, it is not possible, because the berths are 38 inches from the cabin sole. Most boats are designed so that there is a step at the bottom of the vee for getting into the berth. If any kind of filler piece is used, the step is covered, and therefore unusable. To overcome this problem, we mounted a folding step on the bulkhead (Fig. 5-2). We chose a folding step so nothing would project into the walkway during the day. If there is room, a permanent step can be installed. Since stepping on a cold metal tread is unpleasant in bare feet, we carpeted the step with a scrap from the cabin carpet. Ours must be the ultimate in folding steps.

More and more boats are being designed with a double berth, because more and more people want one. Sometimes boats without them can be rearranged to make a double berth. If you feel it is absolutely necessary to have one, be sure you can convert an

Figure 5-2. Folding step to facilitate climbing in and out of forward double berth. Carpeting protects bare feet.

existing berth or construct a double before you buy the boat. In most of the smaller boats, the double is made by converting the vee berths forward, but this means the whole forward cabin is a big berth and nothing else while the filler piece is in place.

Another common double-berth arrangement is a dining table lowered to settee height. Cushions, usually from the backs of the settees, are designed to fit exactly on the table, thus forming a very satisfactory double (Fig. 5-3). Sometimes a double berth can be made by pulling out the seat part of one of the settees so that it is double its normal width. The cushion that forms the back of the settee is placed on the extended part of the seat to form half the mattress. The settee seat cushion is the other half (Fig. 5-4). The only drawback to doubles such as these is that they must be dismantled and made up every day. For some, though, they are better than no double at all.

Whiffle did not have any provision for a double berth when we bought her, but we were able to solve that problem. We filled in the vee, but not completely, and we used a nearly rectangular filler (Fig. 5-5). This can only be done successfully if one of the athwartship bulkheads that forms the forward cabin is wider than

Figure 5-3. A dinette/double berth conversion on Fisher 37. Support column for table is removed, and table top is lowered to seat level, where it rests on sturdy cleats.

the other. It will not work if they are of equal width. And the bulkhead must be wide enough to accommodate a filler piece large enough so that when it is coupled with the existing berth, it makes a reasonable-size double. A boat has to be rather beamy to have an arrangement such as this. Our single berth measures 25 inches by 79½ inches; with the addition of the filler piece, it is 45 inches wide. This is only nine inches shy of a regular double bed's width, and it is very satisfactory if you and your roommate are at all compatible. If you are not, a double berth probably isn't important to you anyway.

With a double berth such as ours, twin-bed sheets (flat, not fitted) are big enough to cover the whole bunk and still be tucked in. If you have even a little sewing talent, you can make custom-fitted top and bottom sheets from the flat ones by making tucks or sewing elastic at the necessary corners. We never have felt the

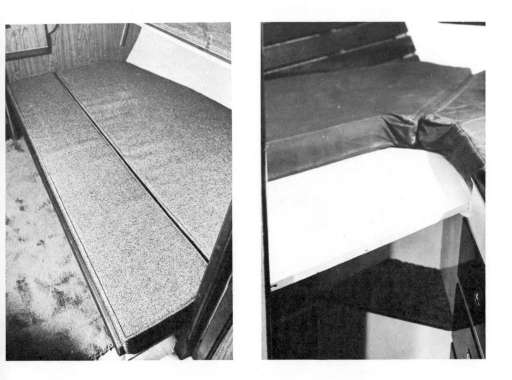

Figure 5-4 (left). Double settee berth on the 31-ft. Bombay Clipper. When double berth is not in use, extension slides under settee cushion and is completely out of the way. Figure 5-5 (right). Whiffle's special filler board, which is used to convert forward vee berths into a double. (Cushion is not shown.)

need for this, however, because the sheets stay put when they are tucked in. If a double is made by filling in the entire vee, larger sheets will have to be used. Some of these huge doubles need king-size sheets to cover them entirely.

During the day, the filler piece and cushion are removed from our berth and leaned against the hull on the starboard side. Happily, they fit snugly under a shelf there and never fall out of place, even in the roughest seas. The bed linens on the starboard side are flopped over onto the port berth and smoothed out. Since we sleep with our heads forward, the pillows are moved aft to the foot of the berth, so they are against the wider bulkhead and invisible from the main cabin. We made a "bedspread" to fit the berth shape in a plain blue material that matches the berth cushion covers. When you look forward from the main cabin, it appears that there are just the two berths with no bed linens on them. At night, the filler piece and cushion are put in, and the bed clothes are tossed back over them and tucked in at the foot of the filler piece.

Double berths are a big plus when you are cruising, because only one set of bed linens has to be washed. In very warm climates, however, it is cooler and more comfortable to sleep singly. Paradoxically, it is usually in these same warmer climates where there are few convenient laundries and fresh water is not plentiful, so washing two sets of sheets can be quite a chore. Sheets can be washed in salt water, but they must have a fresh-water rinse to make them comfortable to sleep on or under.

All berth cushions should be at least four inches thick and as firm as possible. Most cushions now are made of synthetic foam, which is not the most desirable material for sleeping on, but it is the most practical for boats. We looked at one 15-year-old boat that had down-filled berth cushions and seat backs. They looked inviting and comfortable, but we don't know how they would have worked out. They would certainly be a problem if they ever got wet, but they would be cooler to sleep on than synthetic foam or foam rubber. If you are buying a new boat and the manufacturer has thick cushions on the list of optional extras, it is worth ordering them for the extra comfort they provide.

All cushions that make up the mattress of a berth must fit together tightly, or they will slide apart and whoever is sleeping on them will slip gradually into the crevices. Sometimes a tightly rolled bath towel can fill a gap, but it should be used only as a temporary measure, and larger cushions should be obtained as soon as possible. Instead of buying or making a whole new cushion(s), you might be able to glue a strip of foam to the existing cushion so that it will make a tight fit. Most cushion covers aren't so snug that they can't accommodate a bit more foam, so you might be able to use the same cushion covers. When we made the cushion for our double-berth filler piece, we couldn't find any foam as thick as the existing cushion it would have to match. We bought two thinner pieces and glued them together with special glue we got from the foam factory.

If the boat's cushions have vinyl covers, plan to buy or make some kind of cloth slipcovers for them as soon as possible. Sitting on or leaning against vinyl is unpleasant, because it gets hot and holds the heat in warm weather; the reverse is true in cool weather. So many of the recent boats are made of so much plastic of one kind or another that real cloth-covered cushions can add much to the homelike atmosphere of a boat, and make her seem less like a coffee shop. The only thing we can say in favor of vinyl cushions is that they are easy to clean, but even that isn't much of a selling point these days; synthetic upholstery materials can be cleaned almost as easily as vinyl, and most have protective coatings to repel dirt and stains. Cushion covers can be made of any sturdy, washable material, such as cotton duck, denim, or even terrycloth. Covers should be zippered along one side so they can be taken off and washed in a washing machine.

Our covers are zippered and made of heavy cotton duck. We have washed them at laundromats several times. Our own preference is for a machine-washable cover rather than the type of upholstery material that must be cleaned with a sponge or brush and a special detergent. We have had saltwater spray on the cushions several times because we weren't quick enough to get the hatches closed, and we have inadvertently sat on the cushions in dripping foul-weather gear. The only way to get salt out is to wash the cover in fresh water. Perhaps dry cleaning would remove the salt from materials that were not machine washable, but it is usually inconvenient or impossible to locate cleaners when cruising, and it is very expensive if you do.

We use a mattress cover directly on top of the bunk cushion covers to save wear on the covers and keep ourselves a little farther away from the foam, which sometimes is hot to sleep on. We have a standard twin-bed-size quilted mattress cover. We cut off the fitted corners and use the cover flat, and we don't need anything to keep it in place. If the heat from the foam gets to you before you buy a mattress cover, put a layer of newspaper under the sheet on top of the cushion. It makes an excellent insulating material.

If you like a softer bed than firm foam offers, you might try using a down-filled sleeping bag on top of the cushions. If you have a double berth, get two sleeping bags — the kind that unzip on three sides and lie flat. These can be zipped together to make a double sleeping bag or used flat as a mattress cover or a blanket.

If you do have to dismantle your berths each day, you might want to make covers for the rolled-up sleeping bags and use them as cushions at the ends of the settees. This also is a good way to store sleeping bags during warm weather when they aren't being used, if you don't have a locker to keep them in. It also saves space if you store regular blankets this way when they are not in use. If you fold the blanket in halves to its smallest size, it usually will be about the width of a bunk. A cover made like a pillow case can then be slipped over it. The cover can be zippered on one end, or it can be left open with enough material to tuck under to hide the open end when the "cushion" is in place at the ends of the settee or berths. If you must make and unmake the berths each day, you might consider storing the bed linens in a similar cover.

In addition to sheets, our inventory of bed linens includes two lightweight cotton blankets (the kind referred to as "sheet blankets"), one cotton thermal blanket, and two fairly heavy Acrilan blankets. We spend quite a bit of time in cool and cold areas. If you do not, you will not need as many blankets as we have. We have sleeping bags, but we have used them only once, as a blanket, when the temperature was well below freezing. They are stored out of sight in a locker. We didn't sleep in sleeping bags when we lived ashore, and we see no reason to use them now. So many people think you have to use sleeping bags in a boat, but we are not "camping out" in any sense, and neither should you. The boat is our home, and we don't live here any differently than we would in any other kind of home.

Synthetic blankets are the most practical, since most resist mildew; should they get wet or have to be washed, most will dry more quickly than blankets made of natural fibers. You can't beat the natural fibers for warmth, however. Avoid blankets made with rayon, because this synthetic takes a long time to dry. As for sleeping pillows, use any kind you like. Chances are they won't ever get wet, so even down pillows could be used. If you perspire a lot, you might consider washable pillows.

In a seaway, neither the forward berths nor a double berth, wherever it is, will be suitable for sleeping. Forward, the motion is too pitchy, no matter how good a sailer the boat is, and in a double, there is too much room to roll around. This assumes that one of your crew of two is sleeping and the other is at the helm. We don't have any information about sleeping double in a seaway, but neither of us would want to be the leeward person.

A leeward quarter berth makes an excellent sea berth. If you don't have any quarter berths, you will have to make bunk boards (sometimes called "storm rails") for the berths best suited for use in a seaway. These usually will be the berths in the main cabin.

Some bunk boards are made of a wooden board that runs the length of the bunk and can be fitted into slots at each end. They are built in in some boats, and the design of the berths provides for convenient stowage of these long boards. If this is not a feature in your boat and you need bunk boards, you can fabricate them out of canvas or some other sturdy material, or buy them ready-made from West Products in Boston. Even when made of cloth, these devices still are referred to as bunk boards. If you already have wooden bunk boards, you still might prefer the cloth kind. If you do any rolling around, it is more pleasant to roll into cloth than a solid, unyielding piece of wood.

A bunk board is a rectangle or trapezoid of material about three-quarters of the bunk's length long, and high enough to keep a person from rolling out of the bunk (Fig. 5-6). Grommets are put in all four corners, and two or three more grommets are affixed along the edge that is attached under the berth cushion. This edge is secured to the bunk with screws through the grommets. A rope is attached to each of the two upper corners, and the ropes are led through eyes in the overhead and tied off, so that the material is vertical and forms a side for the bunk. The eyes must be attached securely to the overhead and be sturdy enough to hold up under the weight of a heavy person being thrown against the bunk board. Some boats have grab rails located where the ropes could be lashed to them. It is easy to stow cloth bunk boards. They can be laid flat under the bunks they service. Needless to say, in a seaway, the leeward bunk is the one to use.

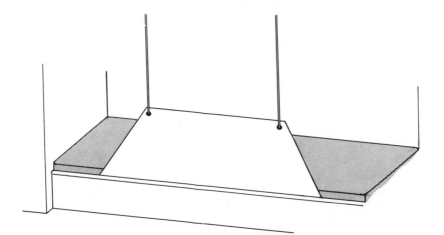

Figure 5-6. Berth equipped with bunk board made of strong cloth. Ropes at top of bunk board are secured to eyes or to grabrail on overhead.

Not only must each person living aboard have a comfortable
place to sleep, but each person must have a comfortable place to
sit when everyone is sitting. No one should have to give up a seat
so someone else can sit there. Although the crew's comfort is
uppermost, there also should be comfortable sitting places for any
guests you might have aboard. This is not as easy to arrange as it
might seem. If more designers concentrated on decent places to
sit, instead of cramming so many sleeping berths into a boat, we
all would benefit. One wise person said, "It's not how many a
boat will sleep that's important, but how many she will feed."
Our boat has one of the more sensible arrangements for sleeping
six, but why anyone would want to sleep six in a 32-foot boat is
beyond our comprehension. The backs of the settees in the main
cabin form two of the berths: they are hinged at the top and
swing up to make upper berths. When down, they are in the right
position and are high enough to provide very comfortable backrests, and that is all they are ever used for on *Whiffle*.

In most boats, there is room for the bottoms of several people
to fit comfortably on the seat cushions, but often there is nothing
to support their backs. Small boats with trunk cabins have the
most tortuous sitting arrangements. Most of the seats are fine, but
when you start to lean against the backrest, you can lean back only
as far as the trunk part of the cabin will let you. This is usually
far from the backrest. The berth was designed to sleep on, and to
be wide enough for sleeping, the backrests are so far under the
cabin that they are useless for anything but decoration. So you
perch there for as long as you can stand it, with your head resting
against the trunk cabin and the rest of your body angled out
toward the backrest but never touching it.

There usually is a shallow storage area along and under the backs
of these berth/settees. To make a better sitting arrangement, this
area could be deepened and brought out to where it would be
flush with the trunk of the cabin. This would provide lots more
space to stow things, as well as a comfortable backrest. This altera-
tion might make the berth too narrow to sleep in on a regular
basis, but it could turn it into an excellent sea berth with the
addition of a bunk board.

There are smaller trunk cabin boats that have a dinette arrangement that looks as though it would seat two people on each side.
In reality, it seats only one-and-a-half persons on each side, unless
the person sitting closest to the hull can get his hip under the
trunk and bend the upper half of his body out and around the
trunk in a "lazy S" position. A quick cup of coffee is about all
that can be consumed before this position becomes intolerable.

Although the lack of good backrests is one of the most dis-
agreeable features of so many boat seats, a close second is the

depth of the seat itself. It often is so deep you couldn't lean against a decent backrest even if it were there. Or, if you do get your back against it, you have to sit with your legs straight out in front of you, because the seat is too wide to allow your knees to bend normally. This phenomenon occurs often in larger trunk cabin designs where your head *does* clear the trunk part of the cabin and you can sit upright under it. Again, you are sitting on a seat that was made wide enough for sleeping. We aren't trying to malign trunk cabins just because our boat is flush-decked, but we have experienced all of the above seating arrangements, and they were uncomfortable in varying degrees. Only recently, though, we were sitting below in a friend's trunk cabin boat in perfect comfort. It was well designed for sitting as well as sleeping.

Be wary of narrow bunk/settees with vertical backs. They aren't comfortable to sleep on or sit on. If you adhere to the philosophy that a berth should be only a berth and a settee should be only a settee, you should come up with good sleeping and sitting accommodations.

Every seat in a boat doesn't have to be comfortable, since some of them are used only for a few minutes at a time, but your own special place for reading or whatever must be as suitable as possible for your shape and size. And guests really should not be expected to bend themselves out of shape when they visit. If you can seat two, three, or four extra people comfortably, then only invite two, three, or four guests at a time.

Along with the sleeping and sitting, we all have to eat sometime, so it is important to arrange a comfortable place for eating meals, at dockside and underway. This means you should have a sturdy table and ample leg and headroom. The dining table also seems to be an afterthought of many designers. We recently saw a 40-foot cruising boat that had no permanent dining table. At meal times, they jury-rigged a board with table brackets to one of the bulk-heads or balanced their plates on their knees.

A few years ago, we met another couple about to move aboard their new boat-home, which did not have provision for a dining table of any kind. When we asked about it, they said they planned to eat all their meals in the cockpit, so they didn't need a table below. Living aboard for them was going to be nothing but clear sailing — no rainy days, no windy days, and no cold days.

If you cannot make room for a permanent dining table, you might be able to make one that folds down from a bulkhead. The Bermuda 30s and Offshore 31s have such tables (Fig. 5-7). When it is down, it is a rigid table that can seat four easily. Folded up, it is completely out of the way. It is attached to the hanging locker door at the forward end of the main cabin. The table is folded in half when in place on the door. To use the table, the door is

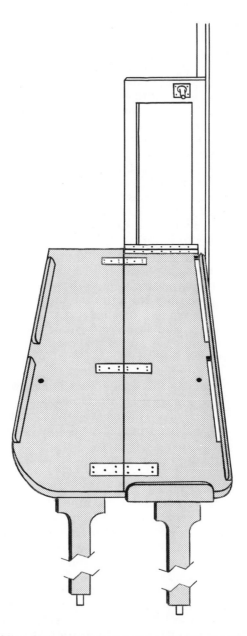

Figure 5-7. Folding dining table used in Bermuda 30s and Offshore 31s. Legs fold up and lock under table, which then folds over and up against hanging locker door, where it is secured with barrel bolts. While table is in use, locker door is held open by sliding wooden bar that pulls out from locker.

opened and the two barrel bolts that hold the table against the door are released; the table, attached to the door by hinges at the forward end, is lowered to a horizontal position. One of the legs, hinged to lie flat along the bottom side of one half of the table top, is released by the turn button that holds it in place. A pin on the bottom of the leg fits securely into a hole in the cabin sole. When this is in place, the other half of the top is unfolded and its leg is released and put in its socket. Built-in fiddle rails are attached permanently to the table. When it is folded up, everything nests together so well that it projects only 2½ inches from the door.

If you get a gimballed dining table in the boat you buy, it probably will come in handy sometime; but if your boat does not come equipped with one, don't worry. A gimballed dining table rarely is needed. We have met many cruising people who have crossed oceans and who have designed and built their own boats, and none of them has a gimballed table or plans to install one.

The same designers who forget the dining table almost always include a chart table. If there is one thing a cruising boat doesn't need, it is a chart table. If you are doing coastal piloting or navigating rivers and waterways, the chart must always be where the helmsman can see it instantly, which means next to him in the cockpit. If you are sailing across an ocean, you plot your position on small plotting sheets and transfer the markings to the one chart that covers whichever ocean you happen to be crossing. You never will need a place specifically to lay out a large chart. Use the dining table if you have to plot any courses. If you are like most of us, the plotting is done in advance, even though that may mean only the night before. Most dining tables are big enough for a large chart, and you can sit down and do your plotting, which is something you cannot do at many chart tables. Racing boats, with their full-time navigators, definitely need both a chart table and a dining table, but on any boat other than a real racing machine, a chart table is a waste of valuable space.

There seems to be a certain mystique about having a chart table; nearly everyone who buys a boat, either to live on or just to cruise in occasionally, thinks he needs one. Perhaps it evokes romantic ideas about man crossing uncharted (by him anyway) oceans, and would-be navigators picture themselves at their chart tables working and plotting at their charts so their vessels will sail safely and surely all over the world. Humbug.

Our boat has a chart table that doubles as the top of the ice chest. It is a good size, measuring two feet by three feet. There are lockers above it where the sextant and other navigating equipment are stowed. All in all, it is a tidy arrangement. Originally, there was no light above it, other than the regular overhead cabin light, but this was too high for reading a chart. We figured we needed a chart light — one of those gooseneck affairs that uses a high-intensity bulb and can be aimed directly at a particular part of the chart. So we put one in. That was more than five years ago. We have used the chart table and its expensive light once: the second day after we had begun cruising more or less full-time. Probably the only reason we used it then is that we thought we should. It is so much easier to sit at the dining table to do any necessary plotting underway. If we had had a chart table that was only a chart table and didn't do double duty as something else, we would have long since ripped it out and replaced it with something more practical.

Even more ridiculous than the chart table are the massive drawers on many boats for storing charts (sometimes six or eight of them). Some of these actually are big enough to store charts without folding, and most are large enough to store a chart that is folded only in half. Why should any small cruising boat be expected to store charts the way a big ship does? It is not practical, and it certainly isn't necessary. If your boat already has these big drawers, they can be partitioned into smaller, more practical compartments and used for storing lots of items that you need to keep within easy reach. (Chart storage is discussed in Chapter XI.)

Every person aboard must have a place where he or she can have a little privacy for sleeping, when others are up and moving about, when dressing or when he or she just wants some time alone. This can be achieved simply by closing off the forward cabin in most boats, either with a curtain or a door. A rigid door that is used only to close off a cabin usually is a nuisance in small boats. It is more practical to be able to open the head or hanging locker door and fasten it athwartships for closing off an area. If a boat isn't arranged that way, you can install a folding vinyl door, such as those used in houses and trailers. It is especially important to be able to close off the forward cabin when you are tied up stern-to in a slip or alongside a dock. It is everyone's inclination to look down into a boat, and there are certain things all of us want to do away from prying eyes.

All the privacy you want can be achieved with permanent bulkheads, but if there are too many in a small boat, they chop up the cabin area to the point where you lose more than you gain by having them. They also make adequate ventilation difficult, and the boat always has the appearance of being cramped and cluttered. In a small boat, it is good sense to have as few bulkheads as possible. Well-fitted curtains that aren't too full can close off compartments satisfactorily for most purposes, and in warmer climates they let more air circulate than solid doors would. Since so many good curtain tracks and sliders are available, something can be found that will be satisfactory for any installation. Much of this type of hardware is made of synthetic materials, and it never will rust or corrode.

Any curtain should have a provision for tying it back so it won't billow. If there is enough headroom, the curtain can be designed to be pulled up or rolled up and stowed above its opening — out of the way and perhaps out of sight. A curtain such as this could be designed so it could be lowered only part way, to allow more air to circulate.

Some boats are designed so the settees have a berth above and in back of them (Fig. 5-8). With an arrangement such as this, a curtain can be run the full length of the bunk for complete privacy. If one long curtain bunches up at one end when it is pushed back, it can be split down the center so that half is pushed to each end of the bunk and secured there.

When it comes to curtains on ports, most men would prefer not to have them, lest they be considered sissified and not proper yachtsmen. This is another holdover from the days when tradition

Figure 5-8. Main cabin of Russ and Evelyn Goldman's Alden ketch, Horizon. *Pilot berth at right has curtain mounted on sailtrack for privacy.*

was favored over common sense. There are few land homes without curtains, so why should boat-homes be different? No one would ever want to put organdy cottage curtains in a boat, but the right kind of curtains can help make a boat more of a home.

The ports of boat-homes need to be curtained for privacy from the ever-present "dock peepers."   We have been porthole-to-porthole close to other boats in slips in marinas, and curtains are needed there, too — especially in the head at night, when a light is on.   Even though we don't have large, easy-to-see-into ports, we close the curtains if we are leaving the boat for a period of time, especially in large cities. If thieves cannot see what there is to steal, they might concentrate on a boat that has things in view.

Wherever we travel, the sun always finds a convenient port to blaze into when we are cooking, eating, or sleeping. No doubt you will encounter this phenomenon in your boat, too. If you have curtains, you can pull them over the offending port until the sun goes away. If some of the ports don't open, curtains can be pulled across them to keep the sun out and keep the cabin cooler.

The larger the port, the more it is likely to need a covering. Some of the Golden Hinds have venetian blinds over some of the ports, which is not as impractical as it might seem. If they are anchored firmly at top and bottom, venetian blinds can be a very good way to cover any nonopening ports.

VI. LIGHTING

AND VENTILATION

As mentioned before, plenty of natural lighting is of prime importance below decks. Every compartment should have enough daylight to see by. If the boat does not already have enough light-admitting devices, you can add to the natural light in several different ways. Hatches that are solid on top can be replaced by translucent or transparent plastic such as plexiglass or Lexan. If it is not feasible to replace the whole hatch, you can cut a small port into it and insert plexiglass there. Even the wooden slides in the main companionway can be replaced by ones made of plexiglass — all of them or just one or two. If you don't want to replace any of the slides, you can install a small port in one of the slides. If the companionway has doors instead of slides, it is easy to cut small ports in them to admit more light.

If the hatches are not opaque and there still isn't enough light below, deadlights can be set flush in the deck itself. A deadlight is made of clear plastic or glass and is rather small — a circle measuring anywhere from four to eight inches in diameter or an equivalent rectangle. For its small size, a deadlight does a superb job of illuminating the cabin. We saw one boat with very little light from any source other than deadlights. There were four deadlights in the main cabin, and the light level was nearly the same as if it had come from small ports. Many of the older boats have very small ports, and these are the boats that benefit most from deadlights. Just one deadlight installed in the head or a hanging locker will usually provide adequate visibility. Some of the older types of deadlights are prisms, which let in more light, because they have more light-gathering surfaces than a flat piece of glass. These once were quite common, but nowadays they are hard to find.

Since deadlights are always set in flush with the deck, they will be walked on at times, and both glass and plastic are slippery when wet. Unless properly installed, deadlights are a potential source of leaks; they must be well bedded and sealed.

There are only a few places where additional ports can be installed without disturbing the looks of a boat. One place where a port should be, but often isn't, is on the forward part of the trunk cabin. Unless this part of the cabin is extremely curved, a port, no matter how small, could be installed there and prove to be very valuable. Aside from the light it lets in, it allows you to see forward without going on deck or raising a hatch and looking out. If this is an opening port, so much the better; it is an excellent source of air. Any port in this location must be sturdy and watertight.

Sometimes there is enough of the trunk cabin over the forward vee berths to allow a port on each side, if they are not there already. If the aft end of the trunk cabin on either side of the companionway is not taken up by too many instruments, ports can be put in there, too.

The solid tops of Dorade boxes can be replaced with clear or frosted plastic (Fig. 6-1). This will provide as much light as a deadlight, and it is easier to install if the Dorade boxes are already there (unless they are molded-fiberglass boxes). This is a way to provide more light in the head, since most heads have a ventilator.

While skylights provide a lot of light below, they leak if they are not constructed properly, and they offer little in the way of

Figure 6-1. Dorade box with clear, plexiglass top.

ventilation, since the openings are port and starboard instead of fore and aft. While all ports and deadlights should be big enough to allow a decent amount of light to enter, they should not be big enough to leave a huge, gaping hole if one or more should be stove in by a bad sea. Smaller holes are easier to plug.

Many openings that let in natural light are sources of ventilation as well. The ideal seaworthy boat should have lots of *small* portholes — small so they won't be bashed in by an angry sea. They should be opening ports that can be securely and firmly dogged down so that no seawater or rainwater can ever get in.

Boat manufacturers tend to skimp on installing opening ports. One 33-foot fiberglass boat that costs in the neighborhood of $35,000 has *no* opening ports and *no* ventilators. This one example (there are others, too, unfortunately) comes to mind because the people who were sweltering in it were once marina neighbors of ours.

If you have a boat with a flush deck as we do, you must be doubly sure the ports are watertight. With a flush deck, excessive heeling means that the ports will be under water. All ports should have a rubber gasket on all sides and sturdy screw-type dogs to hold them shut tightly.

Most boats have ports that are hinged at the top and are held open with hooks and various other devices. On some older boats, you may find ports that are just open holes with gaskets around the inside edges and a wooden frame on the sides and bottom (Fig. 6-2). When the ports are closed, the glass or plexiglass is held against the gasket by wooden wedges inserted between the

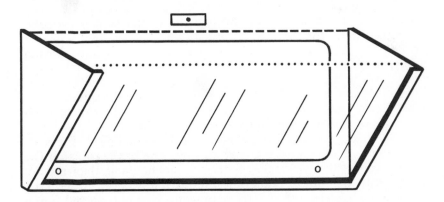

Figure 6-2. Opening port with removable glass or plexiglass. Dashed line shows glass in closed position; dotted line shows open position. Port can be opened during rain, allowing air to enter at top, or glass can be removed completely in good weather.

glass and the frame. Occasionally the glass is held in place with turn buttons. When the ports are open, the glass is removed completely, or it can rest against the frame at about a 30-degree angle from the opening, allowing air to come in only at the top. These ports leak more readily than the type that are screwed shut, and you have the additional problem of stowing all the glass when the ports are completely open.

We saw one boat in which all the ports were of this type; there were eight of them and they all were larger than the usual port size. When all the ports were open, the owner had a large cardboard box full of eight plates of glass (and it was glass, not plexiglass), which he stored on a high, open shelf. When we met him, he had just acquired the boat and he was satisfied with this arrangement. We wonder if he is as pleased now after encountering rainy weather and sailing heeled over with his box of glass.

Personally, we would change ports like this to the hinged type. Who wants to take up valuable space with a box of glass, when the hinged types take up no stowage space at all? The advantage to this type of port presumably is that it can be tilted back into the cabin at its top edge when it is raining to let in air and keep out rain. Most hinged ports have a small projecting lip outside to keep out rain, and this is sufficient in all but a driving rain, when the other ports are useless, too.

Sliding ports are being used frequently on many new boats. They are better than nothing at all, but rain and seawater will fill up the channels and leak. Another disadvantage is that in the open position, only half the port actually is open.

Good ventilation throughout a boat-home that is lived on year round is not as necessary to prevent dry rot and the other bugaboos that attack boats stored through the winter as it is to make her comfortable for those living aboard. To achieve this, a proper air flow must be established. This is accomplished by having enough headroom for the air to circulate freely and enough openings to allow the air to enter and exit. To catch the most air, hatches should be opened no more than 45 to 60 degrees. Any hatch cover that is removed completely or opened more than 60 degrees is completely useless for catching any breeze.

Most boats have forward hatches with the opening side forward. This seems to be the logical way to open the hatch to catch the breeze, especially when the boat is at anchor and thus usually headed into the wind. Sometimes, though, it is better to have the opening facing aft. If the wind blowing past the angled hatch creates a vacuum, the warm air will be pulled out of the forward hatch while cooler air is pulled in through the open companionway. If the sides of the hatch are closed with flaps, the vacuum effect will be greater. Hatches that can open in both directions are best.

You then can determine by experimentation which method works best on your boat.   The air flow can be checked with a lighted candle or cigarette smoke.

One hatch in addition to the companionway hatch is absolutely necessary, and two or three would be better still.   Aside from ventilation, a hatch of adequate size provides another way out of the boat in case of fire or another disaster that might block the main companionway.   There should always be at least two ways to get out of any boat in an emergency.   A decent hatch must have a device to hold it open at the proper angle and a way to dog it securely in bad weather.

An opening hatch that is set in flush with the deck will leak — always and forever.   The only kind of hatch that is leakproof is one that has an upright inner coaming over which the hatch cover fits (Fig. 6-3).   The better fiberglass boats have the inner coaming incorporated in the deck mold, but most of them aren't high

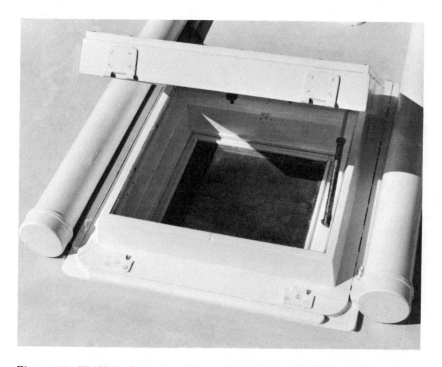

Figure 6-3. Whiffle's forward hatch with 3-in. inner coamings. Hatch is designed to be hinged on either forward or aft side. Whiffle's capped sewer-pipe stowage compartments (Chapter XI) are on either side of hatch. Pipes are 10 ft. long and extend back to companionway hatch coaming.

Figure 6-4. Tubular wind scoop with wings to catch wind. Scoop, sometimes called "wind sail," is hoisted on a convenient available halyard.

enough to keep all the water out. The inner coamings on our hatches are three inches high, and they don't leak. The hatches can be opened slightly in a driving rain without letting in any water.

A wind scoop (or wind sail, as it sometimes is referred to) can bring more air into the boat. This device has been used in the tropics for many years, but we think it has a place on boats that are used in more temperate climates. There are several variations of the most familiar design, which is a tall tube of flexible material designed to be suspended over an open hatch (Fig. 6-4). It has an opening on one side at the top, which is faced into the wind. The bottom of the tube goes into the hatch. The wind flows into the opening, down through the tube, and into the cabin. Most of these scoops have "wings" or "arms" attached to the sides of the opening, and these appendages are stretched out so they can capture even more of the wind. This kind of scoop is quite efficient for bringing air into the cabin. Its two major drawbacks are its cost (about $80, because it is complicated to manufacture) and the fact that there is no satisfactory way to screen off the bottom to keep out insects.

You can construct the tubular type yourself and save a considerable amount of money, but there is another design that works just as well as the tube and is not nearly as difficult to make. It is simply a rectangular piece of material, as tall as you need and want, with two triangular sides (Fig. 6-5). The front is completely open. The three sides fit over the hatch instead of down into the hatch opening. It is secured at the bottom by snap fasteners that are attached to the deck or a strip of Velcro fastened to the inside of the hatch coaming. There are fasteners or Velcro on all four sides of the hatch, so the open side of the scoop can be adjusted so it always faces into the wind. This design allows a screen to be attached over the hatch opening. A ready-made scoop of this design costs about $40.

Air flow must be maintained during rain or heavy weather when hatches and the companionway must be closed. This is achieved by ventilators such as Dorade boxes (which are the most efficient and watertight) and dome-top or mushroom types, which are not as good for bringing in air and keeping out water. Any type of ventilator that must be capped to keep water out is virtually useless, since that is when they are supposed to serve the purpose

Figure 6-5. Simple, easy-to-make wind scoop. Note batten across top, where 2 triangular side panels end.

they were installed for.   The box part of the Dorade type of ventilator usually is about six inches tall; a cowl type of ventilator is mounted on top of the box. The taller the cowl, the more it will pick up air and keep out spray. Some of these cowls are more than a foot high, and, in this size, they certainly don't add anything to the overall attractiveness of a boat. No Dorade ventilator is a thing of beauty, but it is very necessary; every live-aboard boat, no matter how small, should have at least one. Our 32-footer has three: one in the head, one in the main cabin, and one in the forward cabin.   All the cowls screw or snap into the boxes so that they can be turned into the wind or out of the direction of driving rain or spray.

A Dorade ventilator should have a cap that can be inserted to close the ventilator if the cowl is removed. If you do any serious sailing, you might encounter a storm so severe that you would want to close any opening where water could get below. In a situation like that, survival is more important than getting lots of fresh air, so the ventilators should be capped. Cowls are likely to be swept away if the storm is really violent. The chances of your being caught in such a storm are very slim, but don't lose track of those caps. You never know.

A man we knew who built his own boat, a 40-footer, had no ventilators at all. He felt they would ruin the looks of his boat. He wasn't thinking about the boat's appearance on the sweltering day we talked to him in Florida. He was thinking about how hot it was below. He had also neglected to put in any opening ports. He had only the companionway and one hatch forward for ventilation, and both had to be closed when it rained.

A dome-top type of ventilator will only keep out water that is not wind-driven, so this is not the most desirable ventilator. This design has an upright inner lip and a top that can be raised or lowered by screwing it up or down from inside the cabin. The top, in its lowest position, comes down over the inner lip to make a watertight closure.

There are several ventilators available that are modern, low-profile designs. These, too, are better than nothing, but they are very poor in air-gathering capability, because they are so close to the deck, and the openings that catch the wind are not high, as the cowls on a Dorade box are.

If the boat is closed entirely, a single ventilator will not cause the air to flow through her. There must be an intake and an exhaust. One should face forward and the other aft.

Proper and adequate ventilation is absolutely necessary when you are using kerosene or propane stoves and heaters. These, as well as solid-fuel (coal and charcoal) stoves, heaters, and fireplaces, burn up so much oxygen or create enough carbon monoxide that it would be fatal to be in a closed cabin for any length of time. Fireplaces and heaters must always be vented, and it is desirable to have some sort of ventilation over the cooking stove. A 12-volt fan could be used to exhaust the fumes and odors if provision were made to keep water out of the installation. A turbine smoke-head is an excellent ventilator over a cooking area as well as on a smokestack.

Good air flow is necessary to prevent rot in wood and mildew in everything. Every locker or storage area should be fixed so that plenty of air passes through it. This can be done by cutting small air holes at the top and bottom of each locker. They can be round holes or rectangular slots; or, if you are handy, the cut-outs can be appropriate designs, such as anchors. An easy yet decorative design we use is made with two different sizes of hole cutters. We use the design shown in Figure 6-6 at the tops of lockers with only one small, unobstrusive hole at the bottom so air can flow in and out. Louvered doors on lockers would provide excellent ventilation, yet there are very few boats that use them anywhere.

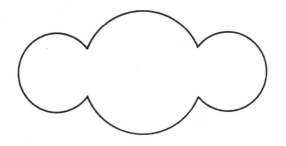

Figure 6-6. Simple, easy-to-do ventilation hole for locker doors. Hole is made with 2 sizes of hole saws.

Ceilings on boats are equivalent to the inside surfaces of the walls in houses. They usually are panels of wood and are attached to the ribs of the hull, thus creating an air space between the hull and the ceiling. In order to get a proper air flow, the ceiling must not reach all the way up to the deck, nor all the way to the cabin sole. An inch or two must be left open at the top and bottom, or several holes should be drilled at the top and bottom edges. Our ceilings are slatted — three-inch-wide strips of mahogany nailed lengthwise with ¾ inch of open space separating them (Fig. 6-7). This type allows maximum air flow, and we are never bothered by mildew, since these ceilings run the entire length of the cabin and are at the back of every locker. Small items occasionally slip down

Figure 6-7. Whiffle*'s mahogany slatted ceiling.*

behind them, but these can be retrieved without much difficulty. We have seen a few boats in which pegboard has been used for the ceilings. Though not traditional, it provides excellent ventilation as well as offering the opportunity to gain some unique stowage space by using special pegboard hooks and other attachments.

Almost every live-aboard will experience condensation or sweating inside the hull sometime during his tenure on a boat. This is caused by heat in the cabin when the temperature outside is quite a bit cooler. A wooden boat sweats the least; a fiberglass boat sweats so much it can be like living in a damp cave. Our steel hull doesn't sweat excessively unless it is quite cold outside (32 degrees or below) and the cabin is heated enough for shirtsleeve comfort. Because of the ceilings, we aren't aware of any sweating. Whatever condensation occurs, runs unnoticed into the bilge. One year we wintered in North Carolina during their coldest winter in a century. Some of our live-aboard neighbors who had fiberglass boats had a miserable time with excessive sweating of the hulls. All their lockers and bunks were right next to the hull itself, with no ceiling between; therefore, when the hull sweated, everything in the lockers got wet, and so did the people in the bunks, if they touched the hull. The hulls also were very cold. One poor fellow had a persistent drip from a shelf over his bunk, and he claims he didn't get a decent night's sleep all winter.

Some fiberglass-boat manufacturers realize the problem of condensation, and they are using carpeting on the sides of the hull next to the bunks. This is better than wet fiberglass, but much of the carpeting is attached directly to the hull with no air space between.

The carpeting absorbs the condensation, so instead of wet fiberglass, you have damp carpeting. Both are unpleasant. Styrofoam placed between the hull and the carpeting makes a better insulation.

If we should ever live aboard a fiberglass boat, we will install slatted ceilings, just as we have now. Vertical wooden strips can be glassed to the hull at regular intervals, just like ribs, and then the wood strips that form the ceilings can be nailed to them. It wouldn't be one of the easier jobs to do, but it would be worth doing, no matter how difficult.

In Chapter VIII, we explain the different ways of installing and using the electrical system. Here we are concerned only about the quality and quantity of artificial light.

Whatever form of artificial illumination is used below should be as good or better than sunny daylight. If you are cruising, it is easy enough to get up and go to bed with the sun; if you are not cruising but still living aboard, you should be able to stay up as late as you desire and have adequate illumination to do whatever you want. We have noticed that many new boats have hardly any cabin lights. This is another area where manufacturers feel they can skimp.

The minimum number of lights in the cabin should be: an overhead or bulkhead light in the galley, one on both sides of the main cabin so there is light over the dining table, a light in the head, and one or two in the forward cabin. Additional lights that we have and feel are necessary are: two good reading lights on bulkheads in the main cabin and one reading light in the forward cabin, a light in the hanging locker, and an extra overhead light in the head directly over the mirror.

All cabin lights should conform to the boat's voltage, which might be 12, 24, or 32 volts. All of the built-in lights that came with our boat, and those we installed ourselves, are 12 volts. A 12-volt system is the most common today, and it is the easiest to obtain bulbs and fixtures for. It would be unusual to find a new American-built boat with anything but a 12-volt system.

The light fixtures must be big enough to hold a bulb that will produce a sufficient amount of light, yet when on battery power, not enough to drain the batteries quickly. Naturally, only the lights that are being used should be on. Our reading lights are the ones that draw the most. They take a 25-watt bulb and draw a little over two amps. The cabin lights use a 15-watt bulb and draw 1¼ amps.

Fluorescent lights have become popular on many European boats, and they are found occasionally on American-built boats. They put less drain on the battery than incandescent bulbs; in fact, they will continue to burn even when it seems that the batteries are dead. But the light they give is very harsh and objectionable to some people.   Since the fluorescent fixtures are long and slim, they can fit into many places where other fixtures might not.   If you object to the light of fluorescent lamps, you might install them only over work areas and for reading lights, and use incandescent lights for general lighting.

Any serious cruising calls for the use of kerosene lamps, unless you can run the engine each day to charge the batteries.   There should be several oil lamps, or at least several brackets, so that a few lamps can be moved to different locations when they are needed.   Hurricane-type oil lamps certainly won't spoil the looks of any boat.   They are handsome to look at and give a very pleasant light, even if it is not as bright as you might prefer at times.

Oil lamps do give off heat.   If it is chilly, the heat is welcome, but if it is very warm, they will make the cabin uncomfortably hot.   The smell of the burning oil is supposed to keep mosquitoes and other flying insects away.   Sometimes it does and sometimes it doesn't.   For those who don't like the smell of kerosene, there is an odorless oil available.   Naturally, it is much more costly than the "smelly" regular kind.   If a low grade of kerosene is used, the lamps will smoke too much.   They will dirty the overhead and bulkheads and fill the cabin with unpleasant fumes.

Even if oil lamps are gimballed, as they must be, the glass chimneys probably will break now and then, so spares should be readily available.   Oil lamps require much more attention than any kind of electric lighting.   If the lamps are used with any frequency, the chimneys have to be washed clean of smoke, the lamps filled with oil, and the wicks trimmed.   Cutting off the charred portion of the wick will result in a brighter, cleaner flame.   If the lamps aren't used often, the fuel tends to evaporate.

Oil lamps that use a mantle and operate under pressure give a very bright light — the equivalent of a 100-watt bulb or better — yet they consume very little fuel.   Lamps of this type are rather large and sometimes difficult to stow when not in use.   Perhaps one could be hung from the overhead and tied off so it would not swing violently and crash into a bulkhead or the overhead.   Lamps of this type are not gimballed, because they are so large they would have to have a bracket that projects too far out from the bulkhead to make gimballing feasible.   These lamps usually come with shades, so that they look much like a small, 115-volt table lamp and are about the same size.   This type of lamp gives off so much heat that it can warm up a small cabin quickly, a considera-tion when you are deciding whether to use one in warm climates.

All pressure mantle lamps need periodic cleaning, and the mantles must be replaced frequently.   The glass globes on these lamps are quite large and subject to breakage because of the difficulty in stowing the lamp.

Pressure lamps that use gasoline should *never* be used aboard any boat!   There are propane pressure lamps that are safe enough if the propane cartridge isn't leaking, but it is a rather expensive form of lighting for day-to-day use.

Battery-powered lamps sometimes are adequate for cabin lighting on a limited basis, but they should not be considered for long-term use.   If you want sufficient light, there always is a huge drain on the battery, which can wear out within hours.   A well-found boat should have four types of lighting: 12-volt, kerosene, and battery-powered lights; and candles to use when everything else fails.   Big, fat candles that can stand on their own bases are best.

Running lights usually are included with any boat you buy, new or used.   They normally are electric, and they are run off the 12-volt battery system.   If the running lights are used on long offshore passages, the engine will have to be run periodically to charge the batteries, even though there is only a slight drain.   The only way to avoid this is to use kerosene running lamps, which are very expensive.   They have been known to blow out, so they must be checked constantly.   Most sailors don't use the running lights at all in midocean; they reserve them for use near land or when in shipping lanes.

Aside from the cabin and running lights, there are other special-purpose lights that are nice to have, such as spreader lights. These are invaluable when it is dark and something has to be tended to on deck at sea, or in an anchorage.   In poorly lighted marinas, spreader lights make nice "porch" lights when guests are coming and going. There should be one light on each spreader. Most types can be angled to aim their beams wherever necessary; we have one angled forward and the other aft.

Consider putting a small, 12-volt, explosion-proof light in the engine compartment.   Even though it can't be directed to exactly where light is needed, it is better than no light at all.   To supplement this, you should have both 12-volt and 115-volt worklights with a long cord and hooks to hang them on in the area where you are working.

Small, out-of-the-way lights could also be installed in cockpit lazarettes, so that you can locate needed items and seacocks in a hurry without bothering to find a flashlight.

If you have trouble seeing at night, there are small, shielded, red or white lights that can be used as night lights, since they cause only a slight battery drain. These can be installed in various walkways and also low in the cockpit, so they will not disturb the helmsman's night vision.

We know of many yachtsmen who use their masthead light for an anchor light, but why drain the ship's battery when there are so many lights that can be used that have their own batteries? Our anchor light is one of these. It uses a six-volt battery and has never failed us in the 12 years we have been using it. A kerosene lamp used as an anchor light has the same disadvantages that kerosene running lamps do: they can blow out and they need more maintenance.

There should be plenty of waterproof flashlights in handy locations throughout the boat, with spare batteries and bulbs for each of them. At least one of the flashlights should have a beam that carries a minimum of a half-mile. The boat's lighting inventory should also include a bright, long-range, 12-volt spotlight. We have one that plugs into a special waterproof, 12-volt outlet in the cockpit, since that is usually where you will be when the need arises for a spotlight.

VII. THE GALLEY

AND ITS EQUIPMENT

There are many theories about where a boat's galley should be located. Unless a boat is very old and the galley is still in the fo'c's'le, don't let the galley location determine whether you buy the boat or not. Some say the galley should be amidships, because there is less motion there. We like the galley to be right by the main companionway, where it usually is light and well ventilated, and easy to get out of in case of fire. (No matter where the galley is in your boat, figure out how you would get out if you had a fire there.)

The galley should be compact enough so that you can strap yourself in to cook in extremely rough weather. There should be plenty of counter-top work space for the kind of cooking you will be doing. If there isn't enough work space, perhaps you can install a hinged counter top that folds up for use and folds flat against a bulkhead when not needed.

One of the best galleys we ever had was in a 30-footer we once owned. The stove was recessed so it was below the level of the counter. It had a "lid" that fit over it and was hinged on the forward side. When this lid was in place over the stove, it formed a continuation of the counter top. When the lid was opened to expose the stove, it was flush with the counter top and formed a flat work area at the side of the stove. It was held up by a small bracket that folded out from the galley bulkhead.

Another way to gain work space is to have sliding leaves that double as bread or cutting boards and can be pulled out when needed. These take up so little space that they can be installed nearly anywhere.

Fortunately, most modern boats have plenty of working and stowage space in their galleys, but usually the spaces must be

111

modified to some degree to suit the needs of the cook.   Even though there may be plenty of storage space, many of the individual storage areas are too cavernous to be of real use.   They should be partitioned to accommodate the foods and utensils you will be using.   It won't do to have to move everything on top to get to things on the bottom, no matter how rarely the bottom items are used.   Anything stored in a big open area can rattle and bang and sometimes break when at sea or when the boat is hit by a wake at dock.

Decide what you are going to put in each locker, and construct the partitions accordingly.   This sounds easy, but just when you have decided on an arrangement, you are bound to think of a more workable one.   It takes many months of living aboard to determine the best way to stow anything. We are *still* working on some of our lockers.

When stowing something in a locker, in the galley, or anywhere else, consider whether it will land in your lap if you have to open the locker while heeling.   We didn't think of this when we stowed some of the galley items when we first moved aboard.   One blustery, cold day underway, we did not have soup for lunch, because taking one can of soup out of that locker meant about 25 other cans of food would have spilled out. Luckily we realized what would happen before we opened the locker. All lockers should have a guard rail on each shelf, even if there is a door, and they all should have doors.   Open shelves in the galley or anywhere else in any boat are worthless.   Even a low rail holds most things if the angle of heel is not too great.

Only the tiniest of lockers is best left without a partition or shelf of some kind.   Most galley items are fairly small anyway. The dish and glass racks that are built into some boats usually are convenient and practical, although sometimes they are hung on bulkheads and give the galley a cluttered look.

Hooks are handy for cups, but they should be the type that has a spring steel closure over the open part to hold the cup so it will not slide off.   It is not a good practice to hang up pots and pans or skillets by their handles.   They are bound to swing and scar paint or brightwork.   In rough weather, they won't stay on their hooks.

The items used most frequently should be at the front of the most accessible lockers. Pack all lockers tightly: there should be no room left for things to slide or fall over.

Because space is limited in most galleys, there usually are lockers of some sort behind the stove.   Items needed from these lockers should be taken out before a stove using liquid fuel is lighted, because it is dangerous to reach over an open flame.   The worst galley arrangement is one with the sink located behind the stove.

The most important piece of galley equipment is the stove. It should be gimballed so it will always be level. We feel that if a stove is not in gimbals, it does not belong in any boat, at sea or dockside. There are many who do not share this opinion, because there are lots of ungimballed stoves around. Rails that grip pots securely on the burners are not enough — the stove also must be free to swing. When the boat is heeling excessively, the rails may keep the pot on the burner, but there is no way to keep the contents of the pot from spilling out. We mention a boat's heeling as the usual culprit in the galley, but we have been tied up at dockside and experienced wakes that make normal heeling seem mild. Even if you never intend leaving a dock, you had better find a wakeless berth or put the stove in gimbals.

If you ever venture out to sea, you will have to have some method of gimballed cooking when the going gets rough. If your regular stove is not gimballed, or even if it is, consider installing a Sea Swing stove for use in rough seas. This is a one-burner unit with high sides all around the burner (Fig. 7-1). A pot no more

Figure 7-1. Whiffle's *double-gimballed Sea Swing stove with Optimus silent kerosene burner installed to replace original roarer burner.*

than 6½ inches in diameter fits snugly into it and will not fall out
if the stove can swing freely. Regular boat stoves can only be
gimballed athwartships, but the Sea Swing is fully gimballed — both
athwartships and fore and aft. The burner can be obtained for use
with alcohol, kerosene, or a can of Sterno. The stove itself is
rather cumbersome, but its bracket is small, so it can be mounted
nearly anywhere, and the stove can be unshipped and stowed away
when not needed.

The most common boat stove in the United States is a pressure
type fueled with alcohol. It is clean, efficient, relatively safe, expensive to buy initially (but then, all boat stoves are expensive —
most of them ridiculously so), and burns the most costly fuel. As
mentioned earlier, "marine" alcohol is selling for $8 a gallon.
"Other" alcohol can be found at about $4 a gallon. It makes no
difference to the "other" alcohol manufacturer whether you use
his fuel in a boat stove or not, but the manufacturers of the
"marine" alcohol claim you must use their product in your boat
stove or you will have all kinds of problems — 't'ain't so.

When we had alcohol stoves, we always bought the cheapest
alcohol we could find and never had trouble with it. It did not
clog, spit, sputter, or fail to burn, as we had been warned it would.
We always tried to purchase the alcohol in regular hardware stores
located far from the water. In a boating supply store, any alcohol
will be more expensive, whether it is labeled "for marine use" or
is the same brand you can buy in ordinary hardware stores.

If you decide on alcohol, you will have the largest selection of
stove models to choose from, whether you want to buy a new
stove or replace an old one. If you plan to cruise outside of the
United States for any length of time, you must be able to store all
the alcohol you will need, because it is virtually impossible to
find in most areas of the world, especially the Caribbean islands.
If you are able to locate alcohol in faraway places, its cost is
astronomical.

A stove that uses kerosene for fuel is the most practical for a
live-aboard cruising boat. It is a little dirtier than alcohol, but for
us its low cost more than offsets the gray film that will build up
over a period of time on the overhead above the stove. It cooks
food almost twice as fast as alcohol, thus making it even more
economical. And the faster the cooking, the less the cabin heats
up. Kerosene is available all over the world, although in many
places dirt must be filtered out of it before it is put into the tank.
Most of the fuel purchased in the United States is clean.

Both alcohol and kerosene stoves can be gimballed. They come
in one-, two-, or three-burner models. Some of the two- and
three-burner models also have ovens. Because alcohol burns at a
lower temperature than kerosene, it takes longer to warm up an

alcohol oven, thus using more fuel; depending on the oven's insulation, it may never be able to attain the higher temperatures.

Alcohol generally is considered to be the safer of the two fuels, just because the fire it creates can be extinguished with water; however, it is four times more flammable than kerosene, so the risk of fire is greater with alcohol. Kerosene fires can be extinguished easily with a fire extinguisher, which every galley should have handy anyway. A fire extinguisher is ready for use instantly, whereas it takes valuable time to draw enough water to put out an alcohol fire. (Some claim that water tends to spread an alcohol fire faster than it puts it out.) Both alcohol and kerosene have odors that are objectionable to some, but since the cooking time is shorter with kerosene, its odor is not around as long. Odorless kerosene can be burned in a stove as well as in lamps. Even with the additional processing necessary to remove the odor, kerosene still is cheaper than alcohol.

There are two types of kerosene burners available: silent and roarer. Most recent and new stoves are equipped with the silent type, although the kerosene Sea Swing has a roarer burner. If you plan to buy a new or used kerosene stove, it would be wise to find out what kind of burner it has. The roarer burner is aptly named; it sounds like a blowtorch when it is lighted, and it makes for very noisy cooking.

All kerosene burners need more maintenance than those using alcohol. The roarer burners need cleaning a little less often than the silent type, but the cleaning is done so easily with the modern self-pricking burners that this reason should not prevent you from getting the silent type. Cleaning the burner means turning the handle counterclockwise as far as it will go, then turning it back again. We make it a habit to clean every burner each time it is used, and we have no problems. Some older burners are not self-pricking, and they must be cleaned with a special tool.

Most kerosene stoves must be primed with a small amount of alcohol to get the burner hot enough to vaporize the kerosene so that it will ignite. It is only a minor nuisance to have to carry two kinds of fuel, and it is not necessary to carry a lot of alcohol. A gallon of alcohol goes a long way when it is used only for priming. Optimus has recently introduced a kerosene stove with a "quick lighter unit" that does away with alcohol priming entirely. This stove is not available with an oven.

Flare-ups are another reason many consider kerosene undesirable, but if the burner is primed with enough alcohol to get it good and hot, there never will be a flare-up. Fill the priming cup all the way to the top and let it burn until there is barely a flame left, then open the valve for the kerosene; it will ignite instantly with no flare-up. If the flame does not light the burner because it has burned too low, use a spark gun held at the burner and pull the trigger as you open the valve. Many new stoves have a wick attached to the side of the burner. When all the alcohol in the priming cup is burned up, a small flame appears at the top of the wick next to the burner. When this flame appears, the valve is opened and the flame ignites the kerosene. We went through the usual period of adjustment to kerosene and its idiosyncrasies; but once we got the hang of it, we found it was as easy to use as any other fuel, and we are very satisfied.

If you should have a flare-up, which is always possible until you learn to use a liquid-fuel stove, consider that the flame may flare up to the overhead. Keep flammable items out of that area. Paper towels, curtains, or anything else that is apt to catch fire should be well removed from the stove.

Until a couple of years ago, kerosene stoves were not popular in the United States, and only a few manufacturers offered them. The incredible price increase for alcohol evidently made most of the manufacturers realize the need for stoves that would burn a low-cost fuel. Now nearly every major stove manufacturer offers a model that will burn kerosene. For many years, only Shipmate stoves, manufactured by Richmond Ring Company in Souderton, Pennsylvania, had a kerosene model with an oven, but this is no longer the case. The Optimus burner, which is manufactured in Sweden, is the burner used in all kerosene stoves.

There are several companies in Great Britain that make kerosene stoves, but none of the stoves has an oven. In Europe and many other parts of the world, kerosene is called "paraffin," and alcohol is referred to as "methylated spirits."

Stoves that use propane gas are becoming increasingly common on boats. They have been used in trailers and campers for years, and now they are seen more frequently on boats. Without a doubt, propane is the cleanest, easiest to use and quickest-cooking fuel. The fuel is inexpensive and relatively easy to come by, but it, too, has its drawbacks. The only reason we would not have it aboard is that the fumes are heavier than air, and if there were a leak, the highly explosive fumes would settle into the bilge. There is no way to get them out of there, short of blowing up the boat, and that is what usually happens anyway. The tiniest spark will set off the fumes, so an electric blower never can be used to suck fumes out of the bilge.

To be as safe as possible, propane installations must have the tanks either mounted on deck or located in a compartment that is vented at the bottom, so that any fumes that might escape are carried overboard. There must be shut-off valves at the tanks. There should also be a shut-off valve at the stove itself, in case the tank valves were to leak. Valves can vibrate open or closed when the engine is running or when you encounter heavy, rhythmic seas for an extended period. The proper procedure for using propane stoves must be followed closely every time the stove is used, or disaster surely will result. You cannot be absentminded or forgetful when using propane on a boat.

Propane is available nearly everywhere. Europeans have been using it for years, and it is becoming easy to obtain in the Caribbean. The tank should have a conveniently adequate capacity, and you should carry one or more spares, depending on the length of a voyage. In any case, you should have one spare, whether you cruise extensively or not. A propane stove can be gimballed if flexible tubing is used, but this type of installation creates another spot that must be checked constantly for leaks.

We filled our 2½-quart whistling teakettle with water, and heated it to the whistling stage with each of the above-mentioned fuels. All burners were turned to their maximum heat. The water boiled in 10 minutes with propane, 15 minutes with kerosene, 20 minutes on the electric stove, and 25 minutes with alcohol.

There still are some boats around with coal or wood stoves, but these are big, old-fashioned units, and they are used as much for heating the cabin as for cooking. Needless to say, in warm weather the cabin does not need to be heated, but it is unavoidable when these behemoths are fired up for cooking. Even diesel-fueled stoves are found occasionally. These are large, too, and they heat up the cabin in warm weather. They burn the same fuel that is used in a diesel engine. None of these stoves can be gimballed successfully. If you have a boat equipped with one of these large stoves, you should buy a small, quick-cooking type for most of the cooking.

Whenever we are at a marina, we cook exclusively with electricity. Electricity usually is included in the dockage fee; since you are paying for it anyway, use the electricity to conserve the other fuel you have to use when at sea or in an anchorage. Our two-burner electric stove fits inside the guard rails on top of the gimballed kerosene stove, so in effect, our electric stove also is gimballed. Ours has Calrod heating elements, just as a regular electric range does; they are completely adjustable to any temperature. Sears, Montgomery Ward, and J. C. Penney have excellent models that sell for about $25. They have a trim design and are good looking. Some of the cheap hot plates on the market are cumbersome and ugly, with poor-quality heating elements that cannot be regulated to any temperatures other than on and off.

We often use an electric skillet, and also a toaster oven. Electric cooking keeps the cabin cooler than cooking with other fuels, and if it is too hot for cooking in the cabin, the appliances can be used in the cockpit. Of course, if you have a generator, your electric appliances also can be used when you are not at dockside. If you have favorite appliances and plenty of room to store them, by all means have them aboard if you use them often enough. If you are in doubt as to which to keep and which to leave behind, bring aboard as many as you can. Then, after living aboard for awhile, you will be able to decide which ones you really want and need and which ones you can eliminate.

One couple we encountered had an all-electric kitchen. They had a three-burner electric stove with an oven (not gimballed), a blender, an electric coffee maker, a waffle iron, and a toaster. Even in a marina, they had to use their own generator when cooking because their stove's amperage requirement usually was too large to be carried by the marina's electrical system. In a peaceful anchorage, they had to start the generator to cook, even to heat water for a cup of coffee. Everything depended on the generator. In rough weather, they couldn't cook anything. You should always have two ways to cook, even if the back-up system is primitive or awkward.

New alcohol and kerosene stoves cost upwards of $300. Ungimballed propane stoves with ovens can be purchased in trailer supply stores for about $150.

Nearly everyone would like to have an oven; some galley cooks cannot function without them. If you have space and can afford it, a stove with an oven is the ideal arrangement. The oven can be used for storage when not in use. We keep the electric skillet in ours, but the space could be used for storing boxes of cereal or crackers, baking utensils, or pots and pans. The two-burner alcohol or kerosene stoves with ovens will fit into a space measuring about 21 inches deep, 24 inches high, and 24 inches wide. These measurements allow for the swing when gimballed.

Any gimballed stove with an oven must be able to be locked in place so it *cannot* swing when the oven door is opened. If the door is opened while the stove is swinging freely, anything in the oven will slide out. A barrel bolt is good for holding the stove in place (Fig. 7-2). Every time the oven door is opened, the locking device should be used to avoid accidents. If the oven door needs to be opened for checking progress during baking, lock the stove in place with the barrel bolt before opening the door, but use a pot holder: the bolt will be as hot as the oven. A hook and eye is another, but less satisfactory, device that can be used to keep the stove from swinging.

If you want an oven and do not have the space for one, you might consider an oven that fits on the stove top. There is a stainless-steel folding oven designed for use over an alcohol or kerosene burner. It has a thermometer on the door, and the temperature is controlled by the flame on the burner. It is not

insulated, so the whole oven will be as hot as the door thermometer indicates. Since it is designed to collapse flat for storing,
it is not especially sturdy when it is set up.   This oven is wide
enough for a nine-inch baking dish or pie tin. It costs about $35.
The oven will bake satisfactorily, but the temperature seems to
need constant regulation. This oven is very difficult to use without
burning yourself.   It is not practical if the boat is pitching or
rolling at all, even if the oven is on a gimballed stove.

If you do not have an oven, you still can do baking and roasting.
It is possible to bake delicious bread and cakes in a pressure
cooker. An electric skillet does a superb job of baking and roasting. It is possible to bake meat loaves, potatoes, and all types of
casseroles in a toaster oven.   You can even bake cookies, if you
have the patience to bake only six or eight at a time.

*Figure 7-2. Whiffle's gimballed Shipmate kerosene stove with barrel-bolt lock
to prevent stove from swinging when oven door is opened.*

Some live-aboards have a portable electric broiler/roaster oven in a size to suit their needs. Some of these ovens are quite large, and others have small interiors that will not hold a big turkey or roast. We thought we were the only ones who carried a ruler to the supermarket to measure the height of a roast or fowl to be sure it would fit into our electric skillet — until we saw a marina neighbor of ours doing the same thing one day. She said she had been measuring meat for years.

The pressure cooker has been favored by sea cooks for years, and rightly so. It probably is the most versatile single pot you can have. Under pressure, it is a roaster, baker, braiser, steamer, and stew and soup maker. Without the pressure control, it is a good sturdy saucepan with a lock-on lid. Some models also can be used for canning.

The cooking utensils you need can be determined only by you. Most people start out with too many, and eventually they weed out what they find they are not using. We moved aboard with three graduated sizes of heavy cast-iron skillets that had been well seasoned by nearly 15 years of use. On the boat they performed as well as they had on land, but they were so heavy to get out of the locker that we began finding excuses for not using them. We replaced them recently with two lightweight Teflon-coated skillets. A whistling teakettle is a good boat item, not because it whistles, but because it is a self-contained unit with no unattached lid that might fly off. Its opening is small, so water is not likely to spill out. One of our favorite items is a cast-iron waffle maker that fits over one burner on any type of stove. We wouldn't change it for an electric one — ever. The waffles it makes are superior to any we have ever had.

Pressure water in boats today is not at all as uncommon as it once used to be. Its advantages are obvious. The disadvantages are that you invariably use more water than if you have to pump it out by hand, and excessive use of the electric pressure pump will run down the batteries if the engine is not running. Neither of these situations would be good on an extended cruise; at dockside, there is no problem. Water tanks can be refilled when needed, and electricity always is available for charging the batteries.

There is no reason not to have pressure water if you want it, but it is not a good or safe idea to have pressure pumps as the only access to the water. At least one hand pump should be installed somewhere. One sink can have a pressure faucet and a hand pump, too. This is the arrangement we have on the galley sink (Fig. 7-3). The hand pump once came in very handy in an anchorage when the batteries were almost dead. Just recently, the pressure pump itself gave up the ghost, and we had to rely solely on the hand pump until we could locate and install a new pressure pump.

Figure 7-3. Galley sink on Whiffle *includes faucet for pressure water system and separate hand pump to draw water from tanks if electrically operated pressure system fails.*

When cruising, we almost never use the pressure water, since the hand pump is perfectly adequate; even at dockside, the hand pump gets a lot of use. It is wise to carry a spare hand pump; with constant use, even the best of them will wear out.

Almost all pressure water systems require that you turn on the faucet with one hand while you wet the other. On land, it does not matter if you let the water run while you wash the other hand. It is too wasteful to do it that way in a boat. We have a foot-operated push-button system for pressure water that lets you put both hands under the faucet, so only the water needed is used. The faucet is turned on, and the flow of water is started when the button is stepped on. This button, which is a standard horn button, is mounted on the floor board near each sink; it is wired into the existing pressure system (Fig. 7-4).

You can install an excellent water pumping system if you can find a place to buy a foot pump. The installation we saw was in an English boat, and the owner had obtained the foot pumps from a trailer supply company in England. We have never seen them for sale in the United States. All that is needed for this installation is a hollow length of pipe for the faucet. The pipe is curved so that the open end is over the sink and mounted in the counter at the edge of the sink. A flexible hose is attached to the pipe. The hose runs to the foot pump, the pedal of which is at the base of the counter. A hose from the water tank to the pump completes the installation. You get the same flow of water from this system as from the usual hand pump, but this one leaves both hands free. It is a good idea to recess the pedal under the counter slightly, so you will not step on it accidentally when working in the galley.

Another good idea has come to us from England. It is not uncommon to see two hand or two foot pumps on the same sink on British boats. One is for fresh water and the other for seawater. If the water you are sailing in isn't too dirty or polluted, the seawater pump frequently can be used in place of the tank water. If you are trying to conserve water, why draw fresh water and put salt into it for cooking, when seawater already has the salt in it? Just about everything can be washed in salt water as long as you

Figure 7-4. Special step built in galley area to eliminate standing on curved part of hull. Switch in corner operates pressure water.

give it a freshwater rinse. It is very convenient to be able to pump the seawater you want, instead of hauling it in over the side in a bucket. In the long run, seawater is bound to add to the conservation of the freshwater supply, because it is just as easy to use.

Most boat sinks are stainless steel, unless they are fiberglass and molded right into the counter unit. Both materials are easy to keep clean. The sink should be big enough to wash dishes in and large enough to get a big pot in under the faucet to fill with water. It should be at least six inches deep and have both a plug or other means for holding water and a waste strainer.

If the sink is not high enough above the waterline to allow natural drainage, a pump will have to be fitted so the sink can be pumped dry. Even a sink that drains by itself when the boat is level may have to be pumped out when a certain degree of heel is reached. Many people install a pump on the drain line whether the sink can drain without it or not. This arrangement prevents water from siphoning back into the sink when the boat is heeling; on a long passage, sometimes you are heeled over for days at a time.

Boards that fit over sinks to make them a continuation of the counter top might just as well be chucked overboard. There isn't any galley chore that does not involve the use of the sink sooner or later, so unless the sight of an open sink really offends you, you will be better off without these always-in-the-way, hard-to-stow boards. If your boat has a double sink with covering boards for each, one of them might be covered without its being too much of a nuisance.

This seems to be a good place to discuss drinking water. Every live-aboard boat should have tanks large enough to hold an adequate water supply, whether you go to sea or not, purely for convenience. We have known live-aboards who had to fill their tanks every two or three days while at dockside. They were not making an effort to conserve water, as they would have if they had been at sea. This might not seem like a problem, except that many marinas have water that you wouldn't want to put in your tanks. This is especially true in the South, where so much of the water is sulfur water. One winter in Florida, we had the misfortune to stay at a marina where this was quite a serious problem. Not only was there sulfur in the water, but there were also black and gray particles (we never found out what they were) that colored the water and settled to the bottom. It smelled and tasted terrible.

The people in the marina who had small-capacity tanks were forced to fill them with this stuff often and endure it as well as they could. Fortunately, we had just topped off our tanks before we had arrived for our planned six-week stay, and we did not run out of water. (Even if we aren't at all careful of how much water

we use, our 80 gallons will last us more than a month.) When we
felt we were getting low on water toward the end of our stay, we
took several jugs into town, filled them with the good water
available there, and then transferred this water to our tanks. This
is the most extreme example of bad water we have ever encountered, but there have been many other places where we have
decided not to top off our tanks because of unappealing water.
Our tanks impart no "tank" taste to the water, and we don't
want to put in any with its own bad taste. We always taste water
before putting any of it into the tank — after we pour some into a
clear glass to see if anything is floating in it.

If you are going offshore or to an area where fresh water is
scarce, you will have to plan your water consumption in advance.
If your tanks will not carry enough, they will have to be supple-
mented with plastic jugs, and places will have to be found to stow
them. If you only do coastal cruising, it still is a good idea to have
some three- or five-gallon jugs filled with good water. You may
have to put in at some "bad water" places when your tanks are
getting low.

If the water tanks in your boat are not "sweet" to begin with,
it will be very difficult to eliminate the tank taste. Water purifiers
or sweeteners normally won't help. The insides of the tanks usually
have to be coated with something that will not impart a taste to
the water, or the tanks will have to be replaced with ones made of
a more desirable material. In many fiberglass and steel boats, the
tanks are molded or welded in and are part of the hull, so it is not
easy to replace them. Sometimes it simply cannot be done.

New fiberglass tanks have the most undesirable taste, but it will
disappear as the boat gets older. If you cannot wait that long, you
will have to work out some method of getting the tank steam
cleaned. This is supposed to remove the taste, but we have never
talked to anyone who has used this method, so we have no way of
knowing how effective it is. If the tanks are removable, they can
be taken to an auto repair shop that does steam cleaning. If the
tanks are molded into the hull, as so many of them are, you will
have to devise some way to steam them on your own or live with
the taste until it goes away.

The design of many boats forces the galley slave to work with
his or her feet slanted at the point where the cabin sole meets the
turn of the bilge. Depending on how the cook is standing, one
foot is on a slant or the toes are pointing up at an uncomfortable
and unsafe angle. So it was on *Whiffle*, but only for a short
time. We built a small, raised platform out over the curved area so
that footing is level at all times (Fig. 7-4). We enclosed the two
open sides of the platform, and thus created a serendipitous
storage space underneath. Of the two boards that form the plat-

form, one is fixed and one is removable for access to the stowage area.   On boats with scanty headroom, this idea might not be practical, since our platform turned out to be four inches higher than the cabin sole.   But ducking your head slightly might be less unpleasant than having your feet slip out from under you, as ours used to do.

After a few weeks of trying to keep our large ice chest continuously cool with ice that, at that time, cost 60 cents for 12 pounds, we were convinced that we wanted mechanical refrigeration.   After we installed our refrigerator, we invited everyone in the marina to taste our first homemade ice cubes — liberally surrounded by the liquid of their choice.   Luckily it was a small marina.

Mechanical refrigeration systems on boats seems to enrage and then defeat many people who ordinarily are calm and intelligent. Some have been known to rip them out and do without. If they had installed the simplest system available, perhaps they would have had the same trouble-free operation we have had. The first thing needed for successful installation is a top-loading box. If you use an upright box, you will lose everything you have gained in the way of coldness every time the door is opened. It is not as easy to find and remove items from a top-loading box, but when the lid is opened, the food does not spill out, as it often does in the upright box, after the contents have been shuffled around by wakes or rough seas. The second requirement is a well-insulated box. When you have taken care of these two considerations, then you can begin to hope that your system will work efficiently.

In our top-loading, very-well-insulated box, we have installed a marine household-type, 115-volt refrigeration unit, which consists of a freezer compartment, a compressor, copper tubing to connect it all together, an electric cord to connect the thermostat switch to the compressor, and a cord to plug into the 115-volt system. The evaporator (freezer compartment) is installed in the box. The compressor can be installed wherever it is convenient and where it will have good air circulation.   Ours is in the forward end of the cockpit locker that is closest to the ice chest, although the compressor can be located as much as 12 feet away from the evaporator if necessary. The copper tubing, which is precharged with Freon at the factory, is attached; the thermostat/compressor/electrical connection is made and plugged into the 115-volt system; and then you can go out and buy ice cream and frozen food. Our freezer compartment holds nine standard ice-cube trays, and it keeps everything frozen.   Our unit, which is the nine-to-twelve-cubic-foot Marvel brand, can be purchased for under $200. We spent only half a day installing it.

A system such as our 115-volt unit can be had for only 12-volt operation, or it can be obtained as a combination 12- and 115-volt unit. The latter type is the most expensive. We converted our existing ice chest to a refrigerator, but if you cannot or do not want to use the ice chest, other types of refrigerators can be purchased with the freezer compartment and compressor all in one unit. Some of these look like regular household refrigerators, except that they are much smaller. Most of them are upright models, but a few are top-opening.

There are small freezers that can be installed in addition to the refrigerator, if you have room. Also available are portable refrigerator/freezers that can be plugged into either the 12-volt or the 115-volt system. For the full-time live-aboard's needs, many of these units are really too small, but one could be used to supplement another refrigerator. Norcold manufactures a compact, one-cubic-foot, top-loading model that runs off a 12-volt or a 115-volt system, and it can be used either as a refrigerator or a freezer.

A refrigeration system that runs on 115 volts dockside and 12 volts elsewhere, might seem ideal for a boat. It probably would be, except for one thing: when running on 12 volts, the refrigerator requires so many amps to cool it properly that an elaborate bank of three, four, or more batteries is needed to run it for a reasonable period of time. All these batteries need to be charged with a larger alternator or generator than might normally come as standard equipment on the engine.

The best type of refrigeration when a boat is not at dockside is the eutectic holding-plate system. This type is the most expensive to install ($1,000+), but it will keep the box colder longer with less energy than any other type. At dockside it runs off 115 volts; otherwise it runs directly off the engine with a belt from the engine to the compressor, or with a standard generator. One to two hours of running the compressor will cool the holdover plates enough to keep the box cold for 24 to 48 hours.

Propane and kerosene refrigerators are not satisfactory for boats, since they must be level to operate efficiently. They generate a lot of heat and there is always an open flame to worry about.

We know of many live-aboards who do not have mechanical refrigeration. Like so many of us on limited budgets, they cannot afford ice, so they simply do without cooling of any kind. You will have to decide for yourself whether you want a refrigerator or not. Having ours certainly has made our life easier and more comfortable, but we would do without it, too, on long offshore passages and extended voyages.

If you have a freezer, you always must be conscious of the fact that it could break down. At dockside, you can go out and easily buy more food. At sea, a breakdown might be a serious problem if you did not have enough foresight to take along plenty of canned goods to replace any ruined food.

For dockside use, especially for the refrigerator, we have installed a simple power-failure alarm system that buzzes if the 115-volt power goes off. An incredible number of boating clods think nothing of unplugging *you* to plug *themselves* in. We hope the idiot will hear the buzzer and realize he has done something wrong. If he doesn't hear it, we will. Then we will unplug *him*.

If you are going to stick with only the ice box that is built into the boat, let's hope the box isn't too big. Some of the larger chests need lots of ice to keep them cool. Before we converted ours, it held 200 pounds of ice and was much too big for use as an ice box. A small ice chest or refrigerator is better, because it is more economical to keep cool.

The ice chest should drain overboard or into the bilge. Some fiberglass chests are molded into the hull and have no drain. If yours is one of these, install some sort of drain, or resign yourself to bailing out the box every day. It is a simple job to drill a hole in the lowest corner of the chest and attach a small hose that runs into the bilge, where the water can be pumped out easily.

If we are anchoring out night after night and do not want to bother running the 115-volt generator to cool the refrigerator, we often use it only as an ice box. We are always prepared for this eventuality. Since our ice chest is so large, we always keep the bottom lined with seven or eight 46-ounce cans of fruit juice. On top of these cans, and tucked in odd corners, are a few cans of soda pop. When these are used, they are replaced as soon as possible. The cans are only put in when they can be cooled by electric refrigeration at dockside. All the remaining space is filled with ice, except for the space taken up by the normally refrigerated items we carry, such as butter, milk, and mayonnaise.

At first we bought ice to fill any empty spaces, but now we make our own ice when we have electricity. We can get six meatloaf-size pans into our freezer compartment, and we use them to make our own block ice, which lasts longer than cubes. We chip drink-size pieces from the blocks when we need them. We keep making ice blocks until we have enough to fill all the vacant spaces. Then we freeze six more and leave them in the freezer compartment. You get more efficiency from your ice chest by putting more into it.

Making our own ice justifies what we pay for dockage, in some instances, since we don't have to buy ice, because we use the electricity on the dock to make it. The heavy, disposable aluminum-foil pans are satisfactory for freezing the blocks. They are good for many freezings before they become too wrinkled to use or develop pinhole leaks. Our homemade block ice lasts for several days, even in warm weather.

Ice is not readily available in any of the Caribbean islands, and it's expensive if you do find it. Nor is dockside electricity common. If you are planning a long stay in the islands, don't count on having any kind of cooling. Buy your foods accordingly.

VIII. THE ELECTRICAL SYSTEM

Electricity contributes so much to our comfort and convenience ashore that there is no reason not to enjoy it when afloat as well, especially if you are living aboard.

The main electrical system on most boats today is 12 volts DC. These days, even the smallest boats normally have a 12-volt system built in as a matter of course, and the price of this system usually is included in the base price of the boat. If a 115-volt system is available as optional equipment, there is an extra charge.

The heart of the 12-volt system is the battery bank, which consists of one or more batteries wired in parallel. Each battery has an ampere-hour rating, and all the batteries should have the same rating. They should also be the same age. If you have a two-battery bank and one battery wears out, replace both of them.

The batteries are wired in parallel so that the ampere-hour rating will be accumulative. Two 75 ampere-hour batteries, wired in parallel, have a total of 150 ampere-hours in the battery bank.

The size of the battery bank you need will depend on the size and number of lights and other electrical equipment you intend to run off the batteries. We have an old tube-model VHF radio that uses 4.8 amps on stand-by (receiving) and 8.5 amps for transmitting. This means that with a two-battery bank, with a total capacity of 150 ampere-hours, approximately 31.2 hours of monitoring the radio would drain the batteries completely. This is purely theory, since the radio would be affected by the accompanying voltage drop and would probably cease to function long before the 150 ampere-hour capacity was used up.

This same example can be applied to navigation lights. *Whiffle* has two running lights and a stern light, each of which draws .5 amp. We could operate the navigation lights for approximately

100 hours before charging the batteries, if the navigation lights were the only drain on the battery during that time.

The best way to figure out the battery size needed is to add up the ampere rating roughly for each of the electrical items you intend to use in a given time. Then multiply that total by the number of hours you think they will be used between battery charges. This will give you a rough idea of the total number of ampere-hours your battery bank will need. We have found that an overnight passage using the navigation lights, compass light, some cabin lights, and periodic monitoring of the radio can put a considerable drain on a 150-ampere-hour system. It is easy to understand why many people use oil lamps exclusively for their lighting needs on extended sea voyages; however, for coastal cruising, electric lights are better for both convenience and trouble-free operation.

The battery bank should be located where you can reach it easily to check the water level in the batteries; they should be checked weekly. The batteries should be stored in a container where they are protected and held securely in place above the normal bilge water level. No salt water should be allowed to get to the batteries. The combination of battery acid and salt water produces chlorine, a poisonous gas. Adequate ventilation is necessary, too, since batteries, when they are charging, emit a very explosive gas that must have room to dissipate.

Close to the battery box should be a master switch capable of handling the full amperage load of the entire battery bank. This should be located on the ungrounded conductor, or plus (+) side, of the battery, and as close to the battery terminal connection as practicable, so that the current can be cut off in an emergency. The switches should be vapor-proof; they occasionally will serve as battery selector switches (Fig. 8-1). A selector switch gives you the option of using one battery at a time. One battery can be reserved for engine starting, and the other used for the cabin lights and other electrical equipment, or both batteries can be used together. Since the batteries are charged by the engine, the indicator on the switch can be set to whichever battery needs charging. To avoid burning out the alternator, never turn the switch from one position to another while the engine is running.

A fuse or circuit breaker should be installed after the master switch for each circuit on the boat. For your own safety, all wiring should conform to SAE (Society of Automotive Engineers) standards. Follow their recommendations for the gauge and insulation of each circuit.

We like to have as many appliances and lights of the 12-volt type as possible. We have installed special 12-volt outlets throughout the boat, so we can use this equipment wherever it is convenient (Fig. 8-2). We have one such outlet in the forward cabin,

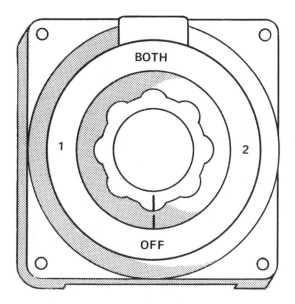

Figure 8-1. *Twelve-volt battery-selector master switch. With appropriate setting, either one or both batteries can be used or charged.*

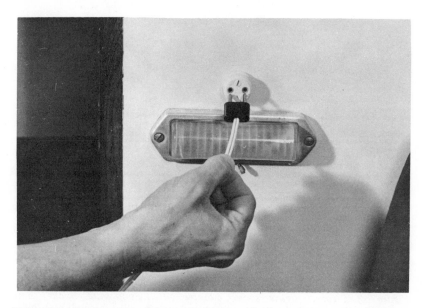

Figure 8-2. *Twelve-volt outlet and plug at end of appliance cord. Different-size prongs ensure proper polarization of DC appliances.*

one in the head, and four in the main cabin. One in the main cabin is near the companionway, so we can use 12-volt equipment in the cockpit if we wish to do so.

The outlets are made in England, but they can be purchased in the United States from West Products. They take a plug with two round prongs. One of the prongs is larger than the other, to ensure proper polarization; it is impossible for them to be plugged in the wrong way. Many items that are run off DC circuits will not work unless they are plugged in with the correct polarity.

Every year brings more appliances and tools that use 12-volt power. The Sears Mobile Home Catalog offers, among other things, a 12-volt hand mixer and an electric shaver. Sanders, drills, and soldering irons are available in 12 volts from many sources; and 12-volt televisions, radios, tape and cartridge players, fans, spotlights, and vacuum cleaners are easy to obtain.

In many American-built boats with both a 12-volt DC and 115-volt AC system, the manufacturers have seen fit to use the same type of outlet for both — the standard outlet that accepts a plug with two flat prongs. A tiny label usually identifies the voltage of each outlet. Unfortunately, the labels can fall off, or you can make the mistake of plugging a DC appliance into an AC outlet, and vice versa. You run the risk of electrical shock, appliance

Figure 8-3. Cigarette-lighter socket adapter with 12-volt plug. Socket can be wrapped with electrical tape or, as shown here, installed in small plastic box, which is available at electronic-supply stores.

damage, or a nonworking item. There is no way to identify the proper polarity with these plugs and outlets, short of marking them with tape or a pen, and these markings rarely last long. The above is an awkward, inconvenient, and extremely unsafe method of electrical installation that ought to be discontinued and replaced by a better system.

The only standard 12-volt plug that is common in the United States is the type that fits into the receptacle for an automotive cigarette lighter. Most of the above-mentioned tools and appliances come with the cigarette-lighter plug, and to use them on a boat would necessitate the installation of several automotive cigarette lighters. Instead of using this expensive and complicated solution, simply cut off the cigarette-lighter plug, and replace it with the West two-pronged plug. A word of caution: although most of these cigarette-lighter plugs are only the electrical connection, some of them contain fuses for the appliance. If there is a fuse incorporated into the plug, do not replace it; make an adapter that has a West plug on one end and a cigarette-lighter socket on the other end (Fig. 8-3). You can then use the appliance wherever you have installed a West outlet. In the case of a radio or tape player that is a nine-volt unit, you will have to have a step-down transformer to utilize the 12-volt outlet (Fig. 8-4). These adapters are available in any radio or electronics supply store.

Any 12-volt DC system is only as good as the means of charging its batteries. A boat should have a generator or alternator with enough amperage capacity to charge the batteries, after moderate

Figure 8-4. Six/nine-volt radio and/or cassette-player adapter, which can be plugged into cigarette-lighter socket and used with 12-volt system.

use, with only one to two hours of engine operation. Alternators are more efficient, and they will charge faster than a generator, but a generator will do a good job if it is large enough.

If you think your alternator or generator is not charging the batteries as quickly as it should, perhaps the voltage regulator can be set for a higher charging rate. Usually generators and alternators are capable of delivering more amps than the voltage regulator allows. Adjusting the voltage regulator is tricky, so have a competent mechanic do it.

Because many live-aboards spend a good part of their time at dockside and use their 12-volt cabin lights and other 12-volt systems, it is necessary to have a means of charging the batteries other than by running the engine. Charger/converters are available to keep the batteries charged automatically (without overcharging, to ensure longer battery life). These units also provide the power to run 12-volt lights, radios, pumps, and other 12-volt equipment.

Our charger/converter is a small 10-amp unit that we installed along with our 115-volt system just after we moved aboard. It has been one of our most useful pieces of equipment. For a time, our generator was not charging the batteries properly, and after a couple of days at anchor, they were low and not getting a full charge from running the engine. Until we replaced the generator's brushes, the cause of the problem, we would tie up at a dock every other day or so, plug in the 115-volt electricity, and the batteries would be brought up to full strength in minutes from the charger/converter. The only effort required of us was plugging it in.

Whiffle has a separate battery for starting the engine that is charged by its own separate engine generator. This arrangement is a good one, provided that you have a means for monitoring the state of charge in the battery. Each generator or alternator should have its own ammeter for checking the charging rate. We also like having a battery-condition meter for each battery bank. Since a measurement of voltage potential is an indication of battery charge, these meters (which are an expanded-scale voltmeter reading between 10 and 15 volts) indicate the percentage of charge in each battery and tell whether the batteries need charging or not. Battery failure can be anticipated, and avoided, by checking these meters regularly.

Sometimes the engine battery needs to be topped off with a small charge after it has sat idle for awhile. We can charge this battery, as well as the cabin batteries, with the charger/converter. All that is needed is a double-pole, double-throw switch (of a suitable amperage rating) wired between the charger/converter and each battery bank. For charging, you simply set the switch to the engine battery position and let the battery recharge itself. Then you switch it back to the usual cabin battery setting.

To be really comfortable, every cruising live-aboard boat should be equipped with a 115-volt AC system of some sort, and it should be more sophisticated than just an extension cord run out from the cabin over to the dock. The convenience of an outlet in the cabin is well worth the effort and cost of installing a proper system, not to mention the fact that it is necessary for such amenities as refrigeration.

Such a system should consist of a three-conductor, grounding-type, shore-power inlet receptacle with a suitable watertight protective cover (Fig. 8-5), a main shore-power disconnect, two-pole circuit breaker of suitable capacity, which usually is 30 amps, and the standard three-prong outlet receptacles mounted in the cabin. Ideally, if more than one outlet is used in the cabin, a 15-amp circuit breaker should be provided for each one, as well as for any other equipment that is wired into the system.

Proper installation of the built-in system helps provide protection against electrical shock for people on the boat and people in the water who might be in contact with the boat, as well as those in contact with both the boat and grounded objects ashore.

Figure 8-5. Thirty-amp, 115-volt, 3-conductor, grounding-type, shore-power inlet receptacle with watertight cover. (Photo courtesy Harvey Hubbell, Inc.)

The amperage capacity of the shore-power cable should be greater than the amperage rating of the boat's shore-power receptacle. The heavier gauge minimizes the voltage drop that occurs between the shore and the boat. Sometimes you may have to use an extension cable of 25 or even 50 feet in addition to your regular shore cable, and this will cause even more of a voltage drop. The heavier the gauge, the less the drop. Do not make the mistake, as so many have, of installing a 30-amp receptacle and using lightweight wire for the shore connection. The shore cable should be able to reach from the boat's receptacle at least 10 feet beyond either the bow or stern, whichever is farthest from the receptacle.

We use three-conductor wire of at least 10 gauge for all our dock cables and our 50-foot extension (Fig. 8-6). We have a 30-amp, 115-volt system, which is the minimum amperage for a good live-aboard boat. Since your electricity needs will vary from season to season, and the shoreside installations vary from marina to marina, a 30-amp circuit will provide an ample reserve for electric cooking, heaters, and air conditioners. However, many marinas are not wired for 30-amp, three-conductor grounded service, so you should have an adapter that allows you to plug into a 15-amp, three-conductor grounded dockside outlet (Fig. 8-7). You will have use for this adapter in more marinas than not.

Even when you stay at marinas with only 15-amp service, you can still enjoy all your appliances, such as toasters and air conditioners, if you remember to use them only one or two at a

Figure 8-6. Ten-gauge, 3-conductor, 115-volt, shore-power cable. (Photo courtesy Harvey Hubbell, Inc.)

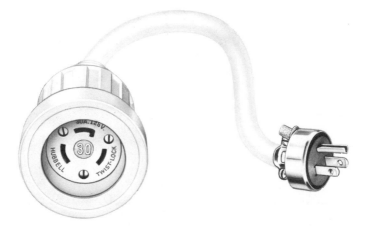

Figure 8-7. Hubbell adapter, which converts 30-amp, 115-volt, 3-conductor twist-lock plug to 15-amp, 3-conductor plug. (Photo courtesy Harvey Hubbell, Inc.)

time.   Unplug or turn off a high-amperage appliance when you want to use another appliance that draws many amps, so you won't load the circuit with more than 15 amps at one time.

One friend, who owned a clamp-on type of ammeter (a device for measuring the AC amperage of a given circuit), helped us measure the amperage load of each of our electrical appliances. With this knowledge, we determined what appliances could be used together or would have to be used alone. Sometimes we have to turn off the heater before we make toast or use the electric skillet. These simple precautions eliminate a lot of chasing around the dock trying to locate the circuit breaker or a new fuse. It seems to be a rule around marinas that when a fuse blows, all the marina employees have just left for home five minutes beforehand and won't be back 'til morning; and, of course, they locked the door to the building where the fuse box is located. If you do a little advance planning, you can use all the appliances you need, and you will never be the one who blows the fuse.

We have installed a 115-voltmeter next to the master switch, and it is surprising to see the voltage variations from marina to marina. In one old marina with ancient wiring, we were getting only 90 volts, but often we have had as much as 130 volts. If we are in a place where the voltage is low, we are more cautious about using too many appliances at the same time, since low voltage could be an indication of inadequate wiring.

We have found that many marina owners, after experiencing overloaded circuits and blown fuses, have "solved" their problems by putting in higher amperage fuses. They don't bother with re-wiring the whole marina, and, more times than not, the existing wiring is inadequate for the increased load. Fuses don't blow in a situation like this; fires start. Plugs burn, and the wiring often gets so hot that it burns, too.

In some of the older marinas, the electrical receptacle still consists of two-prong outlets without any grounding conductor. In such places, we use a standard three-hole ground adapter that fits into the two-prong outlet. A grounding wire comes attached to the adapter. To this we attach a length of wire and run it to the nearest good ground we can find, such as a water faucet or a pipe in the ground. FOR OBVIOUS REASONS, NEVER USE A FUEL LINE PIPE AS A GROUND. You must make certain that the ground you choose is a true ground. For instance, don't use a metal faucet that is attached to a plastic pipe or a rubber hose. We come across ungrounded outlets so often that we carry a 50-foot length of 12-gauge wire for this purpose. It has a battery clip on one end, so it can be attached easily to the ground (Fig. 8-8).

Figure 8-8. Fifteen-amp plug shown here adapts 2-prong outlet for use with 3-prong plug. Two extra lengths of 12-gauge wire are for grounding 115-volt systems in marinas with older-type 2-prong outlets. If longer wire is needed, 2 lengths of wire can be attached with solderless spade terminals.

When using a ground adapter, we check the polarity by using a Hubbell outlet circuit tester. This device has three small neon lights that light up in different combinations to show whether a circuit is wired correctly or is faulty (Fig. 8-9). We check every circuit we plug into, including 30-amp twist-lock receptacles, by using the tester in one of the outlets in the boat as soon as we are hooked up to the dockside outlet. Since we have a steel boat, we are fussier about electrical connections than most people need to be. We have to be especially careful about electrical shocks and corrosion. A "bad" or improper electrical condition can cause severe corrosion damage to a metal hull in a short time.

Not long ago, a marina owner, an elderly man who probably thought he had seen everything, watched us run our 50-foot grounding wire into a nearby shed and up over the rafters to a sink faucet on the far side. He said, as if his feelings were hurt, "Nobody else ever thought my electricity wasn't good enough for them." We explained that we had a steel boat and had to be extra-careful, etc., but he still walked away shaking his head and mumbling.

We think every boat-home benefits from a 115-volt AC generator of some kind. The sailing purists will disagree with us, of course, but some of them don't think a sailboat should have an engine, either. When you buy a boat, she may come with a generator. If

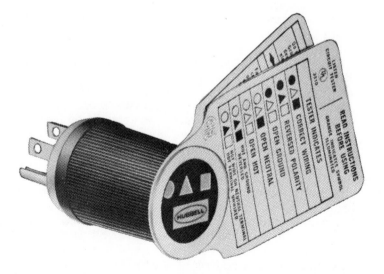

Figure 8-9. Hubbell 5200 Outlet Circuit Tester for testing polarity. It also indicates faulty conditions in 115-volt AC electrical circuits. (Photo courtesy Harvey Hubbell, Inc.)

she does, it probably will be the most common type; the AC generator has its own engine and is completely independent from the main engine. It has its own cooling and exhaust system with the resultant seacocks and exhaust ports. It also has its own electrical starting system, which may or may not require its own battery.

The larger generators can power 115-volt refrigerators and freezers, large air conditioners, heaters, electric stoves, or electric ovens when you are away from dockside hookups. If this type of generator does not come with the boat when you buy her, you might want to install one later. There may be room to install the unit itself, but there also must be room enough around it for good air circulation. It must have the same ventilation as every engine must have to run properly, or, for that matter, to run at all. Independent generators such as these are expensive. The small units cost about $1,200. The installation charges will have to be considered, too, and it is a costly process when it is done by a yard.

Even if you have a good, high-capacity AC generator, don't make the mistake of switching to total electric living. Generators break down and fail just as often as other mechanical devices. If you have the luck that most of us have, the most sophisticated equipment always will break down out in the boondocks, where service is impossible. Don't depend on a generator for too much. It should be only an extra tool to use when necessary.

When installing an AC generator, put in a unit that uses the same fuel as the main engine. Even if the main engine is a diesel, you now can have a generator powered by the same fuel. Until recently, this was not possible, but there now are excellent small, one-cylinder diesel-engine generators in 1½- and three-kilowatt sizes. We once looked at a boat that had a 110-horsepower diesel engine to run the boat and a six-kilowatt, gasoline-operated generator. Ridiculous! One wonders what ever possessed the man, since he had plenty of money and plenty of space to install a diesel generator.

There are other types of generators that might be more satisfactory for your own needs. There are small, portable units, as well as 115-volt AC generators driven by the boat's main propulsion engine. The portable units are available in sizes ranging from a tiny 350-watt output to those with a 1500-watt output. They are all powered by two-cycle gasoline engines with built-in fuel tanks and will run for several hours without refueling. Their capacity is adequate for power tools, pumps, and some appliances. Most of these units also are equipped to provide 12-volt DC power for battery charging.

When an acquaintance of ours is at anchor, he places his portable generator in his dinghy to keep the noise as far away as possible. He runs his small 115-volt refrigerator with it, and he reports that it is just like having dockside power. It appears that he is going to a lot of trouble to get electric power, but his is a good solution for cutting down the generator noise.

Generators powered by the main propulsion engine are of two types. One, the Auto-Gen, has a sophisticated means of regulating the generator's speed for constant 60-cycle, 115-volt AC, regardless of the speed (rpm) of the engine. Small units of this type cost about $600. They will deliver 3,000 to 4,000 watts and are capable of running most electrical equipment within this range.

The other type of generator that runs from the main engine has no control over the voltage or cycles per second, other than the speed at which the engine is operated. We have installed this type primarily because of its low cost ($100) and its relatively high output (3,000 watts). This generator is designed to deliver 115-volt AC at 60 cycles when the generator is turning at 3600 rpm. Originally, we selected 1200 rpm as the speed at which we wanted to run the engine when the generator was in use. This was the closest we could get to idling speed and still have the potential for forward motion. Since the pulley on the generator was three inches in diameter, we used a nine-inch pulley on the engine crankshaft, giving us 115 volts at 1200 rpm. This pulley was specially machined to be bolted on the front of the other belt pulleys. It was combined with them, then balanced at the machine shop. The generator itself is mounted on the engine bed and is driven by a belt from the engine. A voltmeter is mounted in the cockpit and monitored as the engine speed is adjusted to the proper rpm, so that the generator is delivering 115 volts.

Our main reason for installing a generator in the first place was to run the refrigerator just enough to keep food from spoiling when we were at anchor for a few days. We picked the 1200-rpm speed because the engine, at that speed, was much quieter than at a higher rpm, and it would be less disturbing to us and those around us in a quiet anchorage. We have changed our thinking lately and have modified the generator accordingly.

After we hit upon the idea of making our own ice for packing the ice chest, we found that we rarely needed to run the refrigerator at anchor. The ice alone kept the box cool enough for several days. We put a larger pulley on the generator, so that it now delivers 115 volts at 2000 rpm — our normal cruising speed. If we are motoring, we do not have to cut our speed when we want to run the refrigerator. If we have been anchored out for two or three days, we need an hour or two of running at 2000 rpm to recharge the batteries anyway, and we can turn on the refrigerator at the same time. If we are sailing and need to run the refrigerator, running the engine will give us a nice boost in speed. All the time the refrigerator is on, we are making more ice to replace what has melted.

The proper way to modify our generator to conform to our new way of thinking would have been to have another, smaller pulley made to replace the one mounted on the crankshaft. But that would have meant another machining charge and much time spent, again, installing the pulley so that it was in balance. So, instead of getting a smaller engine pulley made, we found a larger, ready-made pulley to replace the three-inch one on the generator itself. It doesn't matter that we found it in a junk yard and that it came out of a 1931 Lincoln. It works.

Both of the engine-powered generators have 12-volt DC exciter fields and draw about 15 amps at 12 volts. This means the DC alternator or generator must be capable of handling this load, in addition to maintaining the batteries. The 12-volt DC circuit should have a double-pole, single-throw switch so you can completely disconnect the field wires from the AC generator. This allows the generator to free-wheel when it is not in use. A double-pole, double-throw selector switch of 30-amp capacity should be used on all 115-volt AC circuits, so that *only* dockside power or *only* the generator is connected to the boat's system at any one time. Any other arrangement eventually will damage the system.

We installed an on-off switch for the refrigerator, as well as a small, red pilot light so we can tell, at a glance, when the refrigerator is on. The switch is used mainly when we are tied up and the dockside power has a very low voltage. When the refrigerator goes on, the initial surge is about eight amps. It wouldn't do to have the refrigerator go on, in a low-voltage situation, if we were using the toaster-oven or some other high-amperage appliance at the same time, so we switch off the refrigerator until we have finished using the other appliance. If we should need to defrost the refrigerator at dockside, we also use the off switch for that purpose.

The pilot light goes out when the refrigerator is not running, and that lets us know when the box has cooled enough so that we can turn off the 115-volt generator. We cannot hear the compressor over the engine noise, so the light is the only way we have of telling whether the refrigerator is running or not.

If you feel you don't need a generator, you might consider an inverter for the occasions when you need 115-volt power and you are away from a dockside source. An inverter converts 12-volt DC from the ship's batteries to 115-volt AC. This can be the least expensive, most trouble-free way of obtaining 115-volt power. Inverters can be found in wattages from 150 watts to several thousand watts, with prices starting at $50. A 350-watt model, which will run most power tools, costs from $150 to $250, depending on the manufacturer. The smaller-watt units provide the power for electric shavers, radios, tape players, and television sets.

The larger the inverter, the larger the battery bank will have to be, so eventually their convenience is canceled out by the attendant equipment needed for efficient operation.

IX. CLIMATE CONDITIONING

Some form of heating is necessary for nearly every live-aboard boat. Homes ashore are heated; homes afloat also should have heat when it is needed. Even if you never venture north of the twenty-seventh parallel, the time will come when you will find it pleasant to have a little heat in the cabin. In Florida and some of the islands, it is only a matter of removing a little chill from the cabin occasionally, and the cooking stove or an oil lamp or two will do nicely.

In northern waters, though, something more effective is needed. The common notion is that anyone who lives on a boat goes south for the winter, and most of them do. But some either must stay, or prefer to stay, in the North, and they get a good dose of winter. There are those who regularly cruise the Pacific Northwest, where it is more chilly than not. Even if you winter in the South, a late start can subject you to bitterly cold weather. We have experienced sleet, snow, and 20-degree temperatures in the Chesapeake in late October.

There are several types and styles of boat heaters available — from potbellied stoves to furnaces with ductwork — to carry the heat throughout the boat. One popular form of boat heating is a portable electric heater. A 1650-watt unit, equipped with a fan or blower, will heat a surprisingly large boat. We wintered in North Carolina one year and had one ice storm that coated everything with a thick layer of ice, another storm that left a foot of snow, and many days when the temperature was in the teens. Throughout all of this, our boat was heated adequately with a 1650-watt heater and a smaller 650-watt unit. The large heater alone was sufficient on days when it was 25 degrees and warmer.

A little shopping around will turn up a heater better suited to a

144

boat than the long, thin baseboard types that are so common. Whatever shape you decide on, pay a little extra to get a thermostatically controlled model.   Our big heater is an Arvin model 29H90.   It is 14 inches high, 10 inches wide, and seven inches deep.   Because it is tall rather than wide, it can be used in many locations where other heaters would not fit.   It also stows well. The metal case is painted mahogany brown, and it blends in unobtrusively with the wood in the boat. This heater automatically shuts itself off if it falls over.   This is a good safety feature to look for in any heater you are considering.   Built-in electric heaters that can be run off a generator as well as dockside power also might be considered.

Adequate wiring is necessary for using electric heaters.   Don't skimp; be sure the gauge is heavy enough.   The use of high-wattage electric heaters for extended periods of time, with improper wiring, has caused too many fires.

Two of the most delightful ways of providing cabin heat are a fireplace and a cast-iron stove.   An old-fashioned stove or a fireplace offers welcome relief from the plastic sleekness of modern boats.   The stoves are quite inexpensive and easy to install.   The Pet model manufactured by the Fatsco Company can also be used for cooking, since it has a wide, flat top.   Fatsco also manufactures the familiar Tiny Tot.

Fireplaces can be plain metal or be faced with colorful tiles (Fig. 9-1).   Both stoves and fireplaces burn charcoal, wood, and coal, and they must be vented to the outside with a flue.   Charcoal must *never* be burned in an unvented heating device, because it gives off carbon monoxide.

A clean, long-lasting fire can be obtained from the use of "logs" made of compressed wood chips and sawdust, such as Presto-Logs. There are many other brands of these "logs" available in supermarkets and hardware stores.   Some are treated to burn with a multicolored flame, which sometimes gives off a rather unpleasant odor in a small place such as a boat cabin.

Any of the processed logs have to be cut down to size so they will fit in a small boat fireplace.   We do this as a matter of course and think nothing of it.   Last winter Bill had a box of logs on the dock and was using a hatchet to chop them into the usual small chunks.   A weekend sailor, sitting on his boat nearby, watched him for awhile, then came over and said, "It's none of my business, but could you tell me why you live on a boat and have to cut up logs?" Bill told him they were for our fireplace, and that answer seemed to confuse him even more.   He had never heard of a fireplace in a boat, let alone seen one, so we showed him ours.

If you want to burn coal, be selective about the grade you buy. The stuff known as cannel coal in New England is ideal.   It is ex-

Figure 9-1. Whiffle's Simpson-Lawrence fireplace. Wood, charcoal, or coal can be used for fuel.

tremely hard — so hard that if you purchase lumps bigger than the fireplace, you will not be able to split them small enough. Because cannel coal is so hard, it is clean and burns slowly. Locating some may be difficult, however, unless you can get to the larger lumber and building-supply yards, where they sometimes stock it or can order it for you.

We once bought some soft coal at a little country store because we couldn't find any cannel coal and had run out of charcoal, which we normally use. We stoked up a good fire one cold day in a marina, and we had plenty of heat and more soot than we could believe. It was all over the cabin and the deck. Our downwind neighbor, who got most of the soot, claimed it was like living in Liverpool.

Even though fireplaces give off the most pleasant and penetrating heat, they are costly to use for extended periods, because all the fuels they burn are expensive. Once, when we were using the fire-place, we were staying at a yard where they built boats, and we were told to help ourselves to the scrap wood pile. So we burned mahogany, teak, and oak with reckless abandon.

Since fireplaces have open fronts, they should be mounted athwartships so there is less danger of anything spilling out when the boat is heeling. Some have been mounted port or starboard or angled out from one side or another. These must have grates with small openings and a firebox cover, so that nothing can spill out. Our Simpson-Lawrence fireplace is set athwartships and has a larger opening than most, but it also has a firebox cover that does its job well. We have had some roaring fires in some heavy seas, but never any spillage. In some installations, fireplaces can be re-cessed into a bulkhead so that two compartments can benefit from the heat.

Simpson-Lawrence fireplaces are made in England. Two American manufacturers, Paul E. Luke, Inc., and Ratelco, make efficient and attractive fireplaces for boat use.

If you want something more than a fireplace or stove, you can install any of several liquid-fuel heaters and furnaces. The heating system can be an elaborate installation that can heat as well as cool, a furnace with ducts throughout the boat, or a self-contained unit that radiates its heat and requires no energy to move the heat, as the others do. The furnaces and self-contained heaters are small and lightweight and may be installed easily.

The liquid-fuel heaters and furnaces burn either diesel or kero-sene. Both produce nearly the same amount of heat for a given amount burned; kerosene burns slightly hotter.

Any fuel, solid or liquid, gives off deadly fumes when it is burned in an enclosed area, so diesel and kerosene heaters must also have a flue. They also must have a fresh-air intake so that all the oxygen in the cabin will not be used up. If a boat has enough Dorade vents, they may be all that is necessary to replace the used-up oxygen. Otherwise, crack a hatch to let in fresh air.

You can figure the amount of BTUs (British thermal units, the standards for measuring heat) needed for your boat by measuring the size of each compartment where heat is needed and calculating the number of cubic feet. If you have a separate galley, or wish to heat the engine room or any other compartment that has a heat-producing device, multiply the number of cubic feet by a factor of 10. For a stateroom, multiply by a factor of 12. An area such as a wheelhouse, which has large windows, should be multiplied by a factor of 15. These figures are based on an outside temperature of 20 degrees and an inside temperature of 70 degrees.

Taylor's Para-Fin pressure kerosene heater is one of the most compact cabin heaters on the market (Fig. 9-2). It is 15 inches high and 6½ inches in diameter, yet it delivers plenty of heat for

Figure 9-2. Taylor's Para-Fin pressure kerosene heater is very popular for small boats in the United States and England, where it is manufactured. (Photo courtesy Taylor's Para-Fin Oil & Gas Appliances, Ltd.)

most small boats. It mounts on a bulkhead and has a small-diameter flue that vents to the outside. Recently Taylor introduced a slightly larger diesel heater similar in design to the kerosene model.

For extended living aboard in cold climates, a built-in forced-air furnace with ductwork to each cabin would be ideal. Today there are several models and sizes to choose from. Wallas-Marine in Turku, Finland, manufactures one of the best-designed furnaces. It is approximately 16 inches high, four inches wide, and 13 inches long. It is kerosene-fired, with an output of 7,000 BTUs, and thermostatically controlled. Its electrical consumption is eight watts. Ducts can be run from the furnace to anywhere in the boat. The flue is a unique design using one pipe, with separate chambers for the fresh-air intake and the exhaust smoke and gases. It will operate at 45 degrees of heel.

A versatile diesel-fueled heater is made by Perkins Boilers, Ltd., in Derby, England. It heats remote areas with hot-water radiators and requires no electrical power. The unit is constructed of polished stainless steel. It is designed for installation in the main saloon or wheelhouse, where it is bolted to the sole. The Cruiser Kit, as this model is called, is not just a heater. There is a hot-water tank attached to it, and the top of the heater offers 63 square inches of cooking surface. A fiddle rail surrounds the cooking area. The rail also holds a removable oven in place over the cooking surface. The Perkins heater can be used when heeling if it is installed according to the manufacturer's directions.

We have seen several boats constructed in the Netherlands that have built-in diesel heaters. They are the same type of heaters used in buses and trucks both here and abroad. They are long and cylindrical, and easy to install where other designs will not fit. Ductwork can be run from these heaters if desired. They are made by Bosch in several sizes and are available from Manhattan Marine.

A boat can be heated when the engine is running by using an automotive heater that utilizes hot water from the engine. These heaters are designed for use in pick-up campers, but they would work just as well in a boat. Sears has a 19,500-BTU model that costs $72.

Catalytic heaters that burn gas or alcohol are not recommended. They cannot be used in a completely closed cabin, because they eventually will use up all the oxygen. There must be some sort of ventilation, which results in considerable heat loss, because the heating capability of a catalytic heater is not as great as other types of heaters. They also give off a "damp" heat, which can be more objectionable than the cold.

If you are living aboard so far north that the water you are in might freeze, you will need something more than a heater or furnace for comfort. A good winter cover is a necessity, more for heat retention than for protection of the decks and hull. A canvas or plastic tarp thrown over a wooden frame won't do. Invest in a good, fitted canvas cover that is held in place by a frame made of aluminum tubing. It must be strong enough to withstand winter gales.

The frame can be engineered so that it is high enough to enable you to stand upright in the cockpit. You shouldn't have to crawl in and out of the boat. The canvas should be white so the area underneath won't be too gloomy. The cover should have a couple of clear vinyl windows in it, so you can see outside. It must also have a person-size flap for a door that can be opened quickly and easily from either side. Heavy-duty zippers are the best closure for the door.

Circulated air, air flow, or cooling, aside from the natural ventilation through the boat, is often desirable year-round in the tropics and in the summer elsewhere. Air circulation can be accomplished with fans. There are several 12-volt fans on the market that do a satisfactory job, although some of them are rather noisy. If 115-volt electric power is available, ordinary household fans also can be used. The square fans that once were referred to as "window fans" seem to work out best for most live-aboards we know. Most of these are at least 20 inches square, but if you are patient and shop around, you will be able to locate, as we did, the more convenient, smaller size that is 14½ inches square.

During the day, the fan rests on the cabin sole or on the wide step just below the main companionway. At night it is placed in the forward hatch above our berth, face down, to bring in cool air (Fig. 9-3). This size fits inside the hatch coaming; it is supported from below by two thin strips of wood on each side of the hatch. Each end of the wood strip rests on a shallow lip that runs around the four sides of the hatch, and the fan rests on these. Not only does the fan cool the cabin, but when daylight arrives, it diffuses the light and prevents the bright sunlight from waking us early.

Some boats do not have hatch openings as big as our 19-inch-square ones, but a fan is just as effective if it is laid across the hatch on deck. The fan might slide off if the boat were hit by a large wake, but it can be lashed in place.

If you want air conditioning in your boat-home, there is no reason not to have it. In Florida and California, it is common to see sailboats with air conditioners. In the North, our air conditioner has always attracted attention when we have used it. Most of our other luxuries and comforts can be tolerated by the sailboat purists, whose usual attitude is: they can have it on *their* boat, but I wouldn't have it on *mine*. Use of the air conditioner, however, seems to infuriate some of these purists, and they speak

Figure 9-3. Small window fan placed in forward hatch over berths for cool sleeping.

curtly to us — that is, if they speak to us at all. They seem to feel that by installing an air conditioner in a sailboat we have done something to besmirch the grand old tradition of yachting. Too bad.   Anyone who isn't a stuffed shirt about sailboats realizes how sensible it really is.

Recently we were spending a week at a marina in Maryland when a cruising sailboat came in for fuel. A woman on the boat saw our air conditioner humming away and called to the skipper, "Come look at this. They have an air conditioner on that boat. What a great idea for cruising the Chesapeake!" The skipper only said, "Humph," and he did his best to avoid looking at it as he walked down the dock.

Our portable General Electric Carry-Cool air conditioner is installed in our wider-than-normal companionway (Fig. 9-4). This is by far the quickest, easiest, and least expensive way to have air conditioning; but the companionway must be wide enough to accommodate the unit, which is 20½ inches wide. Built into each side of the Carry-Cool are panels that pull out to fill in wider openings.   It is 14¼ inches high and only 10 5/8 inches deep, which is much narrower than any other type of air conditioner. It is easy to step over it when entering or leaving the boat, so it does not have to be removed (except for short-legged guests). Removal is easy, however, because the unit weighs only 43 pounds. It is thermostatically controlled, draws seven amps, and the cooling capacity is 4,000 BTUs/hr.   The case is Lexan, so it cannot rust.

Figure 9-4. General Electric portable Carry-Cool air conditioner installed in Whiffle*'s extra-wide companionway.*

When the Carry-Cool is installed in *Whiffle*'s companionway, there are only 4¼ inches between the cool air outlet at the top and the companionway hatch. This is not enough space to allow the cold air to circulate adequately, so we use our fan, which is placed in front of and below the air conditioner, for more circulation. The fan also forces much of the cold air into the forward cabin, which would not be cool enough if we did not use the fan.

Regular household air conditioners often are used in boats, although they are not as convenient as portable ones. The units designed for casement windows are often the right configuration for boats. A boat that has a door, or doors, in the companionway could have a duplicate door made to house the air conditioner, and a casement unit could be mounted in it permanently. In warm weather, you could just take off the original door and replace it with the door with the air conditioner in it.

Some boats we have seen in Florida have household units mounted where a large cabin port used to be, and others have a hole cut in the aft bulkhead on one side of the companionway, with the air conditioner mounted there.

Boat owners in New Orleans seem to favor locating their air conditioners under the bridge deck. If there are no engine instruments or other obstructions there, this location is the most unobtrusive of all (Fig. 9-5). Figure 9-6 shows a deck hatch modified to accommodate an air conditioner. We wouldn't want to

Figure 9-5. General Electric Carry-Cool air conditioner cleverly installed in Ken Mitchell's Dreadnought 32 Pelorus Jack. Hot air goes into engine compartment and is vented through open port in cockpit.

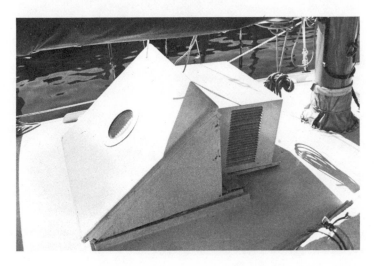

Figure 9-6. Small household air conditioner adapted to work in deck hatch.

guarantee the seaworthiness of any of the above-mentioned installations, except those in which the air conditioner can be removed and stowed below.

There are several air conditioners specially designed for use in boats. Large systems may have separate compressors and pumps, while some of the smaller ones are completely self-contained. Many of the large systems are water-cooled, which means they must have a through-the-hull fitting; but because they are water-cooled, they need no outside air, so they may be mounted anywhere in a boat. On larger boats, ducts can be installed throughout the boat. Some marine units are of the reverse-cycle, or heat-pump, type, and they can be used for both cooling and heating.

The type of air conditioner that is designed to mount over a roof hatch on trailers and campers also can be used over deck hatches on boats (Fig. 9-7). Most of these weigh more than 150 pounds and cost at least $400. All of the above-mentioned air conditioners are powered by 115-volt AC.

If an air conditioner is used in a companionway, it is worthwhile to work out a way to lock the companionway while the air conditioner is still in place, so you can leave the boat but have her cool and unburgled when you return. Our air conditioner wasn't quite as tall as the companionway, and we had to make a small filler piece so we could close it off completely. This worked out well, because it gave us a place to put a hasp (Fig. 9-4).

Figure 9-7. Camper/trailer air conditioner installed on a boat.

A thick layer of insulation under the deck will add immeasurably to the effectiveness of any heating or cooling system. It will also make the boat more comfortable when neither system is in use. *Whiffle*'s deck insulation is four inches thick, which is unusual for a boat of her size. On sunny days, it is never any hotter below than it is on deck; often, it is cooler.

Living aboard your own boat for a time will let you know how well insulated she is. Any wooden boat will retain more heat (or cold) than one of fiberglass, because of the inherent insulating quality of the wood itself. Many of the lockers may provide insulation, because they create air space.

Most boat hulls are as watertight above the waterline as they are below it, but seal any cracks or openings around the hatches, ports, or companionway. In very cold weather, block off any louvers in the companionway slides or doors. Large windows or ports drain off heat quickly, and they might need to be covered with some insulating material when it is extremely cold.

X. THE HEAD

We hope that sometime soon, the controversy over who can use what type of head and discharge what into whose water will be resolved. If you are confused by the above sentence, take heart from the fact that the sentence is much clearer than most of the official opinions and rules that have been foisted on us by the collective city and state governments along the waterways of the country.

All the boating people in the world, using all their heads in tidal waters for a year, could not come close to polluting the water as much as one major city does in a day. Until the cities and large chemical plants clean themselves up, it is sheer nonsense to force pleasure boaters to install elaborate waste-disposal systems. The problem of pleasure-boat heads and the disposal of their contents has been exaggerated — if, indeed, there is a problem. We think not.

Most boating people are perfectly willing to conform to a workable, *uniform* federal law. Presently, nearly every state and many cities have their own laws; in most instances, the laws are far from satisfactory. They have been introduced and passed by legislators who are concerned primarily with the votes they will get if they appear to be staunch pollution fighters. In reality, most of them know little or nothing about the real situation.

As yet, there is no definite opinion from the federal government, but they seem to be leaning toward the holding-tank idea. This is the system where you carry around your sewage until you reach a pump-out station, where you will be relieved of both your burden and a sum of money. Then there is the chance that your sewage will be pumped back into the water you are sailing in, unless municipalities adopt the same strict rules that they impose on pleasure boaters.

156

Besides taking up too much valuable storage space, the waste in holding tanks generates methane gas, which is explosive and self-igniting. It is said that the gas, bacteria, and odors can be controlled by chemicals. We must then assume that the boats that have already blown up from methane-gas explosions did not have these chemicals in their holding tanks.

No matter what laws are passed, they will not be enforceable. Manufacturers can be required to install holding tanks and certain types of heads before they can sell a boat, but the new owner can change anything he wants after he takes possession of the boat. Most boat owners don't make any radical changes. They simply install a Y valve and/or a pump that allows them to pump the contents of the holding tank over the side. We don't know of any boat with a holding tank that does not also have a means for pumping the waste over the side.

We talked to one man who paid $6 for a pump-out and found out, two hours later, that the pump-out equipment hadn't been working properly and his holding tank was still full. He had to discharge the contents overboard, because he could not take the time to go back to the pump-out station, and he was going to be anchoring out for the next two nights.

And what do you do if you are making a long passage at sea in a boat that has a holding tank? For your own protection, you must install a device to pump out your own tank.

When they pass laws to outlaw all the pumps and Y valves on all pleasure boats to stop illicit holding-tank pump-outs, we can go back to the old standby, the bucket, which can be used and dumped over the side in the dark of night or whenever no one is looking. When they pass a law forbidding the use of buckets on boats, we will have to think of something else.

There are several varieties of portable toilets that have a built-in waste compartment. The whole unit can be removed from the boat and emptied into any shoreside toilet. One model of the Porta-Potti, manufactured by Thetford Industries, is arranged so the waste compartment can be detached easily from the toilet. There are positive seals on all openings, so it will not leak, and it has a handle for easy carrying. If a toilet has a waste compartment, a chemical must be used to control odors, gas, and bacteria.

There is no need to use a pump-out station for this type of toilet, but some states require that even these toilets be mounted permanently so that a shoreside station must be used for emptying them. Most of the manufacturers offer permanent-installation kits, so that their products can comply with these states' regulations. If you had to pay the not unusual charge of $6 for pumping out a small, formerly portable tank, which has only a two- or three-day holding capacity, it would be a very expensive proposition.

One family we know had to install one of the portable toilets so they wouldn't run afoul of the law during their summer-long stay in New York State. They didn't want to install one, and it cost them a considerable amount of money and inconvenience. They have named their toilet in honor of the governor of the state.

The chlorinator-macerator might be the best answer to the problem from the boater's standpoint. This device uses the existing head, with an attachment that processes the waste as it passes through. The chlorinator kills any bacteria that might be present, and the macerator grinds the waste into small particles, which are discharged overboard. This treatment is better than that used by many municipalities. One drawback of this system is that it needs electricity for operation.

The recirculating type of toilet that was originally designed for the aircraft industry has found its way into boats. A holding-tank type, it filters and recirculates the flushing liquid, so the holding tank will not fill up too quickly. This toilet also requires electricity for operation.

On a long ocean passage, it is not feasible or sensible to use any kind of electrically operated toilet. The old-fashioned head that requires manual labor to pump sewage overboard is the best for a number of reasons. With a simple adaptation, this model also can function as an emergency bilge pump. (Get a plumber's helper of the ball type. Take the handle off. Cut a hole in the bottom of the socket that held the handle. Attach a hose to the hole. The hose must be long enough to reach the bilge. Insert the ball in the bowl of the head in the normal manner and pump.)

In very rough seas, the head can be used for pumping oil out and onto those troubled waters, and maybe calming them down a bit. Also, the manual pumping is good for you; it is a known fact that sailors on long voyages don't get enough exercise.

After a hard-fought battle across the wild ocean, an intrepid sailor, who has been using his old-fashioned head offshore for all kinds of things, pulls triumphantly into a United States harbor, and feels the need to use the head. What does he do? Use his illegal head and pollute the harbor, and perhaps get fined and thrown into jail? Or try to wait until he can reach a shoreside toilet? Will he have to clear customs and go through quarantine before he can go ashore? Let's hope the problems of elimination are eliminated before they reach this ridiculous extreme.

Since you don't spend too much time in the head, it only needs to be big enough for comfortable use — not just big enough to get the equipment in, but big enough so that normal people can use the equipment. The head itself should be located where it can be used conveniently. Men should not need to hunch over when standing up. The head should have enough room all around for comfortable sitting. Too many boats have the head jammed in tight against a bulkhead or the sink, so you must sit on them at an angle. If you cannot sit squarely, you could get bounced off in a rough sea.

One of the best ways to get the most out of the head without giving up a lot of space is to have it athwartships. The sink is on one side of the passageway with a door across it. The head is on the other side and also has a door across it. When both doors are opened out across the passageway, they form the shower "stall," and there is plenty of room for doing anything that must be done there. In this arrangement, one door usually serves also to close off the forward cabin for privacy (Fig. 10-1).

There should be a sink in the head for convenience as well as for sanitary purposes. The sink should be big enough to accommodate two hands (some aren't that large). It should not be situated under the deck overhang, so that you must bend down and over to reach the sink at all, let alone wash and see what you are doing.

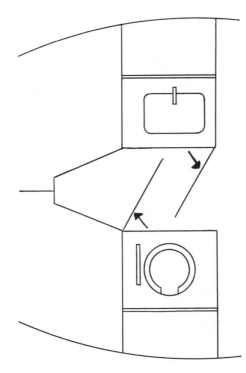

Figure 10-1. Athwartships head. Two doors, opened across walkway, can form shower stall.

The sink should drain overboard. (Some states are considering laws that forbid overboard discharges of any kind!) If the height of the sink is too close to the waterline, it should be fitted with a pump, as described for the galley sink in Chapter VII. Porcelain is easier to keep looking clean than stainless steel, but because porcelain cracks so easily, stainless steel is the more practical material.

If space is limited, a sliding sink can be used. It pulls out for use and slides back into its own cubbyhole when not in use. These sinks are often mounted above, and in back of, the head itself.

A folding sink is not the most desirable type in a live-aboard boat, but it is certainly better than no sink at all. Folding sinks are great space-savers in tiny head compartments.

If you are installing a sink, and if your head pumps directly overboard, you can arrange the sink so it drains into the head. The waste is pumped out through the head. A through-hull fitting is eliminated with a drain of this type. Obviously, it is not a good idea to have the sink drain into a head where the contents are pumped into a holding tank.

A good-quality mirror with a bright light above it is a must. We have added a second light to our small head compartment so that we could have some decent light immediately above the mirror. The mirror should be large, and high enough so a tall man can see well enough to shave without bending over. If the shorter members of the crew have to stand on tiptoe to see themselves, get a longer mirror.

Many boats have a hamper in the counter top next to the sink. These probably were intended for soiled clothes, but they are too big and handy to be used for that in a live-aboard boat. In one boat-home, the hamper was sectioned into a wine-and-liquor cabinet with thick, corrugated cardboard, so each bottle has its own niche. Our hamper has become the linen closet. It holds all of our sheets and most of our blankets.

It is desirable to have several smallish lockers and a medicine chest in the head. They all should have secure closures, especially the medicine chest.

Put up as many towel rods as possible. There is probably a bulkhead where one towel rod can be installed above another, far enough apart so that both towels can hang either their full length or doubled over. You may not ever use enough towels to fill them all, but sooner or later, they will come in handy for drying laundry or spray-soaked clothing.

Good-sized hooks are useful on the inside of the head door and on other bulkheads. Put any door hook high enough so that it is not at anyone's eye level — the higher the better. Then no one can lurch into it in a seaway and cause themselves injury.

A 115-volt outlet should be in the head. We also have a 12-volt outlet, which was installed primarily so we could use the 12-volt fan there.

If you have a shower, you should not have to sit on the head to use it. Only rarely are showers satisfactory in the head compartment. If you could stand with your arms at your sides and your feet close together and somehow get soaped up and rinsed off without moving at all, the majority of them might be more workable.

Still, a shower is one luxury you can and should have — either a built-in unit or a portable one. You cannot always depend on marinas to have showers, and we have seen a few that were so filthy we would have felt dirtier after the shower if we had been forced to use it. However, the majority of marina shower facilities are clean, even though many leave much to be desired in the way of decor. Many times it is easier to use shoreside facilities than to clean up the mess made by trying to shower in the cramped, built-in ones in most small boats. But there will come a time when you will be glad to have your own facilities aboard.

Many of the popular cruising areas now have such dirty water that the traditional dip over the side is not as satisfying, and certainly not as cleansing, as it once was. On a hot day in an anchorage, if you don't want to go over the side, a shower would feel wonderful. Of course, if you are cruising in an area where fresh water is at a premium, you will have to think twice before you use your own water supply for showers.

Since our boat did not have a built-in shower, our solution was to buy a portable one (Fig. 10-2). Ours has a heavy vinyl base that folds flat; the base unfolds to the size of a standard shower stall and forms a semirigid pan, with sides about eight inches high, into which the shower curtain hangs.

The curtain assembly starts with a circular metal plate with a hook, so it can be suspended from the overhead or boom or wherever you want to hang it. Four metal rods are inserted into this round metal device at 90-degree angles. These project out to the edges of the vinyl base. The curtain has a ring on each corner, and each ring is hung on one of the rods. There are dowels in the bottom hem, so that the curtain will not collapse in on itself when it is inserted into the base. This curtain has a full-length opening at one corner.

The showering unit consists of a two-gallon container, marked off in quarts and liters, with a plunger-type pump on the top. A generous length of hose has one end fitted to the water container near the bottom. The other end of the hose has a standard shower head on it. Everything except the container and pump folds flat for easy stowage.

Pressure is pumped up, and the water flow is adjusted and turned on or off by means of a screw ring located at the joint of

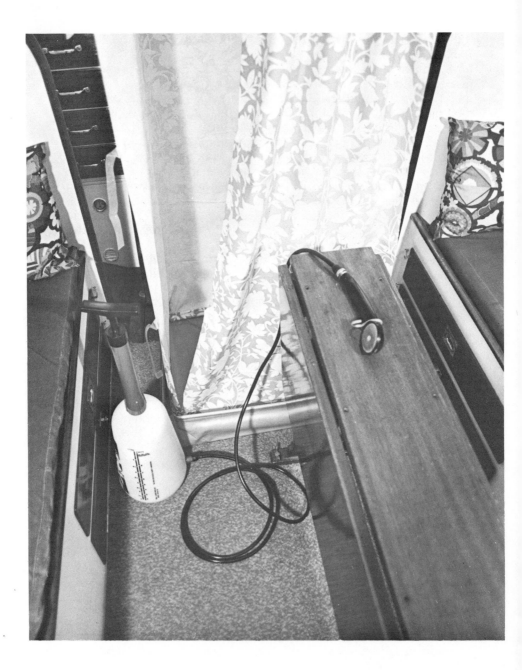

Figure 10-2. Whiffle's *portable shower set up at foot of companionway ladder.*

the shower head and the hose. Very little energy is required to
pump it to the proper pressure. A little pumping at the beginning,
and a little more halfway through, seems to be sufficient for one
shower.   Both of us can shower adequately and wash our hair in
the two gallons, if necessary. If fresh water is in short supply, it is
nice to know exactly how much you are using if you decide to
use it for showering.

The only problem with our shower was what to do with the
shower head when both hands were being used for something else.
It didn't come with any sort of device for hanging it. We bent the
bottom part of an S-hook around the neck of the shower head and
hung the other half over one of the rods that support the curtain.

Just after we purchased the shower, we were not quite sure
where to put the curtain and base when we wanted to take a
shower below.   The first place everyone seems to think of is the
head, which is almost always too small for a comfortable shower
— ours certainly is. We finally decided to hang ours where we had
ample headroom and plenty of side-room to move around while
showering.   That turned out to be in the main cabin at the foot of
the companionway ladder. It may be an unorthodox place for a
shower, but it has proven to be a convenient and workable arrangement. (When we are in a secluded place and it is warm enough, we
shower on deck without the curtain or base.)

Aside from the roominess, we have another reason for using the
shower in the main cabin. We had always felt that emptying even
a gallon of water from the base might be a very tricky operation.
Pumping it out was too involved, and that destroyed the convenience of the shower. We wanted a simple method of drainage.

We hit upon the solution one summer in the middle of a heat
wave, in a marina that had no shower facilities. The marina did
have a store, however, and we purchased a medium-size Delrin
through-the-hull fitting. We put the flat, round part, which goes
on the outside of the hull, on the inside of the shower's base over
a circular hole we had cut. The nozzle end of the fitting, which
hoses are normally attached to inside a hull, was attached to the
outside of the base and projected out like a spout. The fitting was
put in a corner on the floor of the base — not on one of the
upright sides.

After positioning the base where it would be during a shower,
we drilled a hole in the floorboard that was just big enough for
inserting the nozzle end. The deepest part of the bilge is immediately under this hole, and the shower water drains directly into it.
It can be pumped out at our convenience with the bilge pump
(Fig. 10-3). We have carpeting on the floor, so the hole doesn't
show. When we want to use the shower, we simply fold back the
carpet for access to the hole.

Figure 10-3. Drain nozzle in base of Whiffle's *portable shower.*

Most showers that are located in the head drain into a sump, then an electric or manual pump is used to pump the waste overboard.

The simplest portable shower is a rubber bag, such as a hot-water bottle or a syringe type. A shower head with a valve so the water can be turned on and off is fitted into the opening. For use, the bag is hung in a convenient place on deck or above the cockpit. Any suitable plastic or rubber container can be converted into a shower of this type. This is, however, strictly a warm-weather type of shower.

If you use a shower other than the one in your own boat, wear a pair of rubber sandals to prevent foot infections.

It is possible to have automatic hot water for showers and the galley. All marine hot-water heaters run on 115-volt power, but some units have a system for heating water when the engine is running. Hot water from the engine's cooling system is piped to the heater tank, and the water in the tank is heated by a built-in heat exchanger.

We have never felt the need for automatic hot water. When using the stove for cooking, we always heat a kettle of water for coffee or tea and dishwashing. For showers, a half-teakettle of hot water is all that is necessary to warm up two gallons of water to a comfortable temperature. As long as we have a stove that works, we won't need a hot-water heater.

XI. WHERE WILL YOU
STOW IT ALL?

No home needs storage space as much as a boat-home does. Your belongings cannot be left unsecured or strewn about the boat. Some degree of neatness must be maintained, if only for efficiency's sake. If all the lockers, bins, and cupboards are put to good use, it should be relatively easy to be neat without trying too hard.

First of all, do something about any completely open shelves. As we mentioned before, they are worthless in a boat; yet some boats have more of them than any other kind of stowage area. You can completely enclose any shelf to make a cabinet, or put a guard rail along its length to form a bookshelf — or at the very least, put a fiddle rail around it so it can hold small things.

There should be proper stowage for everything you have aboard. "Proper" means that breakable items won't get broken, that water can't leak into storage areas and damage the contents, and that often-used items are handy yet secure.

Clothing seems to be the most difficult stowage problem, mainly because everyone starts with too much of it. Bill moved aboard with 32 pairs of pants and 13 pairs of shoes. Even though we did manage to stow them all, there was still too much, so some things were eliminated quickly.

Hanging lockers are the most convenient place for storing clothes, although with modern crease-resistant fabrics and knits, they are not a necessity. We use our hanging lockers mainly for bulky outerwear.

When we bought our boat, the hanging locker had only one rod that ran from front to back, not from side to side in the usual manner. Since the locker was deep, this rod arrangement allowed for many more clothes than if the rod ran fore and aft. The obvious drawback is that only the garment at the front of the rod is visible and accessible. Soon after we moved aboard, we installed another rod in the locker in the usual manner, leaving the original one in place, and our storage space doubled. The out-of-season clothes are hung on the athwartship rod and pushed to the back of the locker, out of the way. We installed the new rod for convenience, and we did not intend to use the existing rod at all; but this is such a space-saving arrangement that you might consider doing the same thing if your hanging locker is deep enough.

On a long voyage, clothes hung on a fore-and-aft rod will swing back and forth, causing a great deal of chafe. This can be eliminated by putting an old sheet over the clothes and tying a line or two around the bundle. The whole package swings as one unit, so if there is any chafe, it will occur on the sheet and not on the clothes.

Bill's pants (he still has too many) are hung on the hanging locker door, on dowels that have an eye in each end. The eyes are slipped over cup hooks, which are screwed into the door. Each dowel holds two pairs of pants comfortably (Fig. 11-1).

Figure 11-1. Neat, simple arrangement for hanging pants on inside of door. Bin below is used for extra storage space.

The bin under the pants is one of several we have installed wherever we find space. This one holds a pair or two of light-weight shoes. Another bin holds all the small toiletries and medications that are not in the medicine chest. That one is on the inside of a locker door in the head. A white bin is mounted just inside the companionway for small items we need occasionally when we are underway: a wind gauge, a gadget for unscrewing stubborn shackle pins, and the like. Yet another bin is under a cockpit locker. It holds winch handles when we are not sailing, and chafe guards when we are not tied up. There are always so many little items that have to be kept handy in a boat, and bins like this are a good way to solve their stowage problem.

We still seem to have an uncommon number of shoes, so we have attached a small shoe bag inside the door of a small hanging locker and another on an out-of-the-way bulkhead in the forward cabin. If they are not needed for shoes, the pockets of these bags can hold rolled-up sweaters, flashlights, gloves, wine bottles, cameras, etc.

Drawers are expensive to install, so there aren't too many boats with a superabundance of them, unless the boat has been built by the owner. This is unfortunate, because drawers are the best form of storage for many items. Condensation rarely touches items in drawers, because the items are not in direct contact with the hull, as they are in most lockers. If the drawers are installed properly, they will not slide open except perhaps when heeling severely. Many have latches or turn buttons that keep them in place in rough seas. In one method of construction, the drawer must be pulled up and over a lip to open. When the drawer is closed, the lip prevents the drawer from coming open by itself.

We wish we had more than our eight drawers. Two are under each of the forward berths and are used for clothing. One is under the stove recess, and it is used for kitchen utensils and flatware. A small drawer in a bureau is big enough to hold our 60-odd cassettes, and two drawers under the settees in the main cabin are so big, and hold so much, that they are difficult to pull out.

Incidentally, when storing knitted clothes, such as T-shirts, turtlenecks, and light sweaters, in drawers or anywhere else, do not fold them in the normal manner. Fold them in half lengthwise, fold the sleeves back over the garment, and begin rolling at the bottom, making the roll as tight as you can. Rolled clothes take up about half the space of folded ones. Rolling knits tightly won't damage them; they will be wrinkle-free when you are ready to wear them. The garment you want is easier to locate, and the other clothes won't get so messed up when one is removed.

The area above both our port and starboard settee backs originally was a 77-inch open shelf with a fiddle rail only an inch-

and-a-half high along the whole length. Twenty-seven-and-a-half inches of one shelf had a guard rail and was designed as a bookshelf. Twenty-seven-and-a-half inches could not begin to hold our books, so we had to do some remodeling.

First, we built identical cabinets at the end of the shelves on each side of the cabin. They extend right up to the overhead, and they are big enough to have a shelf apiece. These took up only 16 inches; now books take up the remaining shelf space. We put a sturdy rail across the remaining open areas, filling them with books that have yet to fall out. Aside from the nautical books we use constantly, we have the *Columbia Encyclopedia* and *The Random House Dictionary* on the shelf, readily accessible, as well as many other books we often refer to. Our guard rail is a strip of wood about one inch thick. Each end of the strip fits into a notch cut into a block of wood. The block of wood is attached to a sturdy vertical surface. The guard rail is removable when it is lifted, but it won't fall out (Fig. 11-2). Guard rails are easy to make and install, and they help you secure many things other than books, such as RDFs and small radios.

It is not necessary to take up valuable shelf space with a radiotelephone. There are a very few of them that cannot be mounted on a bulkhead. We have both an AM and VHF radiotelephone, and both are mounted on a bulkhead above the bookcase, near the overhead, so books can be stored underneath them.

After partitioning off large lockers and bins (as mentioned in Chapter VII) and filling them with whatever goes in them, you may still have room at the top of some lockers. Cup hooks can be screwed into the overhead of these lockers and be used for cups or whatever else fits there. Two pieces of shock cord — in the shape of an X — might also be secured to the overhead. Pot lids, baking racks, and other flat items can be stored in a very shallow area such as this, flat against the top of the locker.

Don't overlook the inside of the locker door for storage. Both large and small bins, as mentioned before, can be attached to the inside of the doors, as long as you can still close the door. If bins are too wide, perhaps a shock-cord X could be used on the door for lids.

We save any semirigid plastic cases we find, such as the kind bank passbooks come with. These can be attached to the inside of doors with double-faced tape (which we like best) or tiny nails. These cases are useful for holding pens, pencils, small cards, or tablets.

The small plastic flatware holders designed to hang on dish drainers can be converted into handy bins. With a knife, slice off the curved lip. This will allow the holder to fit flush against a flat surface. Attach it where you want it with one or two small

Figure 11-2. Guard rail on open bookshelf. Notch in rail holder is as deep as rail is wide.

screws near the top. The holders usually have a divider across the middle, making two sections. We have one holder in the stationery cabinet to hold pencils and pens in one section and felt-tip markers in the other. These holders are also useful in the head for combs or toothbrushes, since they have drain holes in the bottom.

Chart stowage can be a real problem, especially if you do a lot of cruising to many different areas. Some people throw away their charts when they leave the area covered by them, and buy new editions if and when they return. This is a very expensive practice, because most charts don't change much from year to year, so find a place to stow them. They can be stowed under berth cushions up to a point, but you can't go very far with the number of charts you can fit under the cushions and still have comfortable berths to sit or sleep on.

Regardless of what you may have been told in boating classes, don't think of storing even one chart rolled up. This is insanity on any size boat. And purchasing the overhead racks for storing them rolled up is crazy, too. That is, unless you will only need three or four charts forever. Not only are rolled charts hard to stow, they fight you every step of the way when you try to unroll them for use. When you get a chart, fold it in quarters, printed side out; then think about stowing it.

Some chart tables have a lift-up top and a compartment for charts underneath. Rarely are they large enough to stow charts without folding them at least in half. Usually the compartment is large enough to hold all the charts for any cruising area and they are readily accessible when needed. As convenient as they are, however, the compartments won't hold all the charts you will probably need, so you will have to find an additional place.

A simple chart holder can be made if you have a vacant bulkhead area approximately the size of a chart folded in quarters. Obtain a piece of ¼-inch plywood, slightly larger than your largest folded chart, and attach one side of a piano hinge to what will be the bottom. Cut a strip of 1-inch-by-1-inch wood the same length as the bottom edge of the plywood. Screw or nail the strip horizontally to the bulkhead where the bottom of the holder will be. Attach the remaining side of the piano hinge to the top of the strip of wood. On each side, about two-thirds of the way up, attach a short strap to the plywood. The straps should be fitted with any of the many types of two-part fasteners available. One part of the fastener is on the strap; the other part is attached to the bulkhead. The straps can be unsnapped so the board may be

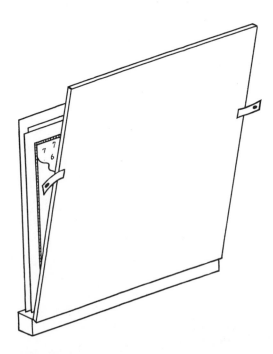

Figure 11-3. Simple chart holder that can be built to fit on bulkhead.

Figure 11-4. Whiffle's *overhead chart compartment.*

lowered on its hinge, and charts may be stored behind it. This is not a very neat system, since everything falls down when the board is lowered, but it is one of the best stowage arrangements when there is a minimum amount of space available (Fig. 11-3).

One potential storage area overlooked by nearly everyone is the overhead. Some of the newer boats have seven-foot headroom. This means that compartments and cabinets can be suspended from above without sacrificing needed headroom. If they are made properly, overhead compartments will not disturb the looks of the boat and might even add to her decor. In trunk cabin boats with ordinary headroom of six to 6½ feet, perhaps cabinets could be suspended over the dining table and the parts of the galley area that are not walkways. There are many places for suspended cabinets in boats with flush decks.

Our chart locker, built in by the manufacturer, is suspended from the overhead, above the forward port berth. It is seven inches high, 28 inches wide, and 29 inches deep (Fig. 11-4). With 130 charts, folded in quarters, it is nearly full. It does not begin to hold all the charts we have accumulated, and we have had to find other places to stow them.

We like the out-of-the-way overhead stowage idea so much we have used it to devise a way to stow charts in the forepeak. A stack of about 70 or so charts, already folded in quarters, is rolled up (as much as you can roll such a bulky package). It makes a cylindrical bundle four or five inches in diameter, which then is secured at each end with two heavy rubber bands. We had some extra pieces of nylon safety netting, which we secured to the overhead in the forepeak to make a hammock for the cylinder of charts. A regular hammock could also be used in this manner, as long as it didn't droop too far. Keep all the charts as close to the overhead as possible, so there is no danger of their being in the way of the ground tackle if it is stored in the forepeak. Depending on the space in the forepeak and how many charts you have, two or three hammocks could be installed.

Several years ago, we read about a dining table that was pulled up against the overhead when not in use. The legs were folded up against the underside of the table and held in place by webbing that was unsnapped to free them. When the table was needed, it was lowered, and the legs, which had positioning pins on their lower ends, were unsnapped and inserted in holes in the cabin sole. The raising mechanism was a small block on either end of the table with a line running through it to a cleat, where the line was fastened when the table was in the up or down position.

We have seen small tables that are raised and lowered on a pipe column, which often is a support for the mast. These tables are held in place with a pin inserted in the column.

We use plastic wastebaskets and dishpans for anything but their normal uses. Our top-loading refrigerator is so big that we had to stop piling in loose food. We created bins with one tall waste-basket and a dishpan. The wastebasket holds pickles, mayonnaise, salad dressings, and the like — mostly items in glass jars or bottles. The wastebasket is rather narrow, so the bottles cannot roll around and break. The bottles don't fill up the wastebasket, so we keep all salad greens in one plastic bag and set it in the top of the wastebasket.   (Incidentally, this is a great way to store salad makings. Lift out one bag and you have everything needed for the salad, except the dressing.   No more hunting through the refrigerator for elusive radishes and cucumbers.)

The dishpan fits on a shelf and holds butter, cheese, and a plastic container of eggs. Cans of juice and plastic jugs of ice water fit around the bins and keep them in place.

Wire baskets, such as those found in freezers, might also be put to good use in a deep bin or large refrigerator or ice chest. Often these are too big and heavy for use on a small boat, but wire bicycle baskets are ideal. We have one of these in the refrigerator, in addition to the dishpan and the wastebasket. We have another bicycle basket in one of the cockpit lockers for various small items.

In the head we have a wastebasket in the locker under the sink. It is full of dust cloths (old undershirts, really), sponges, spray polish, and rug shampoo. The real wastebasket for the head is a plastic bag attached to the inside of the door of the same locker. Two of those handy cup hooks are screwed into the door, and the bag is hung by its two top corners. Fold the top of the bag over so the hooks go through more than one thickness of plastic. The wastebasket items from the head usually are light, so a lightweight plastic bag works well. When it is full, dispose of bag and all. A bag of about 11 by 13 inches works best in the space we have. Bags of this size can be purchased, but supermarket produce bags are just about this size. Since we eat plenty of salad, we never have to buy special bags. All our wastebaskets and dishpans are rectangular, because that shape stows better and holds more than the round type.

At one time we had several tall wastebaskets for storage in the cockpit lockers. They weren't especially satisfactory, so now we have made or found canvas, nylon, or plastic bags that have drawstring closings. These are flexible and thus more easily stowed than rigid wastebaskets.

We don't like to have anything rolling around loose in the cockpit lockers or any other lockers. And we want to be able to find anything with a minimum of fuss and effort — hence our penchant for stowing things in bags or whatever else suits the purpose. We even have a large collection of spare cloth bags that are stored in another cloth bag. All our spare plastic bags are folded up and stored in another plastic bag. There is no reason to tuck spare bags into odd nooks and crannies; keep them all together where they are handy, and you will always know what you've got and where you've got it.

We have a short, heavy-duty electric extension cord, plus 50-foot and 100-foot extension cords, and they are all stored in one bag, instead of snaking all over the locker as they are wont to do if uncontained. Our main electric shore cable isn't in the bag, because it is used too frequently. For a long while, we coiled it up as best we could, and laid it in on top of the contents of one locker. One day, the coiled-up cable was lying next to the canvas ice bag, and we saw that the cable would fit perfectly in there. Now the cable is always stowed in the ice bag when it is not in use. We even store the water hose in a small drawstring bag. We like the new flat water hoses, which can be rolled into a compact ball for easy stowage.

We put our lengths of spare line, 10 feet and over, in one bag. Short lengths are put in another bag, and, believe it or not, lengths of under a foot are put in a third bag! This system evolved gradually with us, and it certainly has paid off in convenience. We don't have to dig around in a big bag of scraps of line to find what we want; we know just where to go to find the right length.

If something isn't in a bag aboard our boat, it is in a box, and usually a plastic box. Various sizes of plastic boxes are so useful it is hard to imagine how the old-timers managed so well without them; it must have been a case of not knowing what they were missing. We store all cereal, flour, pasta, rice, cookies, crackers, instant potatoes, and sugar in plastic containers. Each is labeled clearly. We have many different sizes of the Freezette brand. Their 8½" x 7" x 4¾" container is excellent for cereal. The contents of a 12-ounce cereal box fit into it nicely.

Our canister set and many of our containers are Tupperware. One woman we heard about was so enamored of Tupperware that she designed her galley food-stowage shelves to hold certain Tupperware containers. Since our galley was already there when we bought the boat, we had to experiment with different combinations of containers so they would fit our shelves without wasting space. We started with the containers we already had, then added, eliminated, and switched around until we got them arranged the way we wanted.

Storage of food is only one use for plastic boxes. We have several in the head in various sizes for various items, including a large first-aid kit. We have found Freezette's 3" x 3" x 2-3/8" boxes the best size for our collection of nuts, bolts, screws, washers, and other small hardware. We feel the same way about hardware as we do about line. We don't want to search through it all for a ¼-20 stainless-steel bolt. We have 11 of these small boxes, with stainless-steel nuts and bolts in one, stainless-steel washers in another, hooks in a third, and so on. Putting small items all together in one big container makes it difficult to locate what you want, and it's usually easier to go out and buy what you need instead of searching through a big, messy box (Fig. 11-5).

We have another medium-size box that holds nothing but light bulbs: cabin bulbs, anchor bulbs, flashlight bulbs, compass bulbs, reading bulbs, depth-sounder bulbs, running-light bulbs, and more. We have spares for all our lights, and we want them kept together.

Hooks and shock cord can be used up under the deck, inside the cockpit lockers, in the same way that they can be employed in lockers below. Rarely are cockpit lockers filled to the top, back under the deck. The bosun's chair, for example, can be stored there. Or it might be just the place for a spare anchor that is used frequently. The hooks and lashings for holding it in place would have to be strong, of course, to take the heavy weight of an anchor. Even a small hammock could be hung there, under the deck, to hold sail covers or fenders. The locker's lids can be fitted with webbing straps or shock-cord devices to hold life jackets or sail covers, or the sail bags of the sails in use, or coils of dock lines. Use your imagination. Don't forget the stowage area in front of the transom. Some boats have little extra space in that area, while others are cavernous. Ours, being the latter, has been turned into a lumber yard; it is stacked full of plywood, two-by-fours, mahogany, teak, and spruce. You might ask: "Who needs to carry all that wood around?" We do. And maybe you do, too. After one wild night's ride down the New Jersey coast in a gale, we found we had lost our bowsprit platform. It was made of three teak boards, so we whipped up another one from the teak we had in our "lumber yard." Another time, we discovered a crack in a spreader, and we made a new one from the spruce.

Some forepeaks also are cavernous, and they can be partitioned off for optimum storage space. We ran one partition athwartships in the forepeak, dividing it in half. One of these days we are going to put a fore-and-aft partition in one of the halves to make a chain locker on one side and a place for anchor line on the other. The farthest-forward ribs in our forepeak form a small compartment, and there we stow our tiny artificial Christmas tree.

If your boat is fiberglass, it will take some forethought before

Figure 11-5. With small items separated and stowed in correctly labeled boxes, needed items can be found quickly and inventory can be taken easily.

you can install some of the storage devices we have mentioned. You may have to glass-in wood strips to support hooks and partitions, but it will be worthwhile if you are short of good stowage space.

Nothing, it seems, works smoothly ashore or afloat unless it is slathered with grease or bathed in oil. Even though they are messy to use, impossible to clean up, and difficult to store, lubricants must be carried with you. This is the only area where we feel that land people are better off than live-aboards. Those who live ashore can store their grease and oil in an out-of-the-way corner of the garage and forget about it.

Since all these lubricants invariably will leak onto anything they are stored with, the solution is simple: store them all together in their own container. There they can leak and ooze onto each other, and it won't make any difference. Our grease and oil storage container is a rectangular styrofoam ice chest. This is not the best material for storing lubricants, but we had an old one we were going to dispose of, and it was just the right size. In it we have oil cans and grease guns, pouring spouts, oil for the engine, and many tubes of grease. Just plain old ordinary grease isn't good enough on a boat. There is a different kind needed for every job, and you have got to have them all. A large plastic box with a lid might be a good storage container for lubricants, but the plastic would have to be the right kind, since some types dissolve in certain kinds of petroleum products.

Fiberglass boats don't have much space under the cabin sole for storage, but there is always some. Even if the area is shallow, something will fit there. Wooden boats usually have the most storage area in the bilges. Everyone seems to have a different idea about what should be stored there. Under the main cabin sole we have paint, thinners, brush cleaners, and things of that genre. Most of these are flammable in various degrees, and we prefer stowing them there, away from the engine and the batteries. Also, should they spill, they wouldn't do any damage to anything else stored there. Some of the liquids might dissolve the plastic hoses on the bilge pump if they spilled into the deep bilge and had to be pumped out; but the chances of that are slim, since most of them are stored upright and are packed rather tightly, so there is no room for them to tip over.

Under the forward cabin sole, where the bilge is shallower, we store items like glues, crack and wood fillers, and bedding compounds. These things are packaged in small cans and tubes that fit well into small spaces. If we were going across an ocean, we probably would take out some of the paint and replace it with canned goods. To prevent cans from rusting, coat them with varnish. Varnish can be applied to the canned foods, as well as to any other cans that might rust. So far we haven't had to resort to this, because we have used up everything before rust has had a chance to appear. Varnishing, however, is a time-consuming and rather expensive rust preventative. Before going to such trouble, experiment with Ziploc bags. Put each large can into its own bag and seal it or not, as you prefer. The bags are watertight when sealed, but often it is enough to stand the can in an open bag to keep the bottom dry.

We have three divided areas under the cabin sole — forward, mid, and main. We keep a list in a notebook of what is stored where and how much of it there is. We also keep a list of any lengths of line over 10 feet long. The list gives the length, diameter, and the material of the line. It takes only a short time to make these lists, and they save lots of time when you want to know what you have on hand. It is much more pleasant to read a list to find out where something is than to root around in the bilges.

Sail stowage is a problem on most boats, unless there is a locker or lazarette designed for just that purpose. Try to avoid storing sails on berths used for sleeping; on some smaller boats, however, the only place for them is a quarter berth. Some forepeaks will hold some sails. The small storm sails might be stowed there and, perhaps, some of the larger sails. Cruising boats don't need to adhere to the racing practice of having all the sails ready to be passed up through the forward hatch and dropped down into the hatch after a sail change. But there is nothing wrong with having them there if that happens to be where the sail locker is. In many European boats a sail locker is a part of the forward compartment.

We can get all of our six sails, including the main, into one cockpit locker. The main is rarely stowed, of course; and for coastwise cruising, the jib or the genoa, whichever was used last, is left hanked to the forestay, bagged, and tied securely to the bow pulpit. Some people store their sails on deck if they are cruising in fairly protected waters or are spending time in a marina. Boats with trunk cabins often have a sail bag on each side of the cabin, alongside the mast. Here the bags can be lashed to the grab rails, out of the walkway.

Many good cruising boats have been used for racing, and if you buy one of these, you may find a huge sail inventory included. Unless you are planning to race, you probably can sell half of these sails and never miss them. (We heard of one 35-foot sloop that came equipped with 12 sails.) No cruising boat needs more than the working sails, storm sails, special sails for a particular rig, and one or two genoas. Notice: no spinnaker. If you don't believe us, carry one for awhile and see how much you use it.

We have a large sun awning with metal poles for holding it flat and a sailing dinghy with a two-part metal pole for a mast. Stowage of these unwieldy items presented a problem, but we solved it easily and inexpensively by using sewer pipe. We bought two 10-foot lengths of four-inch-diameter plastic (PVC) pipe. (PVC pipe comes in several colors, and caps can be purchased to close off the ends.)   The awning, rolled up, fits into one pipe and the dinghy's paraphernalia is in the other. One pipe is lashed on each side of the mast on our flush deck, but they could be used atop trunk cabins just as well. Simple wooden holders could be made for them, or they could be held in place with lashings through eyes on the cabin roof. Don't lash them to the grab rails, or the grab rails will be useless as handholds. Mount the pipes in the area between the mast and the grab rails. Sail bags can still be stowed there, on top of the pipes (Fig. 6-3).

XII. BELOW-DECKS

APPEARANCE AND DECOR

Decorating a yacht below may not rate high on your list of priorities, but if the cabin is gloomy and drab-looking, it won't be long before you are feeling depressed and unsatisfied without knowing why. Colors have definite effects on personalities, and because moving to a boat usually is such a drastic change, we should do all we can to make the boat an inviting place to live.

Many older boats are too dark below from lack of natural light or too much varnish and not enough painted areas. Some of the older fiberglass boats are just the opposite, with too much unrelieved white below. The builders of the newer fiberglass boats are trying to get away from the bathtub look, and some have covered every available area with real or imitation wood.

At first glance, a wood interior looks very "yachty" and appealing; but it darkens the interior considerably, even on the brightest days. A happy balance can be found with enough wood for warmth and enough painted areas to make the cabin light and airy.

For some reason, buff has always been the traditional color for painted areas above and below deck. But buff often looks like white paint that has yellowed, and even if the interior has been painted recently, it may have a dingy, neglected appearance. White paint will make the interior lighter. Men, especially, seem to think that a white-painted surface is impossible to keep clean, but a greasy fingerprint shows up just as clearly on buff as it does on white. And it takes just as much time and effort to clean a spot off one color as it does the other.

Paint all the necessary areas white, and use latex instead of "marine" paint, as we mentioned before. Practice on a smooth board to get the feel of latex paint, which is much heavier than other types. Rolling the paint will give you the smoothest surface, but most boats do not have enough large areas for rolling to be practical. It takes a bit of skill to obscure the brush strokes, but it can be done if you practice beforehand. The paint can be thinned with water, which will help to eliminate the brush strokes, but a thinned solution will not cover as well. Since latex paint dries quickly, the prospect of putting on two coats is not so formidable.

Older boats usually have a cabin sole of dark wood, which contributes to the gloom of the interior. Some of these are finished beautifully with inlaid strips of holly wood. But beautiful or not, we advocate covering the entire cabin sole with carpeting. It is more pleasant underfoot, especially when your shoes are off, and is easier to keep looking clean than bare wood. Carpeting also prevents sand and dirt from sifting into the bilges through the cracks in the floorboards. It can add some brightness to the cabin, and often it considerably reduces the noise of the engine.

We had indoor-outdoor carpeting in our previous boats, but it was not satisfactory. It held the dirt, and it was hard to clean unless we took it out, laid it on the dock, scrubbed it with a brush, and hosed it down. Some of the rubber-backed carpeting holds dampness and water and will not dry unless it, too, is removed completely and hung in the sun to dry.

Rugs are not practical for a boat, because they slip too easily, and even carpeting must be attached firmly in order to stay in place in a seaway.

The most satisfactory floor covering we have found is ordinary nylon carpeting designed for house interiors. Our present carpeting is a remnant of some very inexpensive carpeting, because thicker and more costly carpeting has too deep a pile and prevents our doors from opening.

A pure synthetic, such as nylon or polyester, is far more preferable than natural fibers. Synthetics wear much longer, are unaffected by wetness or dampness, and dry very quickly if accidentally soaked. As with blankets, avoid any floor covering made entirely or partly of rayon, because it takes a long time to dry.

We have the entire cabin sole carpeted, including the head, and the companionway ladder. The head is carpeted with a fragment of a machine-washable rug. The stair treads are secured with double-faced tape. Any small carpeted areas should be fixed with tape so the carpet never will slip. Tacking has never been satisfactory. The carpet in our main cabin stays in place without any tape, because it conforms exactly to the irregular shape of the cabin sole and is anchored by the dining table. The carpet is split athwartships wherever there is a split in the floorboards, so the items stored underneath are accessible.

Use a medium shade of carpeting, since it will show less dirt than the darker colors, especially when sand or crushed shell is tracked aboard. It will brighten the cabin and be cooler in the summer. Ours is a solid color in a medium shade of gold; it is completely satisfactory, but a tweed or variegated pattern would show even less of the dirt that inevitably is tracked aboard. A more pronounced pattern, however, is not suitable in small areas such as boat cabins; it will make the cabin look cluttered and much smaller. Most new boats come with carpeting, but much of it is shag, and obviously installed at the instigation of someone who has never had to clean it.

Some thought should be given to the colors used to decorate the cabin, since they can convey feelings of warmth or coolness. White, blues, turquoises, and greens are considered cool colors, while yellows, oranges, reds, golds, and browns are warm colors. The experts discourage the use of warm or cool colors exclusively; they advise using at least one color from the opposite family as an accent. If you use blues and greens, for example, you can introduce a bit of yellow or gold in curtains or pillow covers. Remember that wood trim is some shade of brown, so that can count as your warm color in a cool color scheme. Since most live-aboards spend a good part of their time in warmer climates, the cool colors are a good choice. If there is plenty of wood in the cabin, don't use a warm color scheme.

Most boat manufacturers use a professional decorator's guidance for their interiors. The color advertisements of new boats can be a good guide as to what looks good with what, and the color scheme can be adapted to your own boat.

The main color accent below usually is the bunk cushions, and, unless you want to re-cover them, you are stuck with decorating around the existing color. If the cushions have vinyl covers and you don't like the color, you have a good excuse to have them re-covered with a fabric. If you like the color of the vinyl cushions, invent an excuse to re-cover them in fabric of the same color. Nowadays, most new boats come with fabric-covered cushions.

If you cannot afford to have the cushions reupholstered, learn how to do it yourself, or at least make simple fabric slipcovers for them. Much of today's upholstery material can be cleaned with carpet-cleaning detergents.

A relatively hard-finish material is better than anything plushy. The more nap, the hotter the material will be for sitting and sleeping. It is a good idea to avoid "busy" and predominant patterns on seat and bunk cushions. The cabin of any small boat is bound to look somewhat cluttered with all the normal accoutrements for living aboard. Do not add to the cluttered appearance. Use bold patterns only in small areas, such as throw-pillow covers or curtains.

Curtains of some sort are necessary for nearly every boat. Because most of the ports are small, rather thin fabric should be used. Small pieces of thick fabric cannot be pushed back along a rod or pleated without bunching unattractively. Fiberglass material might seem to be the desirable curtain fabric, since it will not burn, but it is too thick to look good on small ports. Only the curtain on the port immediately above the stove is a potential fire hazard, but if even the least caution is exercised, the chances of fire are slim.

If you decide to use a patterned fabric anywhere, refrain from using any with quaint nautical motifs that would be used only in a child's room ashore. Go easy on the flowers and delicate patterns, too. Remember that you are decorating an adult's living and/or sleeping room.

The patterns of some fabrics may show through slightly on the back side, and if they are hung on a window or port, this is the side that will be seen from outside. Curtains with such patterns should be lined, but linings usually make the curtains too bulky for small ports. When you select curtain fabric, consider how it will look from the outside.

We have curtains of plain-colored permanent-press cotton and polyester. We could have bought regular yard goods to make them, but we purchased a solid-color bedsheet instead. Sometimes this is an inexpensive way to get a quantity of material. The sheet cost $3, and we still have half of it left.

The devices made to hold curtains in boats are varied and expensive; for the most part, they are not necessary. Ordinary dime-store curtain rods will work perfectly well for most installations. Our rods are about 5/16 inch in diameter; they are called sash rods. We bought white ones, and they show no signs of rusting. If there is no wood for screwing in the rod holders, glue small blocks of wood to the fiberglass and attach the rod holders to the blocks. If you do not want to use metal rods, you can substitute painted or stained wooden dowels.

Many people, on seeing our boat for the first time, remark that she looks just like a home. We remind them that she is a home. If she looked only like a boat that people just happened to be living on, we wouldn't be happy living there. We have tried to make her look like a home — a comfortable, inviting one. Mementos of cruises, photographs, and pictures have a place in your boat-home as much as they do in a home ashore. They help create a personal, homelike atmosphere.

Framed pictures cannot be hung in the usual manner on a boat. We always use wooden frames and drill a tiny hole in the centers of the top and bottom of the frame. Hold up the picture and mark where you want it. Insert a thin nail into the top center hole. The nail should be long enough to go through the frame with enough extra to grip the bulkhead, but short enough so it will not go through the bulkhead to the other side. Hold the picture against the bulkhead, on your marks, and gently tap in the nail. After making sure the picture is straight, tap in the bottom nail. The nails are not noticeable in the frame, and it takes only two of them to hold a small picture, glass and all, securely against the bulkhead.

Pictures mounted on fiberglass bulkheads will have to be held on with double-faced carpet tape. Some brands of this tape hold better than others, but none of them will hold if the bulkhead and the items to be mounted on it aren't completely flat and smooth. The tape will hold only lightweight items.

XIII. COMMUNICATIONS, ENTERTAINMENT, AND EMERGENCIES

Every boat needs a radio, but your pocketbook and your cruising plans will determine whether you need a radio receiver or a radio-telephone or both. Our "living room" has four radios, which may be some sort of record. We have both an AM and a VHF radio-telephone, a radio direction finder (RDF), and a multiband receiver. Even if you don't care what is happening in the world, you should have some reliable means of finding out about the weather in your vicinity. Even if you are permanently tied to a dock, you need to know when hurricanes are coming.

The most spartan radio available is tuned to only one frequency and gives only the weather. If that is all you want, buy it and be done with it. Don't complicate your life with the myriad of other types of radios available. Most of us, however, want the news and then some relaxing music to make us forget about the news. And the less independent of us would like to be able to call for help when we need it and stand a good chance of being aided.

As soon as you delve into any radio information, you will be confronted, and probably confused, by the terminology involved with radio frequencies. A hertz (Hz) is a unit of frequency equal to one cycle per second; a kilohertz (kHz) is a thousand cycles per second; and a megahertz (MHz) is a million cycles per second. A meter (m) is the unit for measuring the distance between two cycles. On a given piece of radio equipment, any one of the three designations, or a combination of them, may be marked on the dial. A simple formula will convert one to the other. The meters are divided into 300,000 for kilohertz, and 300 for megahertz.

$$200m = \frac{300,000}{200} = 1,500kHz \qquad 1,500kHz = \frac{300,000}{1,500} = 200m$$

$$200m = \frac{300}{200} = 1.5MHz \qquad 1.5MHz = \frac{300}{1.5} = 200m$$

The chart below lists the radio frequency bands and the radios on which they are found. This may help you to determine what type of radio equipment you need in your boat.

RANGE OF BAND	TYPE OF EQUIPMENT	USES
285kHz to 325kHz	RADIO DIRECTION FINDER	Determination of boat's position by signals emitted from navigation aids
550kHz to 1650kHz	STANDARD BROADCAST AM RADIO RADIO DIRECTION FINDER MULTIBAND SHORT WAVE	Information and entertainment from local and national programming (news, weather, music, sports, etc.)
2000kHz to 3000kHz (2-3MHz)	AM DOUBLE SIDEBAND RADIOTELEPHONE SINGLE SIDEBAND RADIOTELEPHONE RADIO DIRECTION FINDER MULTIBAND SHORT WAVE	Sending and receiving of distress calls (2182kHz); ship's business; other marine communications
88.1MHz to 107.9MHz	STANDARD BROADCAST FM RADIO RADIO DIRECTION FINDER MULTIBAND RADIO	Mostly local music; limited news and weather
156MHz to 163MHz	VHF RADIOTELEPHONE RADIO DIRECTION FINDER	Sending and receiving of distress calls (Channel 16—156.8MHz); ship's business; other marine communications; NOAA weather (162.40MHz 162.55MHz)

Radio direction finders are equipped with a rotating antenna that allows you to determine the direction of signals emitted from navigational aids, radio station towers, or even another vessel, to determine your boat's position. RDFs usually have AM and FM broadcast bands in addition to the low-frequency beacon band. Some have other useful bands as well, such as NOAA (National Oceanic and Atmospheric Administration) weather on 162.40MHz and 162.55MHz.

If you get an RDF, be sure it has the low-frequency beacon band, 285kHz to 325kHz. Some RDFs are designed for air navigation use, and they do not have the bands to pick up signals from marine navigation aids.

If you feel you do not want or need a radiotelephone, the right RDF with a good selection of bands could be the one radio for all your needs.

Standard AM radios are the best for the most diversified programming, although FM offers better reception with less interference. Radios with both AM and FM bands will not be much more expensive than ones with just AM. Any radio of this type should be powerful enough to pick up distant stations, since you may be cruising or living in remote areas at times.

AM double-sideband radiotelephones will be legal until 1977, when VHF will completely replace the AM units in the United States for pleasure boats. Much of the rest of the world, however, including the Bahamas and other Caribbean islands, still will be using AM after that date.

With AM you can select the frequency you want for each of your channels, and a tuned crystal is installed for each individual frequency. There may be four, six, or many more channels on a given radiotelephone. The distress frequency is 2182kHz. The Coast Guard frequency is 2670kHz. Special broadcasts featuring weather and notices to mariners are given daily by many Coast Guard stations on their frequency. The frequency for the marine telephone operator in a given area may be selected as one of the channels, thereby enabling you to make ship-to-shore telephone calls.

You can monitor only the frequencies you have crystals for on your radiotelephone; however, some RDFs and some multiband radios have the 2000kHz to 3000kHz range, and these can be tuned for the whole frequency band. All radiotelephones need external antennas. An AM unit needs a tall whip antenna, which usually is mounted on the deck. An insulated length of the backstay also can be used for the antenna.

Presently, only VHF radiotelephones can be installed in pleasure boats. (Single-sideband radiotelephones can be installed, but not unless you already have a VHF radiotelephone.) On VHF units, as with AM radiotelephones, you select the channels (frequencies) you want, and a crystal is installed for each one. VHF units with 12 or more channels are recommended. VHF transmission is not subject to the interference that is common on AM broadcasting. VHF units have a range of about 20 miles, which can be increased by mounting the antenna as high as possible, such as atop the mast. Our VHF antenna is mounted there, and at night with the right atmospheric conditions, we have had a 60-mile range.

The VHF frequency range includes 162.40MHz and 162.55MHz, both of which have continuous 24-hour NOAA weather broadcasts; it is a good idea to have crystals for both of these frequencies. Channel 16 (156.8MHz) is the distress frequency. Channels 12 and 14 have been used for talking to the Coast Guard, but now channel 22 (157.10MHz) is preferred for routine conversation; 22 also will be used for special weather bulletins. Channel 13 (156.65MHz) will allow you to communicate with drawbridge tenders.

VHF is used mostly in the United States and Canada. Its use elsewhere is limited at the present time. Ship-to-shore telephone calls can be made if you have a crystal for the local marine operator, usually channels 24, 25, and 26.

There are presently three types of radiotelephones for yacht use: medium frequency (MF) 2000kHz to 3000kHz AM double-sideband; very high frequency (VHF) 156MHz to 163MHz band; and the relatively new single-sideband (SSB). SSB units use the same 2000kHz to 3000kHz band as AM double-sideband, but due to a different method of transmission, they are not compatible. The SSB system allows for many more broadcast channels than were previously available on double-sideband.

It seems that regulations concerning radiotelephones, their installation, their use, and their channels are being revised constantly. Radiotelephone modifications must be done by someone who knows what he is doing, and these are the professionals who charge upwards of $15 an hour. Before installing any radiotelephone or modifying an old one, get the most up-to-date information from the Coast Guard and the Federal Communications Commission. Then hope they won't change their minds too soon.

A station license must be obtained for the ship's radiotelephone. The license costs $4 and needs to be renewed every five years. Everyone who lives aboard your boat should know how to use a radiotelephone. Anyone who is likely to use it with any regularity must have a personal license, which is usually the restricted radio-telephone operator's license. This license is easy to obtain, and you need no special qualifications other than an understanding of the rules governing the use of radiotelephones. There is no examination. The license costs $4 and never needs to be renewed.

Citizen's band radios are found on some boats. The Coast Guard does not monitor any CB frequencies, so this radio's use is limited, unless you have a monitoring arrangement with friends who also have citizen's band sets or are within range of a land-based REACT unit.

If you are a ham operator, take aboard as much as possible of your sending and receiving equipment. With this worldwide communication system, a distress call always will be heard by someone somewhere. With AM and FM, you can't be sure. The ham meter bands can be received on multiband short-wave radios.

The Zenith Trans-Oceanic portable radio is a superb instrument that has long been the favorite of many cruising people. While it is not a transmitter, it can receive all the frequencies of all the bands. It is a very powerful set; you can receive news from home when you are halfway around the world. It is operated by internal batteries, 12 volt DC or 115 volt AC.

Other good multiband radio receivers are the Realistic DX-160, which can be purchased at Radio Shack stores, and the Heathkit GR-78, which is a kit that must be assembled. The DX-160 operates on 115 volt AC or 12 volt DC. The Heathkit is powered by a nickel-cadmium battery that can be recharged with its built-in charger from a 115-volt AC or a 12-volt DC source.

The regional *Light Lists* show all low-frequency beacon bands and their signal characteristics in the area covered. Broadcast times for weather and notices to mariners on 2670kHz are given in the regional *Coast Pilot* or *Sailing Directions*. Hydrographic Office publications 117A and 117B (Radio Navigational Aids) and 118 (World-wide Marine Weather Broadcasts) contain useful data and should be included in your library.

Radio stations WWV and WWVH are operated by the National Bureau of Standards; they give time signals continuously on 2.5MHz, 5MHz, 10MHz, and 15MHz. WWV also broadcasts on 20MHz and 25MHz. These signals consist of a tick every second, with voice announcements of Universal Coordinated Time every minute. (Greenwich Mean Time is now called Universal Coordinated Time.) Storm warnings are given three times each hour. WWV covers the United States and the North Atlantic; WWVH covers the Pacific. It is necessary to monitor one of these two stations to obtain the time to the second, which is needed for celestial navigation. Unfortunately, these stations are not received easily without an elaborate antenna and a fairly powerful radio receiver. One or more of their frequencies might be included on any radio you select for your boat, but the stations cannot be picked up unless the receiver has the requisite high power.

Most live-aboards have a television; there is no reason not to. The small transistor sets that use either 115-volt AC or 12-volt DC can be used both at dockside and at anchor. When they are used on a 12-volt system, the power required is slight, so there is very little drain on the batteries. We have a small 12-volt/115-volt Sony portable that has served us well for over nine years.

Aside from the entertainment value of a television set, it can be useful for weather reports. On a cruise in the North Channel of Lake Huron, we often were out of the range of the official weather radio broadcasts, but we always could pick up a television station in the vicinity. Television weather reports are more detailed than the ones you get on commercial radio stations, and they show a weather map, so you can have an idea of what is in store for you.

Getting good reception all of the time can be difficult for the cruising sailor; he often is miles away from the nearest station and reception is miserable at best or completely nonexistent if the set's built-in antenna is used. Some form of external antenna is needed on any boat, and it is absolutely necessary on a steel-hulled boat.

The simplest form of external antenna is a length of bell wire with an alligator clip on each end. One end is clipped to the set's antenna, and the other can be attached outside to the backstay or a shroud, or inside to the bolts holding the lifeline stanchion bases, if they are accessible from below, as they are on many fiberglass boats. This makeshift antenna will pick up distant stations, but it often is awkward to use.

The VHF marine frequency band is midway between television channels 6 and 7, so a VHF antenna also can be used for a television antenna. We installed a two-position coaxial switch. It normally is used for switching from one antenna to another, but we use it for switching from the radio to the television. This arrangement involves a short length of shielded coaxial cable. Two spade-type solderless connectors are attached to the wire and shield. These are then attached to the external antenna screws on the back of the set. A coaxial plug is on the other end of the cable, and this is plugged into the two-position switch. If the VHF antenna is at the top of the mast, you can get good long-range reception. One drawback to this arrangement is that the VHF antenna is not as efficient on channels 12 and 13 as it is on the other channels.

In an electrical storm, disconnect the connectors from the external antenna screws, but leave the two-position switch on the television position. This way, both the VHF radio and the television are protected from damage by lightning.

Garry Saxon of *Jabberwocky III* gave us the ideas for two simple, inexpensive, and very effective antennas. Both are the folded dipole type that can be hoisted to the top of the mast on a halyard, and you can make both of them easily. For one antenna, you will need enough 300-ohm, twin-lead, plastic strip wire to reach from the top of the mast to your television set, plus six feet, and a six-foot three-inch length of ½-inch PVC conduit pipe.   Cut a six-foot length of the wire.   Twist, then solder together, the two wires on each end.   Split one of the wires in the middle so that it makes two leads (Fig. 13-1).

Drill two small holes, 1½ inches apart, in the center of the pipe. Slide the six feet of wire into this pipe. Fish the two leads through the holes, one to each hole, with a thread or string. The leads are then soldered onto the ends of the lead line that goes to the television set.

Cut three lengths of 1/8-inch line as long as the mast is tall. With a clove hitch, tie one line to the pipe near the center next to the lead line, and allow about one foot of line to extend above the pipe.   Tie a bowline in the end of this short length, so it can be attached to the halyard.

Tape the lead wire to the line along its entire length, every 1½ feet, leaving a little slack so that any strain will be taken on the line instead of on the lead wire.

Drill a hole in each end of the pipe and insert one of the re- maining two lines in each hole.   These lines are used to control the position of the pipe and can be tied off on the lifelines or something on deck when the pipe is set where you want it. The side of the pipe, not the ends, must be aimed at the television station.   Another small line can be tied in an inverted *V* to give extra support to the pipe (Fig. 13-2).

Because this antenna is so directional, it can have tremendous range if the atmospheric conditions are right. One year, when we were in Gulfport, Mississippi, we wanted to watch the Sugar Bowl football game on television.   Because some tickets went unsold, the game was blacked out on both the New Orleans and Biloxi stations, which we could pick up easily. It was not blacked out in Pensacola, Florida, 110 miles away.   With the antenna aimed just

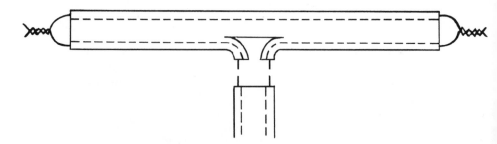

Figure 13-1. After twin-lead wire is inserted in PVC pipe, with each of 2 leads coming from its respective hole, lead wires are soldered onto 2 wires in line that goes to television set.

right, we picked up the game from Pensacola, with excellent reception.

For local stations, the folded dipole antenna is effective when it is secured to the boom by a length of shock cord. It does not have to be hoisted.

When at anchor, the swing of the boat will affect the direction of the antenna; the picture tends to fade and then come back again as the boat swings. If there is a program we really want to see while we are at anchor, we put out a small second anchor to stop the swing, and we pull it up when the program is over.

We did this once when there was a special program we wanted to see. Even though the stern anchor was hooked lightly to stop the swing temporarily, it looked, to an observer, as though we were anchored firmly from the bow and stern. Another boat came into the anchorage, and the skipper dropped the hook in front of us, almost over our bow anchor. Bill told him courteously but firmly that he thought the other boat was too close to us. The skipper of the other boat was unconcerned, and he said, "You're anchored bow and stern; you won't swing into me." Bill said, "But the stern anchor is only my television anchor!" Until that time, the other skipper probably had never heard of a television

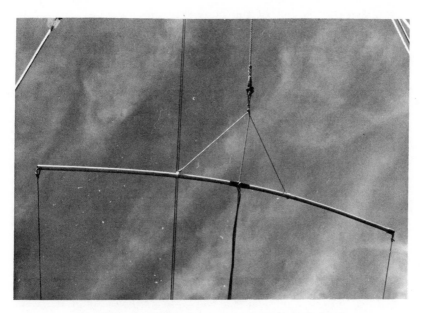

Figure 13-2. Finished antenna, about to be hoisted.

anchor. After Bill explained it to him, he moved away, harboring no hard feelings, and we went back to our program.

The other homemade antenna is omnidirectional, so you will not need a television anchor when you use it. Buy an eight-foot length of 3/4" x 1/8" aluminum bar stock. This can be purchased from nearly any hardware store for about $2.50. Cut off 25 inches and drill two bolt holes in each end and two holes in the center. Bend one inch at each end 90 degrees in opposite directions (Fig. 13-3). This is the center crosspiece of the antenna. Cut the remaining piece of the aluminum stock into two equal lengths, and get two pieces of insulating material, each four inches long. (We used stiff nylon, but wood will work as well.) Bolt each insulator to one of the one-inch tabs with equal amounts of the insulating material on each side of the tabs.

Bend the two remaining pieces of aluminum into half circles, and bolt each to the outside of the insulators, thus forming a complete circle but with the two outside curves insulated from each other and not touching each other (Fig. 13-4). Get a 12-inch length of wood or aluminum and drill a hole in each end; drill two holes approximately eight inches from one end to match the ones in the center of the crosspiece. Bolt the 12-inch piece perpendicularly to the crosspiece. The eight-inch side will be the top of the antenna. Get enough 300-ohm, twin-lead wire to reach from your television set, out of the boat, and up as high as you will be able to hoist the antenna.

Split the lead wire in half for three or four inches and attach each half to one of the bolts at each end of one insulator, thereby connecting them to each of the two half circles. Tape the wire along the crosspiece to the center, where the wire drops vertically to the deck (Fig. 13-5). Attach some 1/8-inch line to the bottom hole of the vertical piece to use as a downhaul, so no strain will be

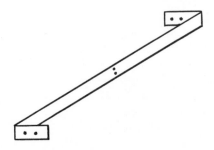

Figure 13-3. Crosspiece of circular antenna. Center holes can be staggered, if desired.

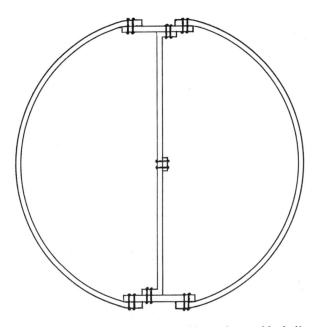

Figure 13-4. Circular television antenna. Short, heavy black lines indicate bolts.

Figure 13-5. Circular television antenna, as seen from deck, looking up. Line at left, outside circle, is secured to forestay. Lead wire is taped to right side of crosspiece. All "raw" edges are taped to prevent chafe, even though antenna is not hoisted when sailing.

put on the lead wire. Tie another short length of this line to one end of the crosspiece, and tie a bowline in the other end around the forestay to keep the antenna from spinning in the wind. Shackle a halyard to the top hole of the vertical piece, and hoist the antenna as high as it can go without touching the mast or stays.

Although this antenna will pick up several stations from different directions, it is not as good as the other antenna for picking up long-distance stations.

Twelve-volt color television is now on the market. The sets are only slightly larger than the black-and-white models, but they draw about three times as many amps. More elaborate antennas are necessary for good color reception, and decent reception from distant stations still is difficult. Different localities and different positions of the boat determine which antenna will do the best job for you.

We had an extensive collection of phonograph records when we were living ashore, and we did not want to give up the records just because we were going to live on a boat. Our solution was to transfer all the records to cassettes. It was an expensive process, but we sold the records and stereo components, which more than paid for the tape we used and the small cassette player we purchased. It was well worth the 90 hours we spent recording on the cassettes.

Our cassette player runs on internal batteries, 12-volt DC or 115-volt AC. Small batteries run down very quickly when they are used to drive cassettes, so a unit that can also be run off the larger ship's batteries is desirable. Phonograph records can be transferred to tape cartridges, but cartridges are larger and take up much more storage space than cassettes.

XIV. NAVIGATION EQUIPMENT

Although this is a live-aboard manual, cruising is a definite part of living aboard. In fact, the cruising aspect is what motivates most people to make a boat their home in the first place. So, assuming you are going to do some cruising, we have included this chapter on navigation to tell you how to get around easily and safely. When we mention navigation, we usually will be referring to the kind of navigation used in the coastwise cruising most of us do before setting off on an ocean voyage.

The most important piece of navigation equipment is the compass, but it must be a corrected compass to be of any real value. If you buy a used boat with a corrected compass, have it checked when you have all your own gear stowed aboard. You can correct it yourself with a sun compass corrector or a hand-bearing compass, or you can have the job done by a professional compass adjuster. Keep the correction (deviation) card handy near the wheel or tiller, where it can be referred to easily. It is a good idea to seal the card in waterproof plastic.

The compass must be mounted so that it can be read easily night and day. Many are mounted so far away from the wheel or tiller they can't be read by the helmsman. The helmsman shouldn't have to twist or bend to see it. The compass should have a red light in it for nighttime use. If you are installing a compass on your boat, be sure to twist the light wires going to the compass to avoid any unnecessary magnetic deviation. (Twisting the wires together breaks up the magnetic field.) Naturally, you shouldn't have cans, knives, cameras, radios, or other metal objects near the compass when you are steering a compass course.

The accuracy of the compass should be checked as often as possible. Pick a couple of buoys or markers in a straight line in the

general direction you are heading. (Only one marker need be
visible.) Measure the course between them with a protractor.
Figure the variation and deviation. Maneuver so that one of the
buoys is directly astern, and steer the course you have computed
for the other one. If your compass is accurate, it will bring you
right up to the other buoy. Try to do this on as many different
headings as you can, as often as you can. That way you will
always know if your compass is accurate on a given heading or if
it has developed any deviation. If you have allowed for any
current or leeway, and your calculated course does not bring you
to the buoy, the compass may be off on that heading and not
agree with the deviation you have established. If too many
headings are different from what they should be, check the compass again and make a new deviation card. Sometimes the re-
arrangement of metallic items in the cockpit lockers affects
certain compass headings.

Believe in your corrected and constantly checked compass as
you believe in nothing else. Remember that it invariably knows
more than you do.

Even the simplest coastal cruising requires a compass at some
time or other. We know of one boat that has her large, antique
brass, never-been-corrected compass mounted on an even more
antique, oriental, carved teak table. As a conversation piece, it
couldn't be better; as a navigation piece, it couldn't be worse.
The skipper of this boat says if he gets into fog, he will drop the
hook and wait until the fog lifts. Luckily, he wasn't with us in
the busy ship channel in Delaware Bay one day, when the fog came
in instantly and the half-mile-apart buoys disappeared as if they
had never been there. We wouldn't want to anchor in a place as
busy as that, even in clear weather! Fortunately, this man's
"cruises" rarely are longer than his dock lines at the marina where
he is currently tied up. Without a good compass, this is as far as
anyone should go — nowhere.

Because we trust our compass implicitly, we have never failed to
navigate through the densest fog and come out where we intended
to be. Learn to plot compass courses and get into the habit of
steering them, especially when out of sight of land or the next
buoy, or when the atmospheric conditions could bring fog. One
minute you can be in clear weather, and the next in fog so dense
you sometimes can't see the bow of your boat. It is a good idea
to have another compass aboard that could be used as a steering
compass in an emergency. Many sailors keep a hand-bearing
compass aboard for this reason.

If the main compass is not removable, make or buy a cover for
it as protection from the sun when you are not underway. Otherwise, remove the compass to a safe, shady place.

Needless to say, the most important navigation item is a proper chart of the area in which you are navigating. Without this, you can't use any of your navigation equipment successfully.

A good protractor is essential. We have found that the more gimmicky they are, the less satisfactory they are. Protractors don't need arms, rollers, or wheels. Our favorite is the "plain" one used by the U. S. Power Squadron (Fig. 14-1). It is a clear piece of plastic 15 inches by four inches with a protractor in the center and several horizontal lines that run along its entire length. To use it, the edge of the protractor, or one of the long horizontal lines on it, is lined up along the course or bearing line. Then slide the protractor so the crosshair is over a meridian of longitude. The course or bearing is read from the protractor where the meridian line passes through it. Latitude lines can be used when the course or bearing you are measuring is nearly north or south. In this case, the result is read from the small inner scale on the protractor. There are no adjustments that have to be made or gadgets to be fiddled with before the course can be determined, nor is it necessary to use the compass rose on the chart. This protractor is easy to use in the cockpit, and, if necessary, it can be used with one hand.

During coastal cruising, we keep the chart in a clipboard, with the protractor also under the clip. Parallel rules, which once were

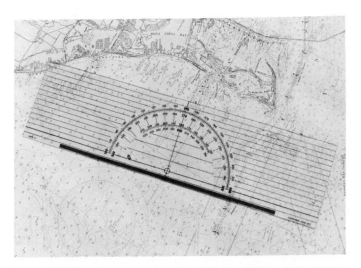

Figure 14-1. USPS protractor. A green strip is visible along bottom when protractor is right-side-up. Strip is red if protractor is placed accidentally on chart upside-down.

used almost universally, can be very inaccurate, and the Power Squadron protractor is now much preferred over them. The chart, the compass, and the protractor are the basic items needed for coastal piloting.

Never skimp on charts. Get the small-scale charts that give the overall picture of a cruising area, as well as the large-scale charts for small craft. If there is *any* possibility that you will be putting into *any* harbor, be sure to have the relevant chart.

As mentioned before, we save all our charts and correct and update them from the *Notice to Mariners*. If you do most of your cruising in one area, use the *Local Notice to Mariners*; if you do more extensive cruising, use the larger, more encompassing *Notice to Mariners*. Both of these publications are free and are issued weekly. The *Local Notice to Mariners* is published by the area Coast Guard Commander, and the *Notice to Mariners* is published by the Defense Mapping Agency, Hydrographic Center, Washington, D. C. 20390.

We make only the chart corrections that affect us directly. For instance, if a ship channel has been deepened to 35 feet from 33 feet, we make no note of it. If, on the other hand, an unlighted buoy is replaced with a lighted one, we indicate it on the chart with the characteristics of the light. As we are cruising, we indicate new landmarks, such as water towers, that might have been built since we last cruised the area.

Most cruising live-aboards tend to cruise to or through the same areas year after year. We have our charts for these areas marked off with the courses we usually follow. We use a permanent red felt-tip marker, so the lines will not be obliterated by rain or dampness. We also indicate the magnetic course and the distance. Traditionally, only true courses should appear on charts, and they should be marked only with pencil. Professional seamen know that when they look at a chart, the plotted courses always will be true. We are the only ones who will be using our charts, so we have them marked for our convenience only. You may find that some nontraditional way is best for you, too.

In many confined channels, especially the Intracoastal Waterway, there are straight stretches that run for several miles, and it is hard to keep track of exactly where you are. To help us, we use an arrow pointer, which is moved along on the chart every time we come to a buoy or identifiable landmark (Fig. 14-2). The arrow is made of masking tape, with the two corners folded back to make a point; each arrow is colored with a felt-tip pen in a color that contrasts with the chart. Or the tape can be cut to a point on one end, and this point is colored. The arrow can be picked up and put down for many miles before you need to make a new one.

Binoculars should be high on the list of needed navigation

equipment. Wide-field, 7 x 35 or 7 x 50 glasses are good for boat use. Avoid the larger magnifications, as they are more difficult to hold steady with two hands, and impossible to use with one hand.

A depth sounder is hard to live without once you have had one. It can be used for many things, but it is most important for letting you know when you are getting into shallow water. Some depth sounders have buzzers that sound a warning. A depth of water safe for your boat is predetermined and set on the sounder. When this depth is reached, the buzzer sounds and you can alter your course accordingly. For example, the sounder can be set to warn you when you are out of the channel.

A depth sounder lets you know how much water you are anchoring in, so you can determine how much scope to use. A depth sounder used with a chart lets you know your approximate position on your course line. A sounder also can be used for position-finding by a series of readings equally spaced in time and distance, plotted on a piece of tracing paper to the scale of the chart. This is laid over the chart on the approximate course line and juggled around until the depths you have marked on the paper correspond with the depths printed on the chart. The sounder

Figure 14-2. Masking-tape arrow with colored point can be advanced easily along a course. Use of this device eliminates checking off each buoy with pen or pencil, thus making chart easier to read on future voyages along the same route.

readings must be adjusted for the state of the tide at the time the reading is taken, since the depths shown on the chart are measured from mean low water. If you want to know how far off you are from a light or headland, check the reading on the depth sounder, find that depth on the chart, and measure your distance off.

Many times we have navigated in fog or haze by using the depth sounder to follow a fathom curve to a buoy or marker. A good depth sounder will let you venture safely into places you might not otherwise go. We have found deep enough anchorages, which weren't indicated on the chart, by venturing in slowly, using the depth sounder as a guide.

If you have to buy a depth sounder, the kind with a pointer or needle will be easier to read in bright sunlight than the kind with a flashing neon light. But the lighted types will register fish under the hull in a less heart-stopping manner than the needle type; fish show as fainter flashes under the bright light designating the depth of the water. With the pointer type, the needle momentarily jumps down to the level that indicates the location of the fish under the hull, which might be just about what your draft is, so it looks for an instant as if you are running aground. You will have to adjust to the way your depth sounder reads.

If you have a sounder with a neon light, or one of the newer light-emitting-diode (LED) types that does not show up well in the sunlight, a simple detachable shield can be constructed to shade it and make the light more visible (Fig. 14-3).

The markings on the scales of many depth sounders are often so close together it is difficult to tell whether you are in 10 feet or six feet of water. The scale below 10 feet is the most important one for most pleasure boats. It is important that the depth sounder have an expanded scale with each foot marked off between zero and 10, so you will be able to see clearly *exactly* how much water is under the keel.

A depth sounder can be used more precisely if you know exactly where the light or needle is located on the scale when you are just barely aground. It will not read zero, because the transducer is located somewhere under the waterline. When we are lightly aground, our depth sounder shows 2½ feet of water under the keel.

Understanding your depth sounder will enable you to turn gunkholing into a fine art. Use of the depth sounder does not mean you will not run aground. We have been aground more times than we can remember, but by paying careful attention to the depth sounder and cutting our speed when it shoals up, we ground very lightly and can back off easily. If anyone tells you he never goes aground, either he is lying or he rarely ventures out in a boat.

A lead and line, the system that has been used for centuries for determining depth, is still a useful tool — a necessary one if you don't have a depth sounder. The lead has a concave indentation in the bottom; in the old days, tallow was put in the indentation so that a sampling of the bottom would stick to the tallow, and you could tell what you were anchoring in. Sometimes it would give you an indication of where you were, if you really knew the area well and were navigating in fog.

One of the ancient mariners claimed that he could tell exactly where the sounding was taken by tasting the bottom material brought up on the tallow. You never will have to be that proficient in reading the lead, because most charts describe the bottom.

The line can be marked off in the traditional way. At the two-fathom point, a leather with two ends is affixed; at three fathoms, a leather with three ends; at five fathoms, white calico is attached; at seven fathoms, red bunting; at ten fathoms, a flat leather with a hole in it; and at 13 fathoms, thick, blue serge. The traditional markings go up to 40 fathoms, but 10 fathoms is all you would ever need for coastal cruising. The reason for marking the line with a variety of materials is to enable the "reader" of the line to do it in the dark, by feel. In these days of spotlights, flashlights, and spreader lights, your line can be marked off with a piece of plastic tape with the depth written on it with a waterproof marker. Where could you find blue serge today, anyhow?

We draw four feet nine inches, and have an eight-foot boat-hook, which we use often for sounding. It is marked off with

Figure 14-3. Depth-sounder shield is made of cardboard and covered with black vinyl. It can be folded flat for easy stowing.

strips of waterproof, colored plastic tape at 4½ feet, five feet, and six feet. When we go aground, we use the boathook to see if the water is deeper on one side of the boat than the other. Often it is, so we have an indication of what might be the best way to get off.

A speedometer or log is handy to have wherever you cruise, and it is necessary for offshore sailing. Built-in speedometers have through-the-hull sensors that might be a paddlewheel, a strut, or a rotor. They register the boat's speed on a dial mounted in the cockpit. Some of the more elaborate units also indicate the distance covered.

One of the features you should look for in a speedometer is an arrangement whereby the sensor can be removed for cleaning while the boat is in the water. The sensors are subject to frequent fouling, so they need to be cleaned often. If you cannot remove the sensor while the boat is in the water, you will have to dive to clean it or be hauled out. Fortunately, many speedometers do have a removable strut or rotor. They fit into a special through-the-hull fitting, and are simply pulled out for cleaning.

Logs, such as the Walker KDO, tow a rotor on a long cord that is attached to the mileage counter mounted on the stern rail. You should have spare rotors (the Walker log comes with one), because fish bite them off now and then, mistaking them for food. Any log streamed from the stern will over-read because of prop wash if it is used when under power.

Unless you are planning an offshore passage, don't be in too much of a hurry to get any kind of speed indicator. Check the speed of your boat, under power and sail, by the time it takes to get from one place to another. You will learn to judge your speed fairly accurately just by watching how fast the water is going by your hull. For coastal cruising, you may need only your judgment for a speedometer.

There are many ways of telling which way the wind blows, from expensive wind-direction indicators to the feel of it on the back of your neck. We prefer a wind sock at the top of the mast and yarn telltales on the shrouds.

Both the expensive wind-speed and the wind-direction indicators are useful when racing, but they are unnecessary for cruising. Our wind-speed indicator is the hand-held model made by Dwyer (Fig. 14-4). It has two scales — two to 10 miles per hour, and four to 66 miles per hour. When the indicator is held into the wind, the air enters a small hole at the bottom of the instrument and pushes a tiny ball up a chute. The figure opposite the ball is the wind speed. When compared to the more expensive instruments, it has proven itself quite accurate. Occasionally the ball needs to be replaced, and additional balls are obtainable from marine stores and the manufacturer. The Dwyer wind gauge still costs under $8.

Our indicator is normally used only to confirm what we already suspected, since wind speed is something else you can become adept at estimating.

Any major offshore sailing will require the use of a sextant. This may be an instrument you eventually will want to purchase, so find a good one. The drum-type scale is easier to read than the old-fashioned vernier scale. On a bouncy boat, a large, high-powered scope or monocular will be difficult to hold steady enough for a good sight.

For coastwise cruising, the sextant can be used to measure the horizontal angle between two fixed objects, which, when plotted on a chart, will give you a circle of position. Two horizontal angles between three fixed objects will give you a fix. The sextant also can be used to measure the angle from sea level to the top of an object of known height. This angle and Table Nine in Bowditch will give you the distance off.

A sextant offshore isn't much good without some means of knowing the exact time. The timepiece can be the traditional chronometer, or a tuning fork, or a quartz-crystal wristwatch —

Figure 14-4. Dwyer wind-speed indicator registers 5-mph breeze.

if it is adjusted to keep the accurate time most of the manufacturers promise. Many navigators have dispensed with chronometers and watches for their time, if they have a radio that is capable of always picking up the time ticks from WWV or WWVH (see Chapter XIII).

The publications needed for celestial navigation are a *Nautical Almanac* for the current year and sight reduction tables for the method of navigation used. The two most common are H.O. 249 (three volumes) and H.O. 229 (six volumes). H.O. 249 is designed for air navigation, but it is adapted easily for sea navigation, and is the easiest system to use. H.O. 229 is more complicated but more accurate. (H.O. is the abbreviation for Hydrographic Office. The Naval Hydrographic Office, now called the Naval Oceanographic Office, publishes the sight reduction tables.)

There are four publications that are helpful for coastal cruising: *Coast Pilots*, *Light Lists*, *Tide Tables*, and *Tidal Current Tables*. All but the *Light Lists* are U. S. Department of Commerce publications. The *Light List* is printed by the U. S. Coast Guard.

Coast Pilots are issued for the United States and its possessions and describe in detail coast features, harbors, bays, rivers, danger areas, anchorages, sources of fuel and supplies, water depths, navigation regulations for prohibited and restricted zones, drawbridge regulations, etc. In short, they include everything you might want to know about a given area.

The *Light List* is exactly what its title implies — a list of every lighted navigational aid maintained by the Coast Guard. There are five volumes covering different parts of the United States and its possessions. The *Light List* describes each light's characteristics, the depth of water it is in, the range of the light, what the structure looks like, and the color of the structure.

Tide Tables enable you to calculate the stage of the tide at any time on any day. Many tidal locations are listed, from north to south, along with the data needed to calculate the tide there. If you are aground (again) and cannot get off, you will be able to tell whether the tide is coming in or going out, and approximately how long you will be stuck.

Included in the data is the range of the tide: how much it rises and falls. This information is useful for anchoring. Figure out the stage of the tide at the time of anchoring. Then figure out how many feet will go out from under you until low tide is reached. It might be that you would be aground at low tide. It is amazing how many sailors never take the rise and fall of the tide into consideration when anchoring. Being high and dry once, though, is bound to make them more prudent.

Tidal Current Tables are similar in format to the *Tide Tables*, but they are used to calculate the strength and direction of the current in a given area. Current tables are as necessary as tide tables. Just because the tide is going out does not necessarily mean that the current is going "out" in the same direction at the same time. Sometimes they coincide; sometimes they do not.

Many places have currents strong enough to delay you severely or give you a nice boost. These currents can be figured out in advance so that you can take advantage of them.

All of the above publications are issued annually at different times of the year. The *Tide Tables* and *Tidal Current Tables* are available at the end of each year for the next year's use.

There are numerous nongovernment books and cruising guides for cruising areas in the United States, Canada, the Caribbean islands, and elsewhere. These publications are very helpful for cruising or planning a cruise. They usually list marinas and their services and sightseeing attractions on or near the water, and they include such things as mileage charts and weather patterns for different seasons.

There are several U. S. Government publications that are useful for foreign cruising, one of which is the *Sailing Directions*. There are 69 editions of the *Sailing Directions*, covering all parts of the world outside the United States. They have much the same information as the *Coast Pilots*, as well as the various customs and regulations of the country or area they cover.

H.O. 111A and 111B through H.O. 116 are the numbers of the seven editions of the publication, *List of Lights and Fog Signals*. These editions have basically the same type of information as the Coast Guard *Light Lists*, except that they cover all the lighted aids in the world.

Two other publications that are helpful for coastal and foreign cruising are *American Practical Navigator*, H.O. 9, usually referred to as "Bowditch" after the author, Nathaniel Bowditch; and *Piloting, Seamanship and Small Boat Handling*, more commonly called "Chapman's" after *its* author, Charles F. Chapman. Bowditch includes everything you will ever need to know about navigation, and also a collection of very useful tables. The title of Chapman's is self-explanatory, and it covers the subjects thoroughly.

XV. DECK WORK

AND STEERING

MADE EASIER

There are many gadgets, both simple and complicated, that a boat can have to make deck work easy. While we are all in favor of making things as easy as possible, we would not go to the extreme that one skipper did. He sat in his big, comfortable helmsman's chair within easy reach of the buttons that controlled everything on his boat. He pushed one button and the engine started — an ordinary enough procedure. He pushed another button and the anchor came up. Not too startling — lots of boats have electrically operated winches. But then he pushed two more buttons and the jib and mainsail were hoisted automatically!

COCKPIT CUSHIONS

Since this is a chapter devoted to making your life easier on deck, let's get rid of cockpit cushions first. Literally get rid of them. They have no place on a cruising live-aboard boat. They are not safe underfoot. They will blow away if they are not secured. They must be removed when you need access to cockpit lockers. If they are not fastened down, they will slide when heeling. When the boat is left unattended, the cushions must be stowed in the cabin somewhere, since that is the only place the unwieldy things will fit. If you need padding under you, get a small, plastic-covered cushion — one that can be stowed in a cockpit locker.

SAIL REEFING

The most common kind of reefing on any new boat these days is roller reefing of one kind or another. Hailed as a great invention when first introduced, roller reefing now causes second thoughts. It is the fastest way to get a reef in the mainsail, and it can be done by one person if a neat job is not expected. Even with two people doing the job, it is very difficult to get the sail to roll up smoothly. And even if a neat roll is accomplished, the sail will not necessarily set properly. Usually it does not.

If a deep reef is rolled in, the boom tends to drop. Any roller reefing works against the natural cut and belly of the mainsail and may cause inefficient sail performance. The reefing gears must be lubricated periodically, but even if they are, they have been known to jam, making it impossible to reef the sail.

Since roller reefing is an accessory not included in the base price of most new boats, give some thought to installing this optional equipment. There is a better, and usually less expensive, way to achieve a reef in the mainsail — by using reef points. We have had three boats with roller-reefing devices, but we added reef points to the mainsails on each when the roller reefing was found to be unsatisfactory.

Reef points have been in use for many years, and they still are the most satisfactory way to reef. Any mainsail or mizzen, or jib, for that matter, can have reef points put on by a sailmaker. There should be at least a double set of reef points so the sail can be well reefed down. Any sail shortened by reef points will set as perfectly as it did before it was reefed.

Tying in a reef is a simple matter. Ease off on the main halyard. Fasten the tack cringle for the reef band desired to the gooseneck fitting on the boom. Haul out on the clew outhaul pennant until the proper tension of the reef band is reached. Tie it off and start sailing. The reef points can be tied in later. They are tied around the bunt of the sail with a square (or slippery square) knot.

On larger boats, it often is necessary to have some mechanical assistance to pull the clew outhaul tight. This can be achieved either by mounting a small winch on the underside of the boom with the clew outhaul pennant led to it, or by the installation of a simple block-and-tackle arrangement on the side of the boom. The clew outhaul pennants should be rove through their respective cringles all the time; the critical part of the reefing can be done from the mast area, and it will never be necessary to work at the end of a bucking, swaying boom. Smaller boats with smaller main-sails would not need blocks and tackles or winches for reefing, but a system such as this should be installed for safety's sake.

JIB ROLLER FURLING AND REEFING

While roller reefing for the mainsail leaves much to be desired, genoa-jib roller reefing can be satisfactory, and using it makes for very comfortable cruising. A few years ago, the jib was only able to be furled. Either it was out all the way or it was rolled up all the way. Now the jib can be let out or rolled up to expose the amount of sail needed, which means, in effect, that it can be reefed.

The first type of jib reefing had the jib winding around its own luff wire. The luff tended to unwind and stretch, allowing the luff to sag to leeward when on the wind. Any effort at reefing resulted in the luff unwinding at the center, and the jib would bag out there while the top and bottom remained somewhat furled. In this position, the sail usually jammed the furling mechanism.

Recent developments have overcome this problem, adding a new dimension to a roller-furling genoa and making it truly a roller-reefing genoa. One method uses a grooved rod for the forestay. The rod, being rigid, does not stretch or unwind. Another type uses a tube that fits over the forestay, and the tube revolves around the forestay. The jib is attached to either the rod or the tube by a bolt rope or barrel slides on the sail. On blustery days, most modern boats sail well under jib alone, so it is very convenient if you are able to let out the sail area you need without venturing to the foredeck.

HALYARDS

If we had our way, we would never have wire halyards. As wire ages, it develops short wire "hairs," which are very hard on the hands. Wire-reel winches can be dangerous, and many people have been seriously injured or even killed when using them. Recently a man was killed by a handle left in a winch. When he released the brake, the winch was spinning out of control. He was standing too close and was hit in the head by the handle.

If there are wire-reel winches on your boat, make sure the brake is in good working order, and always have it *on* when using the handle. Remove the handle first when the brake is to be released. When raising a sail, make sure the wire feeds smoothly onto the drum and there are no overlapping turns, even if you have to guide the wire with your hand. Wire rope taken up around the drum haphazardly and carelessly will snag and surely jam sooner or later.

If wire halyards must be used for strength (Dacron in large diameters is not convenient to handle), the reel winch can be eliminated by splicing a rope tail to the wire. The halyard then can be used on a standard winch.

We would prefer to have all halyards of Dacron, preferably braided, but otherwise three-stranded. The braid wears well and is not as apt to get snagged as the three-strand rope. Wire rope originally came into use because Manila would shrink and swell when wet.   There is little stretch to Dacron, and we have found it to be a satisfactory halyard material.

CLEATS

There is nothing wrong with using traditional cleats for the sheets, but sheets can be handled more easily and quickly if they are secured in Clamcleats (Fig. 15-1). A line can be cleated instantly. The line is simply laid in the trough of the cleat and that's it. The helmsman alone can tack with the genoa in a good breeze. The line is released just as simply by flipping it out. Clamcleats are especially handy when well heeled over. Cleating a sheet in the conventional manner involves leaning over to leeward.

As long as the cleat is properly lined up to take the sheet as it feeds off the winch, it will hold the line just as firmly as the old-style cleats. Some installations will need to have wedges secured under them to line up the cleat correctly. They come in sizes large enough to take 5/8-inch line.

Figure 15-1. Jib sheet in Clamcleat.   Notice that cleat is mounted on pod inside coaming so sheet will lead properly from winch to cleat.

DOWNHAULS

If you don't have roller reefing on your jib, install a downhaul to ease your foredeck work. A downhaul is a simple device to install, yet most boats don't have one. Most likely it is because their skippers have never heard of downhauls.

To make a downhaul, you need a ¼-inch line the length of the forestay, plus the distance from the forestay to the mast, on deck. Attach this line to the halyard shackle and lead it through a small block near the tack of the sail, then to a cleat on or near the mast, wherever it will be handy to the halyard itself. To lower the sail, cast off the halyard and let it slide slowly through your fingers while you pull in on the downhaul. The jib will come down and stay down as long as you have tension on the downhaul. Cleat off the downhaul and the halyard, and the sail can be bagged or lashed down.

If the hanks on the jib are large enough, the downhaul line can be put inside each one of the hanks, along with the forestay, as you are hanking them on. With a downhaul you never will have to go to the bow and wrestle down the jib. A downhaul will also work with mains, mizzens, and other sails that are difficult to haul down.

TOPPING LIFT

It is very disconcerting to have the boom drop into the cockpit as the mainsail is lowered. A topping lift, so easy to install, eliminates this hazard.

One type of topping lift is a line shackled to the end of the boom that runs up through a block at the top of the mast, then down the mast, at which point it is cleated off near the base. This type is the easiest to use if the boom is not too heavy.

Some topping lifts are a length of rope or wire fastened at the top of the mast and run to a block on the lower end of the rope or wire, just above the boom. A line runs from one side of the end of the boom up through the block, down through a cheek block on the other side of the boom, along the boom to a cleat at the forward end. This type gives you a two-to-one purchase and is the best for handling a heavy boom, although it is somewhat awkward to use. All topping lifts should be adjustable, and not the all-too-common fixed type with only a length of shock cord to take up the slack when sailing.

When the sails are up, the boom lifts naturally. Therefore, when the sails are hoisted, take up on the topping lift so that when the sails are lowered and the boom drops, the topping lift will keep the boom from dropping into the cockpit. When the sail is furled, the topping lift can be eased off until the boom is secured in the gallows or otherwise.

BOOM GALLOWS

If you don't have a topping lift, it helps to have a boom gallows, so that when the boom drops it will hit the gallows instead of your head. However, dropping the boom into a gallows with any force is not much better for the gallows than it is for your head. The boom should be lowered gently into the gallows. A gallows is a real help when furling the mainsail. Resting in its notch, the boom cannot sway from side to side with the furler swaying with it. The boom stays put, and you can lean against it to work if necessary.

Most gallows on older boats are wooden and fixed in a vertical position. Some of the newer designs are made of pipe, so they can be folded down against the transom or be telescoped up and down.

LAZYJACKS

Lazyjacks once were a common sight on sailboats, but most of today's sailors don't know what they are. Simply explained, a lazyjack is a couple of lines placed on each side of the mainsail to catch it when it is dropped (Fig. 15-2). The lines are tied off to

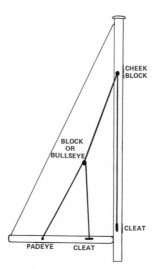

Figure 15-2. Installation of lazyjack on one side of mast and boom. Identical installation is necessary on opposites sides of mast and boom.

cleats on the mast and the boom, so they can be adjusted for different positions of the boom. Lazyjacks sometimes can be used as a topping lift, or they can be used in conjunction with a regular topping lift. Lazyjacks are very difficult to install on a roller-reefing boom.

PULPITS AND LIFELINES

There are many things a cruising boat-home can do without, but lifelines are not one of them. If you run a length of rope from the forestay to the shrouds to the stern, it is better than nothing — but just barely better than nothing. If you ever leave the dock, your boat also should have a bow pulpit. A stern pulpit is not nearly as important as the bow pulpit, but it is very nice to have if you can afford one. If your boat has a mizzen and any part of it extends out over the transom, a stern pulpit is especially useful.

Lifelines should be more than knee high. If you fall backward against a lifeline that catches you in the back of the knee, you can be flipped overboard easily. If the lifelines are more than 24 inches high, they should have a smaller line, parallel to the main lifeline, run through the middle of each stanchion. A high lifeline without the secondary line can allow you to roll underneath and overboard when kneeling on deck.

Be sure to have enough stanchions so that the line will be supported and not go slack between the stanchions. There should be places, both port and starboard, where the tension of the line can be adjusted if slackness occurs. Some lifelines have a turnbuckle at the aft end and an adjusting screw farther forward.

Many of the fancy stainless-steel lifelines are arranged so that the stanchion fits into its base plate and is held there only by a set screw. This arrangement allows the stanchions to pull out if the lifeline is caught under a dock so the stanchions will not be damaged. What preserves the lifeline stanchions, however, is not good for preserving you. If you are thrown against them, they must stay put.

Put the stanchions in their bases, and drill and tap a hole through the base and into the stanchion itself. Insert a good-size, sturdy, machine screw, and screw it tight enough so that the stanchion will never pop out. Try not to run into any docks. Bent stanchions still are easier to straighten out than bent people.

If you can afford it, have pelican-hook gates put in the lifelines. (Gates are expensive because of the hardware needed to install them.) We have one on each side of the cockpit and one on each side just forward of the shrouds. If there is no one to take your lines when docking, jumping over the lifelines is a high, sometimes dangerous hurdle you may have to make. And it is risky to stand on the toe rail outside of the lifeline to make the jump. With a gate, you simply can step ashore.

Some boats have only a bow pulpit and no lifelines. While this is better than nothing, we often wonder about the reasoning behind this arrangement. If the seas are rough and bouncy, the bow pulpit is used to hang onto when changing sail and for other foredeck work. But if the seas are at all rough and there are no lifelines, how can anyone move safely from the shrouds (the last handhold) across the open, unprotected foredeck to the bow? Crawl, maybe. Then there is the trip back.

Lifelines and pulpits do not have to be expensive, since they do not have to be made of chrome-plated stainless steel. Galvanized pipe and cable are just as good, even if they do not look as handsome.

This is a good time to mention the "looks" of a boat. When you are thinking of adding something that you feel will not look right, such as galvanized stanchions, try to remember all the boats you have seen with stanchions made of galvanized metal. Unless you have been very close to a boat equipped with them, you probably cannot remember any boat that had them — but you know you have seen them somewhere. The point is this: you did not remember any specific boat as being good-looking except for those ugly whatsits on her. Don't worry about the looks of little things that only you are aware of, such as fittings you may have put on but are not happy with. Other people will not notice insignificant details about your boat, any more than you noticed theirs. The overall boat is what most people see.

Do think twice, however, about performing unorthodox operations on a noticeably conspicuous item. We once saw a ketch with its masts painted lavender. We noticed and remembered that, and so did everyone else who saw the boat.

But back to galvanized fittings. There is nothing wrong or unorthodox about using galvanized metal for all your fittings, including stays and shrouds. It has been used successfully for years on many boats, and prior to World War II that was all there was for wire rigging. You can make your own lifelines and stanchions and bow and stern pulpits if you are so inclined — from galvanized pipe and wire with just a few tools.

WEATHER CLOTHS AND SAFETY NETTING

When you have the lifelines and pulpits set up, you have a place to hang weather cloths (Fig. 15-7) and safety netting (Fig. 15-3). Weather cloths are strips of fabric lashed to the stern pulpit and/or

Figure 15-3. Common type of awning seen in southern waters. Note safety netting lashed to lifelines.

lifelines on each side of the boat to keep spray from getting into the cockpit. The top edge of the weather cloth can be lashed firmly to the stern pulpit pipe or lifeline; but at the bottom, where it is joined to the toe rail, it should be secured only with shock cord, so it will have some "give" if a heavy sea crashes against it. Unless the weather cloth happens to be rotted, the force may bend the stern rail or stanchion before it tears the fabric if it is firmly lashed down on the bottom.

We have weather cloths that we leave on all the time now, because we found an unanticipated use for them after we initially put them on for an offshore passage. When laying alongside a dock when the companionway slides are removed, they provide an extra bit of privacy below by partially blocking the view into the cabin.

Unless you want the weather cloths for privacy, they are not necessary unless you are going offshore. Neither is safety netting. Sometimes netting is carried completely around the boat, especially if there are small children aboard; but more commonly it is only in the bow area and is used as much to contain the sails when they are lowered as to keep people and objects from falling overboard. Since netting is open, it can be lashed firmly top and bottom.

You can use any kind of net, from ordinary, inexpensive fish netting to the fancy nylon stuff sold specifically for this purpose. We found that our netting was fine on the open sea, but anywhere where you have to keep a sharp lookout for buoys or markers, the netting should be removed, because the navigation aids cannot be seen through the netting from the cockpit. Docking also can be a problem when the view of the dock is obscured by the netting. The netting we use has a fairly close weave, and the openings are only about half the size of those on fish netting, a fact that contributes to the visibility problem. When our net is not in use, we can slide it back along the lifeline and lash it to a stanchion.

AWNINGS AND DODGERS

All live-aboard boats need some kind of sun awning. The most typical kind is a large, flat awning that covers the companionway and the entire cockpit. This type is necessary for use at anchor or dockside. But even more necessary is an awning that gives the helmsman protection from the sun while underway.

The farther south you sail, the more you will see boats with some kind of small, permanent awning rigged over the steering station. Some are nothing more than powerboat bimini tops modified to fit sailboats (Fig. 15-3). Some are custom-made to fit the sailboat's configuration.

We had a logical starting place for our helmsman's awning, since the boom gallows is located slightly forward of the wheel and runs from bulwark to bulwark. The gallows forms the front of the awning frame. We purchased a length of stainless-steel pipe and bent it to the size and shape we needed, a shallow U. We fastened it to the gallows with some stainless-steel straps we fabricated into fittings. These are attached by wing nuts that can be tightened or loosened so the awning can be folded up. We covered the frame with canvas, because that is what we happened to have aboard at that time, and we installed zippers in strategic spots so we could remove the awning for cleaning. We have since added four panels (two in back and one on each side) that can be lowered to keep out sun and, to some extent, rain (Fig. 15-4).

A dodger (or navy top, as it sometimes is called) is another piece of equipment that you will find you cannot do without once you have experienced its comfort. If you are going to add a dodger, go all out and have one wide enough to extend across the whole cockpit. Do not waste your money or effort on one of those handkerchief-size things that fit only over the companionway

Figure 15-4. Whiffle's *awning over steering station.   Four individual panels are rolled up at outer edge and secured with small lengths of line, which are sewn to awning.*

hatch.   The hatch can be closed off to keep spray from getting below.   What you need is something to keep the spray from getting to you.

The bigger the dodger, the better.   If it can be made to extend over the steering station or meet the awning there, so much the better. Maybe you can work out a way to bring the steering station inside the dodger.   Put in windows so you can see where you are going, whether you can steer from under it or not.   A zippered front window is very convenient for air circulation.

Dodgers and awnings should be made of white or very light-colored material so they will reflect, rather than absorb, the sun's heat.

Some motorsailers have an inside steering station, so dodgers and awnings are not needed to protect the helmsman.

RATLINES

Ratlines are perhaps the saltiest-looking items that can be added to a boat.   They are very useful, and a necessity for threading your way through reefs in the Caribbean unless you have another way of going aloft for that purpose.   There are very few rigs that cannot have ratlines installed somewhere on their shrouds.   Ratlines can be made of rope, wire, pipe, or wood. There always will be a little slack in those made of rope and wire, and these will not provide as sure a footing as rigid pipe or wood ratlines. All can be attached to the shrouds by whipping, or with wire rope clamps if pipe or wood is used.

Our ratlines are made of white oak strips, one inch by 1½ inches. Two holes were drilled in each end of each ratline, and the U part of a wire rope clamp was inserted in the holes so that the shroud rests in the curve of the U (Fig. 15-5). The nuts are placed on each end and screwed down enough so that the ratline will not slip, yet not so tight that they crush the shroud. To prevent corrosion, we wrap the shroud with friction tape in the spot where each wire rope clamp will be, before attaching the ratline. This provides insulation between the stainless-steel shrouds and the galvanized clamps.

Our ratlines are 13 to 15 inches apart, the maximum distance we feel we can step safely. If you use wood, you should apply some kind of protection from the weather to prevent splitting. Varnish, paint, or oil will do the job. We have ratlines port and starboard, although many boats have them only on one side, which is not a good idea. On one tack, a single set of ratlines will be to leeward, which would make them unsafe to climb.

Aside from their use for navigating, we have used ratlines for painting the mast and spreaders, changing the bulbs in the spreader lights, and as a perch for getting high-angle photographs. Some-

Figure 15-5. Wooden ratlines secured with wire rope clamps.

times, in the deep land cuts on the Intracoastal Waterway where the banks are too high to see over, we climb up the ratlines just to watch the scenery.

ANCHORS

The easiest way to handle the anchor is with an anchor windlass. If only a chain is used for anchoring, a windlass is the only way to handle it. Whether you have a windlass or not, a roller chock should be installed in the bow (Fig. 15-6). The anchor line will lead directly from the bow, as it should, instead of from the usual chock on the side just aft of the bow; so the vessel will lie to her anchor better. A roller chock eliminates much of the chafe that occurs when a standard chock is used, and the roller makes it easier to pull up the anchor.

A plow anchor (Chapter XVII) stows handily in a roller chock and thus is always ready for use (Fig. 17-19).

A few years ago, roller chocks were found only on foreign-built boats. Several American companies now manufacture them, or you can build your own. A little ingenuity can turn a couple of pieces of welded metal and a rubber boat-trailer roller into an excellent roller chock.

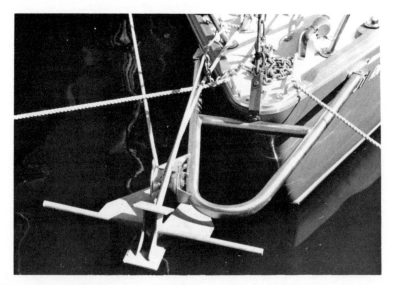

Figure 15-6. Roller chock attached to bowsprit. On boats without bowsprits, roller chock can be installed on bow itself.

SELF-STEERING

One of the nicest ways to be comfortable while cruising is to have your steering done for you. Aside from the comfort aspect, not having to steer means you will have more time to take care of the other things that always need to be attended to while underway. The fatigue that comes from never leaving the helm will be eliminated, and a self-steering device can steer a better course than you can.

Your steerer can be either an autopilot or a wind vane. An autopilot runs on electricity, and the wind vane has to have wind. Neither operates very efficiently in storm conditions, and when the going gets rough, most autopilots draw a considerable amount of electric current. Even though a helmsman is not needed to steer, some sort of lookout must be kept for other ships and obstructions hazardous to your boat.

Autopilots come in many sizes. There are small portable units that fit into the cockpit and steer the tiller by means of a push-pull rod. When fitted to a small boat that is normally easy to steer, and where the steering is done with a tiller, this unit does a good job.

For larger boats with wheel steering, more complicated autopilots are necessary. The autopilot is connected to the wheel by geared chains or cables. They usually steer by a compass heading, rather than the direction of the wind, and for this reason, they are more useful when under power. Many sailors prefer an autopilot over a wind vane because of its ability to follow a compass course. Some yachts are equipped with both, since wind vanes will not work when the boat is under power.

A wind vane is essentially a large weathervane that uses the wind's power to steer a definite course relative to the wind's direction. In order to set a vane, you have to steer the course desired. While holding this course, disengage the vane so that it can weathercock into the wind. Then re-engage it, and the vane will take over steering the boat. If the boat falls off or heads up, the wind pressure pushes against the vane, pushing it over and activating the mechanism of the vane, which brings the boat back on course. Some vanes work by pivoting horizontally, and some by a vertical pivot (Fig. 15-7).

There are four major types of wind vanes now on the market. The least complicated wind-vane arrangement transmits direct power from the vane by lines run through blocks to the tiller. This simple type of vane is suitable for light-displacement, tiller-steered small boats that are well balanced and develop little weather helm. The most popular vane of this type uses a horizontal pivot arrangement.

If a boat is equipped with an outboard rudder, a trim tab can be fitted to the rudder. The wind vane turns this tab, and the force of the water going past the tab exerts pressure, which turns the rudder in the opposite direction. This type of vane usually has a vertical pivot, which simplifies the design of the linkage between the vane and the tab. Since there is no mechanical hookup to a wheel or tiller, this vane can be used with either. This type of vane is capable of steering with some weather helm. Boats 35 feet and under can use this vane successfully.

Another type of vane has its own separate, semibalanced rudder mounted aft of the stern. It usually is operated by a trim-tab arrangement, or the vane turns the rudder directly. This type can be either a vertical- or a horizontal-pivot vane, and it has no hookup to the boat's rudder, wheel, or tiller. This type will work on well-balanced boats of 35 to 40 feet if there is little weather helm.

The most powerful vane is the kind equipped with a servo-pendulum blade. The vane turns the blade (or oar, as it is sometimes called), which hangs straight down into the water. The blade's

Figure 15-7. Duncan MacGregor designed this wind vane for his 32-foot sloop, Gitana. *On most wind vanes, vane is a solid wooden piece, which is much heavier than this tubular-metal one. When this vane is in use, a cloth sleeve is slipped over framework to form "solid" vane. When wind conditions warrant, the sleeve can, in effect, be reefed. Weather cloth/awning/ dodger arrangement is also a MacGregor design. Snap-on mid-section fills space between awning and weather cloth, so entire cockpit can be enclosed. Here, only half of mid-section is snapped in place.*

motion is sideways, due to the force of the boat's movement through the water. The blade swings one way or the other, like a pendulum, depending on which steering correction is needed. This movement is utilized, through linkage to the wheel or tiller, to turn the boat's rudder. A servo-pendulum vane will steer a boat with considerable weather helm; it also is capable of overcoming the friction found in many steering wheels. This vane is suitable for all boats up to 60 feet.

Any type of vane is difficult to fit to a boat. One type may perform well on one boat and be almost useless on another. The best procedure is to write to the manufacturers of the vanes that interest you, and ask them to recommend an installation for your particular boat.

Wind vanes cost anywhere from $150 to more than $1,000. They are invaluable for extended cruising, and many helmsmen also put them to good use for coastal cruising.

XVI. MAINTENANCE,
REPAIRS, AND TOOLS

Approach the upkeep of your boat-home just as you would a land home. Do not let your boat get out of hand and become run down. Avoid at all costs the "hippie" look so many sailboats acquire. Of necessity, a live-aboard boat must have many things stowed on deck, but the deck does not have to look like a junkyard.

A boat can quickly take on the look of a near-derelict if the top-sides are left unattended until the paint peels or wears off, or the colored hull of a fiberglass boat is allowed to fade or develop scars and scratches. Painting of the topsides and bottom is the most frequent major maintenance work any boat owner encounters. The job usually is done every year or so, but, as we mentioned before, you must decide when it needs to be done.

Bottoms need to be painted when they accumulate barnacles or other marine growth, and topsides need painting when they start to look shoddy. Often you can touch up the topsides in the bad spots, rather than repaint the whole boat. There are many live-aboards and other boaters who get their jollies from working on their boats. We would rather spend our time cruising, so we do our maintenance only when it is necessary — never for "fun." We have gone as long as 20 months without hauling out for bottom painting. Of course, since we have a steel hull, we do not have to worry about teredo worms any more than those with fiberglass boats do. Worm protection would have to be the de-termining factor when you consider hauling and painting the bottom of a wooden boat.

Unless you are a painting freak or a die-hard traditionalist, one of the first things you will find you can do without is a boot-top stripe. Most live-aboards merely extend the bottom paint up to what would be the top line of the boot top. Most of us do not want to waste time scrubbing the growth off regular boot-top paint, and using the bottom paint eliminates one more can of paint you would otherwise have to buy and stow. There is also one less line that has to be masked off, so you also save on masking tape.

Nearly everyone knows that hulls of a dark color will absorb the sun's heat, but fewer people consider that the sun will quickly fade the dark colors. This is more obvious with dark-hulled fiberglass boats; the faded paint on wooden boats usually is covered sooner or later, but so many fiberglass boats fade and look more disreputable every day, probably because their owners are convinced there is little or no maintenance to a fiberglass boat. As we write this, we can see a once-red-hulled fiberglass boat that has faded to various shades of sickly pink.

Have a dark hull if you wish, but be prepared for plenty of maintenance work to keep it looking shipshape. A touch-up job on a dark hull will be quite obvious. On white or light-colored hulls, the touched-up spots are often invisible. Since the dark colors absorb more heat, a dark-painted wooden boat can dry out rapidly, the wood will shrink, and the seams will open up — creating more maintenance work.

Brightwork can look disreputable more quickly than anything else, and there aren't too many live-aboards who bother with much of it. Sun is very damaging to varnish, so varnish is seldom seen on boats that spend a great deal of time in the South.

Maintenance time can be cut down if you use the right tools. Paint the topsides in a large swath with a three-inch-wide brush. Invest some money in a good natural-bristle brush, and take care of it. A quality brush enables rank amateurs to do a smooth job with few or no brush marks. Put all bottom paint on with rollers, except at the point where the bottom paint meets the topside paint. We have painted the bottom of our 26-foot-waterline boat in an hour by using rollers. Buy the cheapest rollers and trays you can find. They can be disposed of after each use or saved for the next time.

When you are hauled, clean the bottom immediately before it has a chance to dry. Clean it with water and anything that will roughen the surface — bronze wool or even brushes dipped in the sand that may be under your feet. Then, when you are ready to paint, the bottom will not have to be sanded first. If you use masking tape for cutting in a sharp line, do not leave it on any longer than necessary, and do not let it get wet, or else the tape will be very difficult to remove. Many paint jobs have been ruined by masking tape left on too long.

Decks should never be pure white. In bright sunlight, they are blinding. A four-to-one, five-to-one, or six-to-one mixture of white with a medium shade of gray, blue, or green is enough to take away the glare, yet the deck will still look white.

Mix sawdust, sand, or a commercial antiskid product with the deck paint to give the deck a nonslip surface. The antiskid properties will be in direct proportion to how much deck paint is used. During use, the paint must be stirred often to keep the gritty substance suspended in the paint. Any antiskid deck, whether it be a molded-in surface pattern on fiberglass or the painted-on type, will be more difficult to keep clean than a smooth surface, but it is extra work that must be tolerated.

If there are any gouges or deep scratches in the hull, fill and sand them before painting. After experimenting with several fillers, we have settled on Cuz, a Martin Senour product that can be purchased at National Auto Parts stores. It is an auto-body filler and costs half the amount of similar marine products that do the same thing. It is a two-part polyester product applied with a plastic spatula; it hardens quickly and sands easily. Cuz can be used on wood, fiberglass, ferrocement, and metal hulls.

Whiffle's steel hull, under the paint, is completely plastered over with troweling plaster. As this wears off or gets knocked off (which is usually what happens), we fill in the holes with Cuz. Troweling plaster is affected by temperature changes, which cause cracks to develop around the perimeter of previously filled holes. We have never experienced this with Cuz. Once it is applied, it stays put.

Once, when docking, a protruding bolt gouged a big chunk out of the plaster at the waterline, exposing the bare metal. The damage wasn't worth getting hauled for, yet we could not ignore it. Not knowing what else to do, we slapped on some Cuz. The gouge was damp, and the Cuz got wet before it hardened, but the stuff stuck and stayed there until we were hauled and able to repair it properly.

For a mirror finish, after the Cuz has been sanded and faired, apply one coat of Interlux Boatyard Sanding Surfacer. It dries quickly. Sand this lightly, then apply the topside paint. Sanding Surfacer can be used on wood and fiberglass boats as a prime coat. When sanded with fine sandpaper, it provides an extremely smooth surface for the final coat(s).

Different bottom paints behave in different ways, depending on the temperature, the latitude, and the salinity of the water. A popular brand that works well in one area may not be sold in another area because it doesn't perform well in those waters. Fortunately, the Woolsey Vinelast that was on *Whiffle* when we bought her has worked well in all the waters we have been in. If you have a metal hull and it has the Woolsey vinyl system on it, maintain the paint system conscientiously. Do not change it for another system until you investigate the alternatives carefully. Any problems with metal hulls usually begin because people do not know how to take care of them. The previous owner of our boat started with the Woolsey system, and we have been thankful that he did. It takes extra time to apply all the necessary eight coats of various paints when we patch the holes in the bottom paint, but the excellent protection this system gives to the hull makes the time well spent. We have no rust now, and we never will if we keep up the system. And, with this system, bottom paint adheres to a metal hull. It will not peel or fall off. We have heard of bottom paint coming off in sheets on some metal boats. A new epoxy system, using only three coats, has been developed by Woolsey, and that probably is the wisest choice for bottom paint if you are starting from scratch with a bare metal hull.

Steel and aluminum hulls need a buildup of several coats of special paints to insulate the bare metal from the metallic content of the antifouling paint, which could cause galvanic corrosion if applied directly to the bare metal hull. Wooden boats need bottom paints that will foil both hungry teredo worms and barnacles; but fiberglass hulls can be painted with any bottom paint that works in the waters where you are cruising. Cement boats need extra protection on the bottom, because the cement is porous and allows salt water to reach the metal reinforcing rods and mesh, with resulting galvanic corrosion. Woolsey recommends the epoxy system for ferrocement boats, too.

We hope we have already made our point about doing all your work yourself, which is one of the real keys to living aboard and being able to afford it. Anyone can learn to do the maintenance work on a boat. Start by gathering all the information necessary for the job you are undertaking. Sometimes product labels give you all the information you need. Owner and instruction manuals are helpful. Save relevant magazine articles. The English are great do-it-yourselfers, and their boating magazines are filled with helpful, detailed information. Many articles we have saved have come from them. Most American boating magazines seem to be concerned mainly with getting their readers to buy new equipment from the manufacturers who advertise in their magazines.

Two years before we moved aboard, Bill had nearly every copy of English and American boating magazines from the previous six years. Jan finally put her foot down and said he could keep any articles from any of the magazines, but the magazines themselves had to go. We pasted the articles on loose-leaf sheets and categorized them. We came up with an invaluable collection of easy-to-find information. We still follow this practice, because we still buy many boating magazines. Since we are living aboard, we cut them up more quickly and do not accumulate a large pile of them.

Buy or borrow books from the library that will tell you how to repair and maintain wood, metal, fiberglass, and cement boats; make and repair sails; and do all kinds of splicing. If you really want to learn, you can find information somewhere.

Aside from the money you save by doing your own work, no boatyard employee will care as much about your boat and how the work is done as you will. For this reason alone, you should learn how to do your own work.

Painting is the easiest maintenance task. This is the job always given to the unskilled employees in boatyards. Most of them do not know "how" to paint any more than you do, if you haven't done it before. Why pay them to learn on your boat when you could be learning yourself?

The "mechanic" you hire to work on your engine may be someone who was a construction worker a month ago. Just because someone is employed by a boatyard does not mean they know anything about boats.

Because of the lack of skilled workers, there are more and more yards being set up for the do-it-yourselfer. If you are wise, you will patronize them. But remember, just as with regular yards, there are good and bad do-it-yourself yards. Check with other boating people to find out what experiences they might have had with the yards you are considering.

Do-it-yourself yards charge a fee per foot for hauling. You can scrub the bottom yourself or hire the yard's people and their equipment to do it. The equipment might be a high-pressure hose that can blast off much of the stuff on the bottom so a minimum of scraping will have to be done. If it does not cost too much, we usually have this done by the yard. They can do the job quickly while the bottom is still wet. We are about to be hauled out again, and the yard we are using this time charges from $10 to $25 for the service. The hauling charge normally includes chocking, but check to be sure there is no extra charge for it.

Two or three days "on the beach" are usually included in the hauling fee. Depending on the yard, the longer you stay out of the water, the more it will cost. After a few days, a daily charge is applied for each day up to, say, 10 days. After 10 days, there is a higher daily charge. These charges encourage owners to move their boats quickly in and out of the yard. If you have plenty of work to do that will require you to be out of the water for a long time, try to use a yard where they will give you a special rate.

Usually only the owners of a boat can work on her; you cannot bring in a group of friends to help with the job. To protect yard workers' jobs, some yards absolutely forbid it; others charge an hourly rate for any work performed by outsiders. It usually is expected that you buy your paint from the yard; some yards insist that you buy your paint from them, and unless you do, you don't paint in their yard. Others have slightly more flexible rules.

Reputable yards have a sign listing everything for which you might be charged, so you can figure out in advance how much a normal bottom-painting haul-out will cost. Some yards offer special deals during the slow months when bad weather is just as prevalent as good weather. You can save money by taking advantage of these offers, but not if the weather prevents you from completing your work in the prescribed time.

When you are hauled, be sure the Travelift will take the weight of your boat. You will save money if the Travelift has a gate so the mast will not have to be unstepped before the boat can be hauled. Find out what kind of insurance the yard has, and how much their coverage will cost.

Try to be hauled in a yard that has a shower, a decent head, nearby sources of food and supplies, and, ideally, a place to eat when you are too tired to cook. If there is a good hardware store nearby, so much the better. You may have to buy paint from the yard, but you don't have to buy their other supplies, such as sandpaper.

After having several haul-outs, we now know in advance what supplies we will need. As soon as we are back in the water, we set about replacing the supplies that we have just used up, so we will be prepared for the next haul-out. For example, we need several cheap, disposable brushes for the various paints needed to touch up the holes in the bottom paint. Throwing away a 25-cent brush is much more economical than trying to clean it in a solvent that costs $2 a pint. We watch for sales and buy the brushes we will need for the next bottom-painting session.

It is easy to plan ahead for a haul-out for normal maintenance, but sometimes you have to be hauled for emergency repairs, and you may not be able to choose which yard will do it. This can put you at the mercy of boatyard bandits who try their best to relieve you of all the money you have. One of the more common practices of these unscrupulous yards is to charge you for more time than they actually spend working on your boat. To prevent this, stay at the yard and watch the workers every minute of every working day. One boatyard has a sign listing two different rates for their labor: the standard rate for doing the work, and *double* the standard rate if you watch them doing the work! Either way, you are going to pay much more than you should for anything done in a yard like that.

Once we were forced to use a yard where we could not do our own work, and they tried to bill us for six hours of labor performed *after* the boat had been removed from the yard. We were launched at noon on a Monday, and we then went back to our regular slip in another marina. When we began arguing over the impossibly high labor charges, the manager of the yard produced time sheets from two of his employees that showed they were working on our boat from one o'clock to four o'clock on Monday. Needless to say, we did not pay any of the padded portion of the bill, much to the manager's dismay.

"Are you calling my men liars?" he shouted. We told him we couldn't think of a more appropriate name.

This same yard employed workers who were capable of carrying only one tool at a time. The weak little fellow who was assigned to our boat made four separate trips to the tool shed, in a far corner of the yard, to get the right socket wrench to fit the particular nut he was struggling with.

Our experiences with dishonest yards, along with tales told by our boating acquaintances, would fill another book. All we can do is warn you about the potential traps. If you need major work done, and you cannot do it yourself, try to get a firm price for the job and a written contract to back it up. We say "try" because some slick yard managers will not give you a contract; or if they do, it will have so many loopholes in their favor that it is of little value to you.

Sometimes very busy yards are the best ones to deal with, even if you have to make an advance appointment and perhaps pay a higher hourly rate. Because they *are* so busy, they will do your job quickly so they can get on to the other work awaiting them. Their employees do not have to work slowly and pad time sheets so the yard can show a profit. If their hourly rate is a little higher than other yards, the speed with which the work gets done more than makes up for the cost.

Beware of the man who says, "Sure, I can fix it — no problem." When a nice fee is involved on a transient boat, he will be anxious to "fix" it; but when you discover that your problem still is not solved, you often are far out of the area and cannot bring the boat back so he can correct the problem. Only rarely will you encounter an honest mechanic who admits freely that he doesn't know a thing about your particular problem. It always is best to assume that no one knows as much as you do about your equipment. Even if you know *nothing* about it, that will put you on an equal basis with a horrifying number of "mechanics."

The engine and its failures seem to be the cause of a good deal of unhappiness among sailors. One of the main reasons sailors have so many engine problems is that they do not run them enough. Engines are designed to be run, not to sit idle and rust. The weekender who uses his engine only to get in and out of his slip is just asking for trouble. Has there ever been an ocean sailor who didn't complain about the way his engine misbehaved or failed him? Run the engine everyday when you are underway, and every few days when at dockside, and let it run up to temperature before turning it off. If the boat is tied up properly (and there is no reason she should not be), run the engine in gear. On a long passage under sail, the engine needs to be run every day or so to keep its vital juices flowing and avoid freeze-ups of moving parts.

Follow the engine maintenance recommended in the owner's manual. Do not develop a leave-well-enough-alone attitude. "Well enough" can turn into "unwell" very quickly if you neglect routine jobs. As soon as you have a boat, send for the technician's service manual for your engine. The owner's manual does not contain enough information for complete engine maintenance and repair. The technician's manual discusses valve clearances and other adjustment data and explains how to perform all the work on the engine. The good manuals give step-by-step procedures; if they are at all well written, they can be understood and used by anyone with a minimum of technical knowledge. Much of the work on marine engines requires muscle and brute force anyway. Also order the special tool list, if the manufacturer has one, and the parts catalog, which gives parts numbers and exploded views of the parts to show how they are put together.

Try to establish a relationship with someone at the factory, so you can call them personally for advice and parts. Don't bother writing letters. The few dollars spent for phone calls will be more than offset by the dockage fees saved by finding out what is wrong and being able to fix it quickly.

If the factory cannot get the parts to you because they work only through their distributors, get the name and phone number of the manager of the local distributorship and call him. If he cannot send parts to you personally, obtain a purchase-order number from the marina or yard and have him send the stuff there. All the distributor needs for shipping is the number; the yard can mail the actual purchase order later. If he does not deliver in the one or two days he might have promised, call him again. Don't sit back and assume someone else is taking care of things. Stay on top of the situation until you have the parts you need.

Unless the items are unusually large or heavy, have them mailed first class special delivery or shipped by air freight. Even if you have to rent a car to pick up items at an airport, it may be cheaper in the long run. One sailor needed an engine part, and he called the factory. They said they would send it by United Parcel. A week went by and no part arrived, so he called them again. There had been an oversight and the part had not gone out, but they promised to ship it right away. After another week and another phone call, he found out that the part had been shipped by *parcel post*. He finally got the part at the end of the third week, all the while paying $5 a night for dockage — $105. That $105 would have paid for lots of car rentals and shipping charges, and he would have been on his way much sooner. To make a sad story sadder, the part had been available locally, which he could have found out if he had thought of looking up a source in the yellow pages. Do not assume you have to go far afield for something without first checking all the local sources.

If your engine manufacturer doesn't want to let an ordinary mortal such as you have one of his sacred technician's manuals, tell him you are going to the South Seas, or somewhere where there will be no one but you to fix the engine. That way, he will not feel as if you are infringing on the territory of his authorized dealers and their mechanics. How many engines break down where a dealer is handy anyway?

Frequent visual inspection will catch minor problems before they become major. Check the oil and water (if the engine is freshwater cooled) every other day. When the engine is running, make a visual inspection of the generator belts, stuffing box, water pumps, exhaust system, and anything that might leak oil, water, or fuel. At first we didn't make too many checks on the engine. Then we had a few problems, and some more problems, and we found that the frequency of our engine checks rose proportionately with the number of problems we had with it. But as we checked more frequently, the problems diminished proportionately; we simply caught them sooner.

We check the bilges periodically to see if we are sinking. We started this practice because once, quite by accident, we found out we were in a sinking mode: the stuffing-box cap had backed off completely. It is these almost-disasters that make you more cautious and careful in your routine checks. We look most often for leaks and smoke. The exhaust system on most sailboats usually is poorly designed, awkwardly installed, and especially prone to leaks, so it should be checked frequently.

The minute you buy a new fiberglass boat, you should start your first inspection; probably your first maintenance work will follow immediately. Look at the cleats, winches, and lifeline stanchion bases to see that the bolts are backed up with plates of hardwood or stainless steel. Do not be too surprised if they aren't even attached with bolts. Many boat manufacturers put on the deck hardware with screws. Ordinary screws put through just the bare fiberglass! They might as well have put them on with library paste. If the manufacturers cannot afford to put on the hardware properly, they should be honest and give you a big bag of the necessary hardware when you buy the boat, and then let you put it on yourself. We have had this problem with fiberglass boats we have owned, and nearly everyone encounters it to some degree if they buy a recently manufactured, American-built fiberglass boat. The ports will probably leak, too; test them by squirting a hose on them.

If you are buying a new boat, be sure that all through-the-hull fittings at or below the waterline are equipped with seacocks. On many boats, these cost extra. Either pay the extra amount, or put them on yourself. Every through-the-hull fitting at or below the waterline on new and old boats should have a seacock on it.

Make a periodic check to see that all of the seacocks work easily. If they are stiff, take them apart (when the boat is out of the water) and lubricate them with water-pump grease. If they become stiff and a haul-out is months away, you may be able to free them by applying a product such as CRC or WD-40 and allowing it to soak in. It may take several applications and a few gentle whacks with a hammer, but patience should pay off. Whenever you are in the vicinity of a seacock handle, work it back and forth a few times so it will never have a chance to freeze up.

Check the wiring, plugs, and outlets in the electrical system for loose connections and worn insulation. Check plugs for burn marks. When these appear, they are an indication that you are using equipment of too high an amperage.

Other common maintenance work, in addition to that mentioned above, includes checking the battery water, repacking and tightening the stuffing box, greasing the steering wheel and cable sheaves, and packing and tightening the rudder gland. Periodic and visual stem-to-stern inspections will catch most problems at the stage where they can be coped with easily.

Every time any fitting or piece of hardware is initially installed or reinstalled anywhere where rain or spray can get at it, something is needed to keep water from getting between the item and whatever it is mounted on. This can be either caulking or bedding compound. We prefer bedding compound, because it is much less expensive and easier to use than any kind of caulking, and it does not creep, as caulking often does. We have used Dolfinite bedding compound for many years. When using bedding compound, keep a container of mineral spirits handy to clean up the excess.

Bedding compound looks and feels somewhat like peanut butter, and is applied like peanut butter. Spread it thickly over the entire surface so there are no gaps or holes. Screw or bolt the item firmly, until the bedding compound oozes out on all sides. Run a putty knife around the edges to pick up most of the excess, and clean up the rest with mineral spirits.

When bedding compound is used on fiberglass and metal, it prevents water from leaking through screw or bolt holes. When hardware is affixed to a wooden area, the bedding compound will keep out moisture so no dry rot can start. Bedding compound is not flexible in its dry state, so it never is a replacement for deck and cockpit caulking. You can use caulking for bedding hardware if you wish, but you cannot use bedding compound for caulking the deck.

The only area that needs caulking on *Whiffle* is the teak cockpit. When it starts leaking, we pull out all the old caulking and redo it. We use Life-Calk, a polysulfide caulk material, although some prefer a latex caulk. To smooth either type, and to keep it from sticking to your fingers or your tools, dip your finger or the tool into a heavy concentration of detergent, such as Joy.

Caulking the hull of a wooden boat is a major project; it hardly falls into the category of routine maintenance. There are various techniques for caulking hulls. If you are in doubt about how to do it, talk to others who have done it, read any material you can find on it, and then decide which method you want to use.

Fiberglassing can be done by amateurs, although the job is messy and distasteful, from the initial application of the sticky resin to the final sanding.

Git-Rot or similar products can stop small areas of dry rot from spreading in wooden boats. It should only be used on surface areas, never on structural members, such as ribs or planking. Watch for cracks in the spreaders and the mast if they are wooden. Cracks don't occur only in wood, though. Metal can crack, too, so check for cracks in the masthead fitting, swaged fittings, and even the shackles.

A sewing machine and marlinespike equipment should be included among your tools. The sewing machine can be used to make new sails, awnings, and dodgers from scratch, or it can be used for mending old ones. Marlinespike equipment should include the necessary tools for wire splicing, as well as the more common rope tools. There are several easy wire splices that can be executed quickly and will hold until a proper one can be made.

A rope-to-wire splice can be done by amateurs, and doing your own will save a great deal of money. You may never have to do one, but find information on how to do it and keep it handy just in case. We have two magazine articles and a leaflet from the Samson Cordage Works on rope-to-wire splicing. We *did* have to make a splice of this type once; by following the instructions in our literature, we came up with a strong, professional-looking splice.

Some sailors feel that a hand-operated sewing machine is the only kind to have, and for the ocean sailor who rips his sail in the middle of the Pacific, it probably is the best. When we have a small sewing job to do, we often don't use our electric machine. We sew it up by hand, which is just as good as, and often better than, machine stitching, Modern sailors often lose sight of the fact that at one time everything that was sewn was done completely by hand, from the smallest ditty bag to the huge sails on clipper ships. Unless you have a heavy-duty machine, hand stitching must be done when you need to sew through several layers of cloth.

We have a standard portable machine that, so far, has sewn up everything we have fed into it. If the right needle is used, and all the other necessary adjustments are made for specific fabrics, our small machine can perform amazing feats. Some electric machines can have a handle attached to the wheel so they can be used without electricity, and one English-made machine is designed to be used either way.

Knowing how to do everything yourself isn't going to help you unless you have the tools to do the jobs. The tools you need on a live-aboard boat are all out of proportion to any other equipment needed.   Tools are just like the lubricants we mentioned earlier: a special tool is needed for every repair or fix-it job, just as a special grease is needed for each lubricating job.

Be on the lookout for small and short-handled tools that might make a job in cramped quarters easier. Also look for tools designed for one thing that can be used on a boat for something entirely different. We have a Sears tool that was designed for removing cotter pins, but when we saw it we knew it was just right for removing old caulking from seams. We bought it and have yet to remove a cotter pin with it.

In most live-aboard boats, the stowage of tools is a problem. If you are stuck with some of those large drawers intended for charts, make them into a tool chest by partitioning the drawers into smaller sections. Tools always should be handy. If you can get to the tools easily, you will do simple repair jobs when they are needed, instead of waiting for a big job that justifies getting out the tool box from wherever it is buried.

Try to keep all the "normal" tools (hammers, screwdrivers, pliers, and wrenches) in the cabin somewhere — not in the cockpit lockers. Build a special case for them, as we did (Fig. 16-1), or convert an existing stowage area. Shallow drawers are good for tool storage, because the tool you need is never hidden under a bunch of other tools.

Waterproof plastic boxes are the worst possible containers for tools. If the tools were sealed into them hermetically and never opened, they would be preserved beautifully. Water cannot get into a waterproof box when it is closed; water cannot get *out* of a waterproof box when it is closed, either. If *any* moisture gets into a waterproof case while it is opened, or if any tool is damp when it is put away, the whole box of tools will rust. Opening and closing a tool box in excessively humid weather can let in enough moisture to rust the tools.

Any container that lets in a little air is better than a waterproof box. Until we built a tool cabinet, we used metal cases for tool storage, and neither the cases nor the tools rusted. Large power tools that will not fit into the cabinet are stored in sturdy fiberboard telescoping boxes and secured with a strap of webbing. The cases have been damp many times from condensation or rainwater, but they dry out before the tools inside have a chance to rust.

Many power tools come in plastic cases, and water can collect in these cases, too. Water can leak out of a metal case at the corners and seams, but it has no way of getting out of a molded plastic case. Punch a couple of small drain holes in the bottom, or put a piece of canvas over the cracks at the openings on the plastic cases. We store many of our power tools in the cockpit lockers, and in heavy rains some water gets into the locker. Some of this water always finds its way into the cracks around the lids of plastic tool boxes. To keep the water out, we cut a piece of

Figure 16-1. Whiffle's *built-in but removable tool chest.*

Figure 16-2. Simple cover made of water-repellent material keeps rainwater out of plastic tool case.

canvas larger than the top of each case, with a slit in it for the handle (Fig. 16-2).   The canvas is water repellent, so any water that falls onto it, rolls off.

Don't forget to include electronic test equipment in your tool collection. Having and knowing how to use a volt-ohm-milliampere (VOM) meter will save you a lot of trouble and money.   Also include wire strippers and cutters, a soldering iron, solderless connectors and their crimping tool, and electrical tape.

Keep spares of things that wear out and need to be changed frequently, such as water-pump impellers, fan belts, oil and fuel filters, and a spare plug for your dockside electrical cable. Always carry enough oil for an oil change, and enough disposable containers with lids to drain the old oil into, so you can get rid of it conveniently. Extra topside or deck paint is also handy for minor touch-up jobs.

XVII. SAFETY FOR YOU

AND YOUR BOAT

You do not have to know anything about boats to decide to live on one. Some have done it successfully, learning as they went along, but you will avoid many problems and complications by knowing something about the subject before you make a boat your home. If one partner knows about boating, it is his or her duty to teach the other partner, and it is the other partner's duty to learn.

It goes without saying that every crew member must know how to sail the boat, but they also must know how to stop the boat and how to pick up someone who has fallen overboard. Each must know how to dock the boat and how to handle dock, heaving, and towlines. Each must know how to get off if the boat runs aground, and each must learn how to pilot and navigate. Women should know how to sail and how to start, stop, run, and maintain the engine; men should know how to cook, clean, and do the laundry.

Safety for you, your boat, and her equipment is of prime importance. You won't be especially comfortable living aboard if you suspect the boat is not tied up properly, if the anchor isn't set right, if you are not able to perform work that has to be done to avoid injuries or loss of life.

The cruising sailor cannot count on tying up at protected slips and docks. He will, of course, find many standard docks; but he will also encounter angled docks, zigzag docks, nondocks, too-short slips and docks, and tie-ups with tidal ranges of 10 feet or more. He often will have to improvise because of unusual circumstances and unusual dock arrangements.

Do not bother splicing loops into one end of each dock line. If a loop is needed, a bowline will suffice. When we purchased *Whiffle*, she came with two dock lines with loops in the end, but

236

we soon cut them off, because they were seldom used and they got in the way when we tied up.

Dock lines should be too long rather than too short, and you should have too many rather than too few. Every boat should have an absolute minimum of four lines: a bow line, a stern line, and two spring lines. The lines should be no shorter than one-and-a-half times the length of the boat, and they should be nylon so they will stretch. Lines should be strong enough to hold in any kind of a blow, and thick enough in diameter so they will not chafe through quickly — yet not so thick (or thin) that they are hard to handle.

Long lines allow for tidal ranges, and they often are necessary for heaving ashore if you are quickly drifting or blowing off a dock. We met one cruising couple who could not get a line to anyone ashore until they were within arm's length of the dock. Keep a long boathook handy when docking. You might be able to snag the dock with it if you can't get a line ashore.

Unless we are making a long offshore passage, we leave four dock lines cleated on all the time: one port and one starboard at the bow and one port and one starboard at the stern. No matter how we have to come into a dock, we always have a line ready.

Much damage can be done to a boat at a dock or in a slip if she is not tied up properly. The pounding of wind and waves can cause chafe on the dock lines and on the hull. The boat should be tied up so she does not touch the dock. If this is not possible, use fenders at every point where she does touch. The casual way in which boats costing thousands of dollars are tied off never fails to amaze us. Not only are many of them tied up improperly, but the lines are often too short and made of the wrong material (poly-propylene or clothesline).

In nontidal areas, the common practice is to use only a bow line and a stern line and forget about any spring lines. This will only keep a boat tied to the dock; it will not protect her from anything. Spring lines are used to keep the bow and stern off the dock and to prevent the boat from surging fore and aft. We use spring lines whenever we tie up, but they are especially useful in areas where the current is strong and where a boat is buffeted by wakes from passing boats.

Using enough dock lines is important, but even more important is the way the lines are led. Figure 17-1 shows a boat tied up in the conventional fashion, with a bow line, a stern line, and two spring lines. There is nothing wrong with tying up this way, but Figure 17-2 shows a more effective way to use the same lines. The stern line going to the outside quarter keeps the bow from being blown into the dock if the wind is blowing as shown in Figure 17-3. The bow is the most vulnerable and the hardest to fender. Spring lines

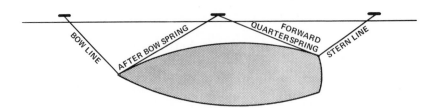

Figure 17-1. Conventional way to tie up to a dock. Spring lines keep down any fore-and-aft surge that might occur with changes in wind and tide. Bow and stern lines hold boat against dock.

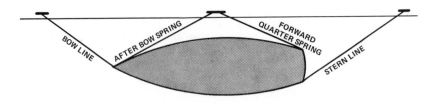

Figure 17-2. More effective use of stern line. Coming from outside, it keeps stern in toward dock and, consequently, positions bow away from dock.

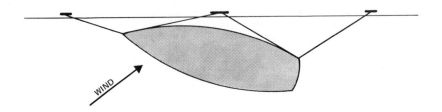

Figure 17-3. In strong wind from direction indicated by arrow, bow will blow into dock unless stern line is led from outside. Since it is almost impossible to fender bow adequately, every precaution should be taken to keep it away from dock.

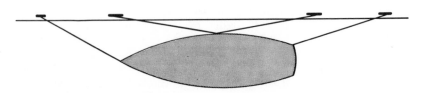

Figure 17-4. Spring lines tied this way, nearly paralleling bow and stern lines, are virtually useless. Springs must work in opposition to bow and stern lines.

used in the manner shown in Figure 17-4 will provide no effective control.

Since pilings on docks are usually equidistant from one another, you may find your boat resting against one of them when she is tied up in the spot assigned to you. By using a fenderboard and leading the lines properly, the boat will not rest against the piling (Fig. 17-5). If all four lines are tied with just a little slack, the boat will ride up and down comfortably with wakes from passing boats and with the tide, if the tidal range is small.

Long lines are especially important for docking in areas with extreme tidal ranges. To avoid surging fore and aft at high tide and to avoid taut lines, or worse — having the boat hung by her lines, out of the water, at low tide — run the four lines out as far as you can, and arrange them so that they all will have the same vertical movement from the boat to the dock. The longer the line, the less the boat will surge (Fig. 17-6).

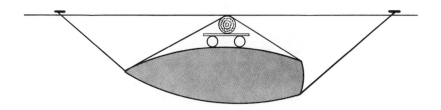

Figure 17-5. When piling is at or near center of dock space, boat must be positioned so piling is opposite beamiest part of boat. Fenders and fender board keep boat off piling.

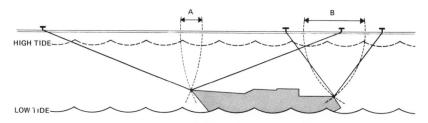

Figure 17-6. Right and wrong ways to position lines where there is extreme tidal range. Bow lines are correct. Stern lines are too short. Dashed, curved lines (A,B) show amount of fore-and-aft surge that can occur at high tide. The longer the lines, the less the surge. Lines that are too short (B) will also permit boat to move in and out as tide rises. This boat would be tied up properly if stern lines were as long as bow lines and tied at same angle as bow lines. If boat is resting against piling (Fig. 17-5), fenders and long fender board will permit boat to ride safely and comfortably up and down with tide.

When you find yourself at a short dock with a minimal tidal range, you might tie up as shown in Figure 17-7. If there is a great tidal range, lengthen the springs to the bow and stern, and move the bow and stern lines farther toward the shore (Fig. 17-8).

Figure 17-9 shows a short dock situation we have encountered several times. The bow line run out to a piling ahead of the boat offers the best control for the bow. This tie-up is only for areas with little tide.

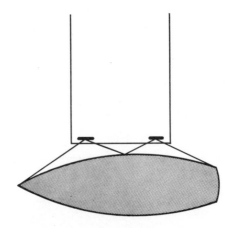

Figure 17-7. If tidal range is 3 ft. or less, and you are tied up at dock shorter than your boat, this is a good way to tie up.

Figure 17-8. Same dock as in Figure 17-7, with boat's lines lengthened and located to allow for greater tidal range.

In some crowded marinas, you may have to raft off another boat; in an anchorage, you may want to raft off a friend's boat. When rafting, use spring lines for the same purpose that they are always used: to keep the boat from surging (Fig. 17-10). Naturally you must use fenders when rafting off another boat, and use them wherever necessary in all the above examples.

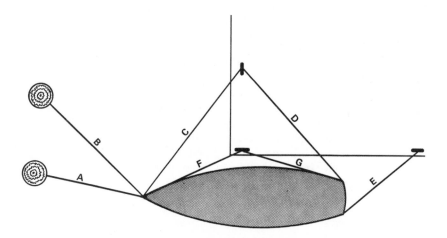

Figure 17-9. When you have only a corner of a dock to tie to, and there is a piling to tie to ahead of the boat, the most secure combination of lines is B, F, G, and E, as indicated in this drawing. We have used just C, D, F, and G when there was no other place to tie the bow. (C and D hold the boat into the dock, and F and G control the fore-and-aft movement.) E is a better stern line than D. An anchor can be used for A or B if there is no other alternative and you feel it is necessary.

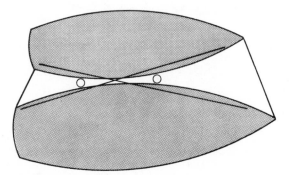

Figure 17-10. The proper way to tie up when rafted to another boat either at dock or at anchor.

Tying up in a slip involves the same principles as tying up to a dock, except that two more lines are involved (Fig. 17-11). If the slip has a finger pier, the two arrowed lines will hold the boat off and fenders will not be needed. You will find slips that are too short for your boat, but it is still possible to tie up safely (Fig. 17-12).

You will rarely, if ever, have to moor stern-to in the United States, but it is a common practice in Europe and some other areas. Figure 17-13 shows one method, and Figure 17-14 shows a much better way to moor stern-to. Cross the stern lines for both to keep the stern from pivoting unnecessarily. If you can put an anchor out, use a four-to-one scope. Fenders will be necessary on the stern. With a strong onshore wind or a large tidal range, the method shown in Figure 17-13 will not be satisfactory.

Often one long dock line can be used for two different functions, such as when the bow line's excess is used for the after-bow spring. In a slip, both the bow lines can be effected with one long line. In any situation where there is excess line, arrange it so that it is on the boat instead of on the dock. Then, if the lines need adjusting, this can be done from the boat. Putting an enticing coil of line

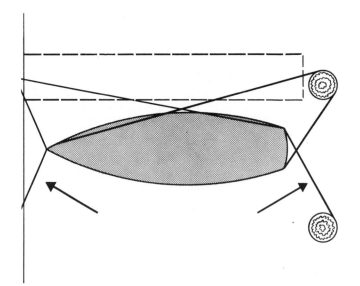

Figure 17-11. Tying up in a slip, with or without finger pier, usually requires 2 more lines than would be used at a dock. Unless slip is very narrow, fenders are not necessary between boat and finger pier if 2 arrowed lines are used. Use loop or bowline on any line that goes to a piling if thumb cleat on piling might prevent line from sliding down. Otherwise, use clove hitch or round turn and 2 half hitches.

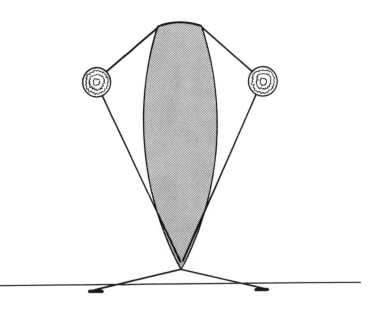

Figure 17-12. If slip is too short, use this method for tying up.

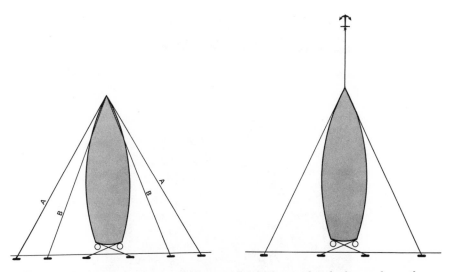

Figure 17-13 (left). This arrangement should be used only in good weather or for temporary tie-up — and then only if stern can be fendered properly. A lines are better than B lines. Figure 17-14 (right). For mooring stern-to for any time, use anchor for bow line and take up on it enough to keep stern off.

out of the way of thieves or mischievous vandals is another reason for keeping extra line on the boat. One friend of ours didn't, and one night all his excess line was neatly cut off and stolen.

Whenever the dock lines rub against the dock or a chock, they must be protected from chafe. A 12-inch-wide piece of canvas can be wrapped three or four times around the line at the chafe points and lashed on with light line. Or special waterproof tape can be wrapped around the line. Rubber chafe guards are often used; these are the easiest and quickest to use, but unfortunately, they don't last very long before they are worn through.

Learn the knots used for tying up: the bowline, clove hitch, and half hitch (Figs. 17-15, 17-16, 17-17). A clove hitch with two half hitches serves the same purpose as a bowline, but it often

Figure 17-15. Bowline tied loosely to show how knot is made.

Figure 17-16. Clove hitch.

is harder to tie and untie from around a piling in a slip. A bowline can be flipped off from a distance.

Learn how to cleat a line quickly so it will hold. Figures 17-18 1, 2, 3, and 4 show the four steps for cleating a line properly. Step 3 shows the important twist that locks the line around the cleat so it cannot slip off. The line must be brought around each horn of the cleat. If the locking twist is done on only one horn, the line may jam when you want to cast it off.

There may be situations when you cannot get a line around the cleat fast enough, and the line begins running out and will soon be off the boat. Let it go. *Don't ever try to cleat a running line.* You can be relieved of a great number of fingers if you do.

Since your ground tackle may be the only real insurance you have, be sure it is more than adequate. Three anchors is the minimum that a cruising boat should have. What type(s) of anchor you use should be determined by what sort of bottom you will be anchoring in. The wise skipper will have a combination of anchors that will hold well in any sort of bottom. They all should be of a weight that will hold your particular boat in any normal situation, and one anchor should be much heavier for storm conditions. Whether you use all chain or a combination of rope and chain is a matter of personal preference and economics; an anchor windlass will be necessary if all chain is used, and chain is initially much more expensive per foot than line.

The one anchor seen most often on cruising boats is the CQR; if you can have only one anchor, it should be this type. It has good holding power in most bottoms except hard clay or rock. The CQR is a plow anchor, but all plow anchors are not CQRs. There are copies of the CQR on the market, but their holding power is not as good as that of the genuine CQR. The CQR is

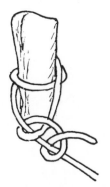

Figure 17-17.   Round turn and 2 half hitches.   (From The Ashley Book of Knots *by Clifford W. Ashley, © 1944. Reprinted with permission, Doubleday & Company.)*

Figure 17-18. Four steps for cleating line. (1) Take line to far side of cleat first. (2) Bring line up far side of cleat, under horn, and back across to far side. (3) Make locking twist to keep line from slipping off cleat or jamming. (4) Properly cleated line. Tied this way, line can be uncleated easily, no matter what strain is on standing part.

manufactured in England, but it can be purchased through many of the larger marine supply companies in the United States, such as West, Fawcett and Manhattan Marine.

The CQR stows nicely in a roller chock in the bow and is convenient for anchoring (Fig. 17-19). Any anchor can foul, regardless of what its manufacturers claim, but the CQR is less likely to foul than any other design. A 35-pound CQR is the minimum size any cruising boat should have as her smallest anchor. The heavier the anchor, the faster and deeper it will dig in.

A good second anchor is one of the Northill type, which is manufactured by the Danforth company and is their Utility model (Fig. 17-20). A Northill is excellent in rock and clay, as

Figure 17-19. Tidy arrangement of 2 plow anchors stowed in roller chocks. Anchor on left is CQR.

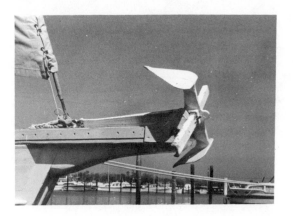

Figure 17-20. Northill-type anchor in roller chock.

well as in most other bottoms. Our reasons for not recommending the Northill as the main anchor are that it is cumbersome to handle and not as easy to stow.

A Yachtsman or Herreshoff anchor is a good anchor for all conditions, and it will hold when many other types of anchors will not (Fig. 17-21). These anchors need special equipment for handling and stowing, such as catheads and anchor davits. They must also be heavier than the plow or Northill for equivalent holding power. For this reason alone, they are not as popular as some of the other lightweight patent anchors.

If the boat is equipped to handle it, chain is the preferred anchor rode. Chain has two great advantages over rope — its weight provides a natural catenary, and safe anchoring can be done with less scope, usually three-to-one. On a recent cruise we took to the North Channel of Lake Huron, there were many delightful, small, deep anchorages where we could anchor only with chain.

A boat can fetch up sharply on chain, causing an uncomfortable jolt, but this can be eliminated by using a 15-foot length of ½-inch-diameter nylon line. The nylon line can be less than ½ inch in diameter, but it should be no larger, because it needs to be able

Figure 17-21.   Yachtsman anchor.   The diamond-shaped flukes are less susceptible to fouling than other fluke designs used on this type of anchor (such as heart shapes or arrowheads.)

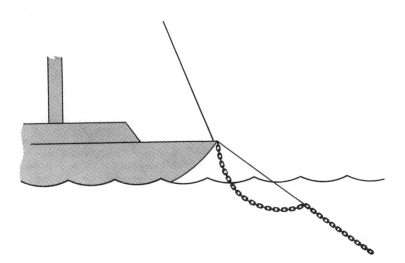

Figure 17-22.   When anchoring with chain in a situation where not enough scope can be veered to achieve a catenary, snubbing that occurs from swells or waves can cause anchor to break loose. Fifteen feet of nylon line tied to chain can prevent this from happening. Use shackle or tie the line to chain with rolling hitch, then slack chain until strain is on nylon.

to stretch. Tie one end of the line to the chain with a rolling hitch, and cleat the other end to the boat. This stretchy line will take the strain, and the chain will be slack (Fig. 17-22).

Chain is self-stowing and cannot chafe. A minimum of 150 feet should be enough for most small boats. On multihulls or very light-displacement boats, the weight and stowage of the chain will have to be considered. Three-eighths-inch chain weighs nine pounds per fathom, and many light-displacement boats cannot take this much added weight in the bow.

Nylon is the material used for most anchor rodes today because of its stretch and great strength. Nylon is fairly resistant to chafe, and chafe is eliminated completely when used in a roller chock. The use of lightweight anchors with nylon rode requires a scope of seven-to-one. If it begins to blow, 10-to-one is the minimum safe scope. Three hundred feet of anchor line for each anchor is the minimum you should have. In 30 feet of water, 300 feet of line will provide only a 10-to-one scope. The larger the diameter of the line, the less it will stretch; so use the smallest diameter recommended for your size boat. For many years we have used ½-inch nylon for our main anchor rode and ¾-inch nylon for our storm anchor.

Nylon line, in spite of its virtues, is worthless without a length of chain between it and the anchor. Most anchor manufacturers recommend only six feet, but 15 to 20 feet should be the minimum length used. The chain provides the weight necessary on the line to give the horizontal pull that sets the anchor properly. Chain also prevents the line from chafing on the anchor itself during tide changes. A long length of chain will not chafe in coral or rock, even if the rest of the rode is nylon.

We recently rode out a bad squall with 60-knot winds with our 35-pound plow, 20 feet of 3/8-inch chain, and ½-inch nylon line with 10-to-one scope. (Had we had any indication that the squall was coming, we would have set our big anchor.) A powerboat in the same anchorage had two Danforths set on nylon line with no chain. During the squall, he dragged onto the rocks. When we talked to him later, we found he had suffered no damage; but he was going to add hefty lengths of chain to both of his rodes.

No matter what kind of rode you use, mark it off in feet or fathoms so there will be no guesswork as to how much scope you have out.

The Danforth, which is the most common anchor seen on powerboats and weekend sailboats, can foul on objects on the bottom and not dig in. If it does dig in, its flukes can bend in a bad blow. If you decide you want a Danforth, find a cast Danforth rather than the standard or high-tensile Danforths. Buy one that is twice the weight recommended for your boat by the manufacturer.

How you anchor will be determined by personal experience and by reading how the "experts" do it. Good, safe anchoring can be done only by feel, so it is something that must be developed by experience. If you have dragged anchor often, you are using the wrong procedure for anchoring or the wrong anchor for the bottom, or you are anchoring in the wrong place.

In places where there are strong currents, such as rivers, anchor away from the bends, where the current runs the swiftest. The bends are usually the deepest part, and often, because of the swift current, the bottom is scoured clear of any decent holding material. If the current is swift and not likely to reverse direction, as happens in tidal rivers, you can use one anchor; otherwise, you should set one anchor from the bow and one from the stern.

Opinions on what is a safe anchoring scope range from four-to-one to seven-to-one. When using one anchor, we never use less than seven-to-one scope, and we often use 10-to-one. The longer the scope, the better the anchor will hold. The freeboard of the boat should be included with the depth of the water when figuring the scope, and the state of the tide should also be allowed for. When anchoring where there is an extreme tidal range, there may be plenty of water for your boat's draft when you anchor, but you could be high and dry at low tide. Always know how much water will be going out from under you.

Our way of anchoring is the same method used by many, and vastly different from the method used by others. There are many theories on the best way to anchor. We pick our spot and slowly go in upwind under power or under close-hauled main alone, rounding up at the right instant. As the boat slows to a stop and begins to fall off, we lower the anchor *slowly* to the bottom. When we *feel* the anchor hit the bottom, we slack the line slightly so the anchor will start to lie in the right direction — with the shank pointing toward the bow of the boat. As the boat falls back, pay out the line to a four-to-one scope and then cleat it off. Back the engine down hard until the line is taut, then pay out to a seven-to-one scope or more. Under sail, as the boat falls off, keep the main sheeted in tight and she will start to sail downwind. Pay out the required scope, cleat the line, and let the boat snub up to set the anchor.

Anchoring with chain is done in basically the same way, paying out the chain slowly until the desired scope is reached, and backing down with the engine or snubbing up under sail. Use force of some sort to make the anchor dig in.

Do not anchor by tossing the anchor and a bundle of line over the side, as we have seen done so many times. At least don't anchor that way if we are in the same anchorage. We do not want to share an anchorage with a fool who might drag into us. Choose an isolated spot where you can harm only yourself.

Two anchors may be needed in small or crowded anchorages where it is impossible to swing with the scope needed for safety, or in exposed roadsteads where security is important. Setting two anchors makes it impossible to foul the anchor with the rode. We anchor with two anchors so often that we have installed a stern roller chock.

There are several ways of anchoring with two anchors. The most common is to anchor in the normal manner but pay out a scope of 14-to-one. Cleat the line. Drop the stern anchor. Take in on the bow anchor line and pay out the stern anchor line until there is a scope of seven-to-one on each. The stern line then can be shifted to the bow so the boat can swing to the wind and take the strain alternately between the two anchors.

Double anchoring with chain is done in the same manner, but the boat must be equipped with two roller chocks in the bow to handle each rode. There also must be some way to winch in both rodes.

We have been in many anchorages where others would come in and know *how* to anchor, but the majority didn't know *where* to anchor. The worst place to anchor is in front of any other boats that are already there. Since you always drop back from your anchor, you may drop back onto another boat, or to the spot directly over her anchor, if your scope is long enough. It is only common sense to anchor downwind of boats already anchored, so you will drop back safely into your own spot. We wonder why so many people don't anchor this way. Even when there is plenty of room in an anchorage, the tendency of most newcomers is to anchor ahead of other anchored boats. This has happened to us innumerable times.

If you are smart enough not to anchor directly in front of another boat so you will not drag into her, then you should be smart enough to know that you should not anchor directly behind her so she cannot drag into you (Fig. 17-23). A wind shift or the tide can change the whole picture; but if you drop your hook astern and to one side, the chances are you will not swing into each other, because the basic relationship between the boats will not be changed.

If, due to lack of space, you must anchor upwind or alongside other boats, anchor so that your final position is not in a straight line with the others, so your boat will have less tendency to swing or drift into them (Fig. 17-24). A little ESP would be helpful here, since you have no way of knowing how much scope your neighbors have out. Make as intelligent a guesstimate as you can, and plot how the others would swing with a wind change (Fig. 17-25). Your swinging radius can overlap, but you are safer if it does not.

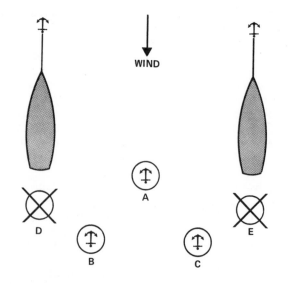

Figure 17-23. Best anchoring position in this situation is A; B and C are second choices; D and E are unsuitable.

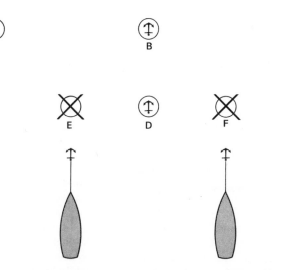

Figure 17-24. For anchoring ahead of other boats, A, B, or C would be best locations, since they provide room to drop back from anchor. D is less satisfactory, especially if long scope is needed. Wind shift would cause boat to swing into another boat. If you anchor at E or F, you will be over anchor of boat behind when you drop back. You could also drag into others.

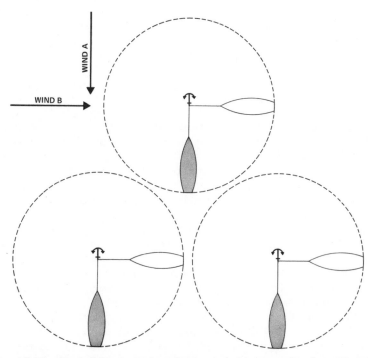

Figure 17-25. Shaded boats anchored when wind was coming from direction A. Dashed circles show swinging radius of boats if all were anchored with equal amounts of scope. If wind shifted to direction B, boats would swing accordingly.

Going aground for the first time can be a very traumatic experience, but it is something you will have to get used to if you plan to do any cruising. After a few groundings, only the inconvenience will upset you. The only groundings that are really serious occur when the tide is falling and it will go out several feet from under you, or when you are aground on a reef, rocks, or a beach where the boat might pound herself to pieces.

We were planning to stay overnight at a small, unfamiliar marina in the Chesapeake a couple of years ago. When we arrived, no one was around to tell us where to go, so we motored slowly to the head of the marina's tiny basin to see if we could find anyone there. The depth sounder informed us it was shoaling up, but the bottom was soft mud and we were proceeding very slowly. At the instant we touched bottom, a lady popped her head out from one of the nearby boats to ask us if we wanted a slip. She shouted in the same breath that it was very shallow where we were. She had that oh-dear-they've-gone-aground look on her face. We backed off the mud instantly with no problem, and went to the slip she indicated. Later she remarked that we had seemed so unconcerned about running aground. We explained to her that we had been aground so often we never let it bother us anymore. She and her husband have since become cruising liveaboards, and they don't worry about groundings either.

The best situation for going aground is on a rising tide. Sit tight for 15 to 30 minutes and you should be afloat. If grounding occurs in an area where there is little or no tide change, you will have to expend a little more of your energy to get off.

Assuming you were cautious, watching your depth sounder, and did not ground at full speed, your first maneuver should be to try to back off slowly. If you can't get off this way, sound around the boat with a boathook marked off as described in Chapter XIV. Often there will be deeper water on one side of the boat; and knowing where it is will help you determine the direction in which you should move the boat.

Try going ahead slowly, fishtailing the rudder from side to side. Then put the engine into reverse for a moment, "steering" for the deepest water. If you don't quite get off, repeat the process several times. Moving the rudder from side to side can cause the keel to twist slightly; in mud, this might break the suction, and in sand it might cause you to slide.

During the forward bursts, the boat may try to turn to starboard or port. If she turns enough, she may pivot so far around that you can power out back toward deeper water. A powerful engine and a three-blade prop really prove their merits when you are trying to get off such a grounding.

If the above maneuvers fail and you are still aground, you will have to launch the dinghy to row the anchor out to deep water, and drop it, using plenty of scope. Kedge off. Run the anchor line (nylon is superior to chain for kedging off because of its stretch) through the bow chock to a windlass. If you don't have a windlass, take the line to a sheet winch in the cockpit or a halyard winch. Winch the line in until there is a good strain on it. Here, again, it might help to fishtail the rudder and reverse the engine occasionally. Normally the boat will move just a little distance at a time. Every time the line goes slack, take up on it.

Heeling the boat will reduce the draft, and this sometimes can be done by setting sail or having someone climb onto the boom and swing it outboard. If she won't heel this way, reeve the anchor line through a block and hoist it to the top of the mast. With the anchor line around one of the halyard winches, try to heel the boat over until she is afloat. Using the engine might help in this situation, but don't count on using it if the boat is heeled so much that the engine's cooling water intake and/or prop is out of the water.

If you can attract the attention of a powerboat, ask them to circle around you and make a big wake. Most of them will love doing this, and it might be enough to bounce you off.

As a last resort, try to find someone to tow you off. During a towing operation, exercise extreme caution to avoid injury and damage to either boat. Very few seamen, amateur or professional, know how to pull off and tow a boat. The usual procedure is to attach a tow line, and then to try to jerk the grounded vessel free, with the towing boat going like hell. This is one of the best ways to kill someone and wreck your boat, and one of the worst ways to get afloat.

If the rescuing boat draws less than you do, have her come alongside and raft up. Coordinate your boat's movements with those of the towing vessel, and the combined efforts of the two engines will serve to get the boat off. This method puts no one and no vessel in danger.

If the rescuing boat's draft is too deep to lay alongside, pass over the end of a sturdy line that you have fastened to a stout cleat or a samson post — a cleat that you know is well backed up or a samson post that is fastened to the keel. Insist that the towing boat slowly, *slowly*, s-l-o-w-l-y take a strain on the line; then try to turn the boat or pull her into deeper water. *No one on either boat should be standing anywhere in the vicinity of the cleat or tow line while it is under any strain.* Stand well away from it. Amidships is good. If the line parts or the cleat breaks off, no one will be injured. Those wire-mesh devices in back of the helmsmen on Coast Guard boats were installed to protect the helmsmen from broken, whipping tow lines and flying hardware.

Pulling a boat off is one of the most dangerous situations on the water for both the boat that is stuck and the rescuing vessel. Never touch the tow line until it is slack, and make sure that the people on the other boat are aware of what you are doing. If signals get crossed and they start to pull before you are ready, let the line go and move out of the way. Don't try to untie a line when it is under any strain. Again, never try to cleat a running line.

If you have to get rid of a taut tow line, cut it off. An ax is recommended for cutting tow lines; its long handle will keep you at a safe distance when the line parts. There aren't many sailboats that carry an ax, and certainly not on the foredeck, so if any cutting must be done, it can be done with a sharp knife. Stand or kneel aft of the tow line and keep your face away from it.

It is especially important to keep the tow line as short as possible, so the towing boat will not yaw or drift off from the grounded vessel. If the boats are close, the prop wash of the rescuing boat may be beneficial to the grounded vessel. A short line also minimizes the danger if the line parts or a cleat lets go. In one miserable incident we would prefer to forget, we were towed successfully over a hundred-foot-wide bar with a 20-foot line attached to a towing powerboat.

If you must have your boat towed somewhere, lash the towing boat alongside, with her rudder aft of the stern of your boat for easier steering (Fig. 17-26). Even a small boat can tow a larger one effectively this way. A friend of ours towed a 57-foot motorsailer with his 37-foot ketch for five miles this way, then he docked

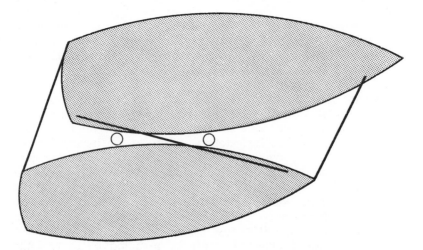

Figure 17-26. Small boat towing larger boat.

her with complete control.   If the Coast Guard is doing the towing, they probably will not want to tow alongside. Insist on this method.

The only justification for any boat being towed astern on a long line is rough seas. In such a situation, the towing line will become alternately slack and taut due to wave action, putting a good deal of strain on the line, the cleat, and the two boats as well. The tow line must be attached to the tow boat forward of the rudder, or the tow boat will not be able to steer. It must be made clear to the captain of the towing boat that he *must* proceed slowly. If a sailboat is towed faster than her hull speed, she will begin to yaw and roll over.   Once we had the Delaware Bay equivalent of a Nantucket sleigh ride at the end of a Coast Guard tow line; they were rocketing along at a good 10 knots before we could get their attention and ask them to slow down.

When the weather is rough (and it can even get very rough in "protected" waterways), put on a safety harness. When steering at night, or in the daytime if everyone else aboard is asleep or below, wear a safety harness even if it is calm and you have no foredeck work to do. Do not worry about whether anyone will think you are a sissy for taking precautions.

Any horseshoe ring that might be tossed to someone in the water should have a long line attached to it. If the ring itself is not caught, sometimes the line is within reach. Use polypropylene line; it floats. And tie a couple of knots in the line, so it can be grasped easily.

There should be an easy way for someone in the water to get back aboard the boat. Most boats suitable for living aboard have too high a freeboard to climb over. Some boat designs lend themselves to having steps attached to the transom or rudder, and this provides a convenient way to climb back aboard. Swimming ladders should be kept within reach so they can be put into use quickly.

A quick-release rope ladder can be stored rolled up on a lifeline stanchion, perhaps held up by Velcro loops, with a trip line rigged through them to release when pulled. The trip line should be long enough so it can be reached easily by anyone who is trying to get back aboard. Often it is possible for a person in the water to reach the toe rail, but on a boat with a high freeboard, the toe rail is much more than a long arm's length above anyone who might be in the water.

If you make frequent offshore passages, an inflatable life raft will give you a certain peace of mind, provided that you don't worry about whether it will really work if you need it. On boats of 30 to 40 feet, anything but an inflatable life raft is impractical. The boat's dinghy, inflatable or not, is never a suitable lifeboat, but it is better than nothing.

It is a good idea to use a radar reflector when sailing in shipping lanes; in bad weather, use one all the time. An aluminum mast is not a good radar reflector, because it is not a design that will reflect the radar waves back to the antenna. When a small vessel is heeled, the radar wave that might normally bounce back may reflect upward from the mast instead. We have talked to tug and ship captains who say radar reflectors do help them to see small boats, although they often are spotted too late to avoid an accident.

A bilge pump is an absolute necessity on any boat; two pumps are infinitely better than one; and three are not too many, even on a boat of 30 feet if you go offshore at all. One pump should be the highest-capacity manual pump you can fit onto the boat, the second might be an automatic electric pump, and the third should be manual. If only one pump is used, it should not be electric. Many boats have been sunk because they depended solely on their automatic electric bilge pumps and then their source of electricity disappeared for one reason or another. If you have a serious leak, you should not have to depend solely on an electric pump. If water gets to the batteries, the pump will cease to function when it is needed most.

Most bilge discharge holes are located at the waterline or below, the worst place for them. They are placed there so no unsightly stains will dribble on the topsides. If you are installing bilge pumps and you are concerned more for the safety of the vessel than her looks, put all the bilge pump discharges well above the waterline. They will be much easier to pump, since you will not have back pressure from the water. The discharge will have a clear, unobstructed shot over the side. If the bilge water should stain, scrub off the stain with a long-handled brush before it can set.

Some sailors have a bilge pump mounted right on deck with the discharge hose over the gunwale. The business of putting bilge pumps in cockpit lockers must be a holdover from some guy who didn't know where to put his pump, so he stuck it in the cockpit locker and everyone else down through the years followed suit. When a boat is taking on water severely, it is usually in heavy weather when the seams may have opened or waves are crashing aboard. This is not the time to be out in the cockpit with a locker open, trying vainly to pump out the water already in the vessel — not to mention all the water that will come in through the open locker.

To be really safe, install one of the pumps so that it can be operated from the cabin below, when all the hatches are dogged down securely. Your stamina will last much longer if you are dry and warm below, instead of on deck both pumping and fighting the elements. Some boats have a bilge pump that can be arranged to discharge into one of the cabin sinks.

Once you have removed the bilge pump from the cockpit locker, install something so that it and every other locker, lazarette, or compartment in the cockpit can be dogged down securely in rough weather.   Engine access covers in the cockpit floor that simply fit over a lip with no fasteners at all are not safe.

If the bilge pump installation exposes any rubber parts to the sun, carry spares for them, since they will deteriorate quickly. Why the manufacturers make these parts of black rubber is hard to fathom, since black-colored items go to pieces so quickly in sunlight.

Sooner or later someone will have to go aloft either for maintenance or to unfoul something.   The "aloftee" should be the lightest weight person on board, so the "alofter" will be able to get the "aloftee" aloft.   Jan does all our work aloft, including painting the mast.   Our ratlines go up to the spreaders, which are about halfway up the 40-foot mast.   Any work done above this level must be done from a bosun's chair.   The chair itself can be purchased ready-made either plain (a flat board with a couple of ropes and a ring) or fancy (with pockets and other devices attached for tools, etc.).   Either kind can be made with a minimum of materials and tools, and, as with any work you do yourself, you'll save money.

To make a bosun's chair, drill a hole large enough to accept ½-inch line in each corner of a 20-by-eight-inch oak board.   A suitable length of this line is passed back and forth through the holes to get the effect shown in Figure 17-27.   Short-splice the ends of the rope on the bottom of the chair (Fig. 17-28).   The four ropes are frapped together about three inches down from the top to make a double loop for the shackle or a heavy ring, which will have to be put on before the rope is spliced.   Pockets and hooks can be added as personal preference dictates.

Jan often lashes a line with a snap hook on it to one of the lines on the chair.   She hangs a good-sized bucket on the hook and keeps all her tools in there.   When painting the mast, she sets the paint can in the bucket; the brush rests across the top of the paint can.   If the paint should spill, it will spill into the bucket, and not onto the deck.

Most sailors who go aloft do not take any more safety precautions than being sure the bosun's chair is fastened firmly to the halyard.   Every time anyone goes aloft, all splices involved should be checked and the halyard itself inspected for signs of chafe.   If the halyard passes through a sheave in the top of the mast instead of a block, there is less chance of the halyard's jamming.

Attach about four feet of 3/8-inch-diameter line to the loop or ring in the ropes of the bosun's chair — the same loop or ring to which the halyard will be fastened.   This line serves as a safety

Figure 17-27. Continuous line goes through all 4 holes in seat of bosun's chair.

line. It is tied in a clove hitch around the mast and is slid up so it is always level with the person in the chair. When spreaders or other obstacles are reached, the line is untied and immediately retied above the obstacle. If the halyard should part, the clove hitch will keep the chair from falling; it also prevents the chair from swinging from side to side while you are working aloft. It takes a little more time to get aloft when using a safety line, but we would not think of doing it any other way. Use this same procedure in reverse when descending.

A reel winch is not suitable for hauling someone aloft, because the "aloftee" cannot be lowered unless the brake is off and the winch handle is used to control the speed of descent. Injury or death could result to both parties if the winch ever got out of control. One person usually can haul another aloft easily, but it is safer if a third person can tail the halyard. On the descent, the halyard is eased slowly around the drum of the winch with one hand, while the tailing is done either with the other hand or by another person.

Whenever Jan works aloft or either of us is working near the rails on deck, we tie a line to any tools we may be using so they will not get away from us. If a heavy power tool is being used on deck, the safety line is tied to a lifeline stanchion or the lifeline itself. The lightweight tools have a two-foot length of string tied to them, and one end is held or wrapped around the hand that is not holding the tool. As an alternative, a hand-size loop can be tied in the string and slipped over the wrist.

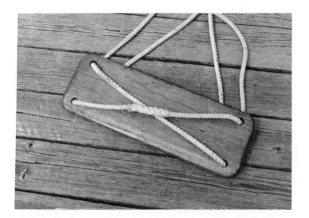

Figure 17-28. Short splice joins ends of bosun's chair line.

When Jan was putting on the ratlines, she devised a way to put a safety line on the socket part of the socket wrench she was using. She taped one end of the string around the socket in the middle; as she screwed the nut on, the string wound itself up on the socket. She just unwound the string and started all over again for the next nut.

Often the companionway ladder and sections of the cabin sole must be removed when working on the engine or in the bilge. If you must leave the boat without replacing these items, be sure no one will be able to go below in your absence. Many people have stepped into a boat expecting the ladder to be in its normal position and the cabin sole to be intact, and they have received severe sprains and broken bones. When you return to the boat, don't *you* forget how you left her, either. To jog your memory, write a note to yourself or erect some obstacle that must be removed before you can go below.

The larger the boat, the longer and steeper the companionway ladder. Put grab rails on the ladder or nearby, so anyone using the ladder will have a handhold for the whole length of the ladder.

If you have long hair, pin it up securely. When you are docking or maneuvering, it is inconvenient and often dangerous to have hair blowing across your eyes. Even worse is the danger of loose hair getting caught in winches or other mechanical equipment. This is the twentieth-century method of scalping, and it is just as effective as the traditional Indian method.

One thing you learn, as you get older and as crime afloat and ashore continues to increase, is that a thief who wants something badly enough will find a way to get it. But this doesn't excuse you from making his work difficult. Keep a list of the serial numbers of everything you own that has a serial number, and keep the list up to date as you buy new equipment. If there is no identifying number, scratch your social security number on it, or write the number on in waterproof ink or paint. This includes your shore cable and each of its detachable plug-in adapters. Do not put the boat's name on it as the only identifying mark. Someone might steal the boat and the name would only prove that it was a piece of the boat's equipment.

Dinghies rate high on the list of items thieves go after, because so many sailors make them so easy to steal. What other piece of high-priced equipment in any other recreation, business, or sport is so often tied up with just a piece of rope and left unattended?

When we are anywhere where dinghynapping is a problem, we usually deflate ours and stow it in a cockpit locker that will be locked. Sometimes, though, we have had to use the dinghy every day or so, and it is too much of a nuisance to inflate it repeatedly. We bought a 20-foot length of heavy galvanized jack chain and a sturdy combination padlock; we now chain the dinghy to the boat when we are in port, whether at anchor or in a marina. Our dinghy has three inflatable seats that are integral parts of the whole. The chain is run under the three seats, so if anyone wants the dinghy badly enough, he will have to ruin it before he can free it from the chain. The oars are always kept on deck.

To avoid chafe from the sharp edges on the links of this chain, we covered the whole 20 feet of chain with canvas. We stitched up a fairly snug-fitting canvas tube and worked the chain into it. When we row into a dock, we use the chain to secure the dinghy there or wrap it around a tree trunk.

Oars can be locked into the dinghy when you have to leave it. A ¾-inch hole can be drilled in the blade of each oar, and an ordinary chain or cable bicycle lock will hold the oars together. The chain or cable can be passed around a seat for further security. A combination lock eliminates carrying keys.

Sails stowed on deck are easy to steal. If you cannot stow them below or in a locker when you are away from the boat, lock them on deck. Run a two-foot length of cable, with an eye spliced in each end, through one of the cringles in the sail. Bring the cable out through the opening in the sail bag, slip one of the cable eyes through the other, and pull tight. The long end of the cable can then be put around the mast or a lifeline stanchion and padlocked either to itself or to the other eye.

Our life raft is mounted on deck with its quick-release webbing straps to hold it securely in place. When it is not apt to be needed, we lock it down. We made up a length of cable, again with an eye in each end, to fit over the raft's canister. One eye is fastened permanently to a pad eye, with the screw heads filed down so the screws cannot be unscrewed. The other eye goes over another pad eye and is padlocked (Fig. 17-29). The padlock is removed when we are underway.

Winch handles and other loose equipment should be removed from the deck when you leave the boat for any length of time. All cockpit lockers and hatches should be locked. Many professional burglars will go after the expensive electronic equipment they know or assume is in a boat, and they are prepared to cut or smash their way to it if necessary. There isn't a whole lot you can do to stop them if you aren't around.

There are numerous types of boat burglar alarms, but they have limited value, because they are set to go off while you are away. These days, few people care enough to pay any attention to your alarm — certainly not enough to get involved with any burglar that is not after their own property.

There are many differing opinions as to whether you should carry aboard any kind of firearm. There are many people who, when pressed, would not be able to use a gun. There are others who feel that if it comes down to Him or Me, it is going to be Him. We feel that having a gun aboard is a good idea. It doesn't ever have to be loaded if you are uneasy about it. But when an intruder looks into the barrel, he will have no way of knowing whether the gun is loaded. A long gun, such as a rifle or shotgun,

Figure 17-29. Life raft locked to deck.

can be used effectively as a club, whereas a hand gun cannot; but the long gun will be more difficult to stow.

Try to work out what you would do if your boat was boarded by intruders. Plan your attack from the cockpit or the forward hatch, and figure out what you would use for a weapon at either location. For instance, if someone were coming down the main companionway, would you try to get out through the forward hatch or stay below and deal with the intruder there?

It is unfortunate that we have to write about stealing and thievery and such, but crime is on the rise everywhere. About 15 percent of the boating people we know have experienced thefts, and two acquaintances have had intruders come aboard in the middle of the night.

XVIII. BOAT HOUSEKEEPING

Because a boat has such concentrated living in a relatively small area, it needs cleaning every day. If you are away from land for several days, the need for cleaning is minimized, since nothing is tracked aboard. There is nothing like a good deck shoe to give you the footing you need, but there also is nothing like a good deck shoe to pick up sand, shell, and dirt — and then release them as you descend the companionway ladder. Save your deck shoes for when the deck is slippery underway. Shoes with a flat, unpatterned rubber sole can be worn at dockside. Nothing will adhere to the sole, so nothing can be tracked aboard. Unless you are clumsy and careless, you are not likely to slip as you get on and off your boat.

The area below that gets the dirtiest is the cabin sole. If left uncarpeted, dirt and dust will show and collect in the corners. Carpeting hides most dirt and is easy to clean. When at dockside, we use a small, 115-volt vacuum cleaner. We have tried numerous 12-volt vacuums, but none were satisfactory. This was several years ago, and no doubt they have been improved considerably since then. It is possible to get 115-volt vacuums that are as small as the 12-volt units, so size no longer need be a consideration. The 115-volt vacuums come with various attachments. The crevice attachment comes in handy in a boat, since there are so many tight corners where dirt can collect.

When away from 115-volt electrical power, we use a carpet sweeper, the Bissell Little Queen. We bought it in a toy store, because that is what it is — a toy. The Little Queen is a miniature of the large Bissell and works just as well. It is a good size for even the smallest boat, and the handle unscrews so the sweeper can be stowed easily. A whisk broom is useful for sweeping dirt from corners into a less confined area, where the carpet sweeper can then be used. A year or two ago, we saw this same carpet sweeper advertised in a marine catalog, but we have not seen it since. It would be a good item for marine stores, since they are more accessible to boating people than toy stores are.

If you have carpeting, you will need something for cleaning it while it is in place. The only alternative is to take it up and shake it, which is not practical if the carpet has been put down with double-faced tape. Naturally a boat carpet will have to be cleaned more often than carpeting in a house, since it is much more likely that horrendous things will be tracked or spilled onto it.

We clean our carpet with a concentrated liquid carpet or upholstery cleaner, diluted according to the package directions. We sponge the carpet with the suds, and it usually is completely dry in an hour. For cleaning isolated grease and oil spots, we use a more concentrated mixture.

When we get paint on the carpet (notice that we said "when," not "if"), we remove it with Kem Brush and Roller Cleaner, which is a cleaner made by Sherwin Williams. We originally purchased a can of it to clean brushes. You dip the brush into it to remove the paint, then wash out the brush in water. The back of the can says the product also can be used to remove oil from driveways and some fabrics. One day Bill put his foot into a puddle of wet bottom paint, climbed aboard, and tracked remarkably little in the cockpit — but he managed to get a big, blue footprint on the gold-colored carpet below. We wiped off as much as we could with paper towels, then removed the rest of it with some Kem cleaner on a cloth. Unless the cleaner is washed out with water, it leaves an oily residue that will attract more dirt. We used carpet shampoo for sponging up this residue. When it was dry, there was no evidence that a spot had been there. Kem cleaner has also been useful for removing grease and oil stains from washable clothes.

A fiber or knotted rope doormat will collect much of the stuff that might otherwise be tracked below. A solid rubber mat must be removed every other day or so to allow the deck underneath to dry out.

Dusting in the usual household sense is not often needed in a boat, since there aren't many large areas to collect dust. But because it is not often obvious, too many boatkeepers let dust collect along ledges and in out-of-the-way corners, until the boat looks unkempt. Often the boatkeepers aren't even aware that their boat looks so shoddy.

Dusting every two weeks or so should be adequate. Use one of the spray waxes if wood is varnished. Use a damp cloth for dusting oiled wood, fiberglass, and imitation wood.   If your vacuum cleaner has a dusting tool, use it to clean the tops of books and similar dust collectors. If you have followed our suggestions about closing off open shelves, there won't be many items exposed to dust.   Also, the boat will look much neater if everything is put away.   The insides of the cupboards and lockers can be messy, but at least outwardly the boat will look neat.

The overhead gets very dirty when you live aboard. Cooking, heating, and especially smoking can leave a dirty film in six months or less. Whether the overhead is fiberglass, vinyl, or painted wood, it can be wiped down with any of the many liquid cleaning solutions on the market. If the finish is shiny, such as fiberglass or painted wood, the cleaner will dull it, but a light wipe-down with spray wax will bring back the luster.   If you don't have a cleaning liquid available, you can use dishwashing liquid or even laundry detergent, which are satisfactory if the area isn't too badly soiled.

One of the most versatile products you can have on board is baking soda.   It is an excellent polish for nearly every metal; it will not scratch even the shiniest surface; and it costs much less than regular metal polishes. Baking soda also removes the greenish deposit that appears when metal has been exposed to salt air. The places you sail and the atmosphere of the cabin will determine how often you need to polish things.   Some people like the look of polished metal and don't mind keeping it up, but we don't want to polish any more than we have to, so we keep tarnishable items to a minimum.

We keep a large container of baking soda in the galley, because it is a good fire extinguisher.   A bit of baking soda dissolved in water to make a paste also stops the itching from insect bites. If you have a bathtub aboard, and you have a sunburn or a lot of insect bites, soak yourself in a tub of water with baking soda added to it — it will relieve either problem.   Take some baking soda when you have an upset stomach. You can brush your teeth with baking soda every day; it not only polishes the teeth, it sweetens the breath.

For clogged drains, pour in a handful of baking soda followed by a half-cup of vinegar.   Cover the drain tightly for about five minutes, then uncover it and run some water. This solution cleans drains safely.   Ordinary drain cleaners are much too harsh for boat plumbing.

Oh, yes — baking soda also can be used for cooking.

Vinegar is another product handy for boatkeeping. When stainless steel becomes spotted, rub it with a cloth dampened in vinegar. Plastic upholstery also can be wiped clean with a vinegar-dampened cloth. If you want to remove an outdated Coast Guard Auxiliary inspection sticker from a port, soak it several times with vinegar. After a few minutes, wipe it with clear water.

If you feel you have been in the sun long enough to get a burn, pat vinegar on the burned areas immediately after exposure to prevent peeling. If baking soda doesn't soothe insect bites, try full-strength vinegar. One-third cup of vinegar mixed with one cup of detergent makes an inexpensive carpet shampoo. The taste of stored water can be improved by adding ½ teaspoon of vinegar to a quart of water. Some say the addition of the vinegar quenches thirst more quickly.

Paint-hardened brushes are reusable after being soaked in hot vinegar for several minutes and rinsed in warm, sudsy water. For sparkling, unstreaked ports, wash them with 1/8 cup of vinegar and ½ cup of ammonia in a quart of warm water. The vinegar helps dissolve any salt on the ports. Pour some full-strength vinegar into the head, and let it sit overnight to remove any salt encrustations, if you have the old-fashioned pump-over-the-side head. (Vinegar, too, is handy for cooking.)

Laundry will be an ever-present chore, no matter how few clothes you wear. There always will be bedsheets, towels, and dish towels that need to be washed. The washing is no problem, if you can find a laundromat and if you can afford it. When cruising the islands, where laundry facilities are few and far between, you may have to do all your wash by hand.

If fresh water is scarce, soak the laundry for several hours in a bucket of salt water with a good detergent. Joy works very well in salt water. After soaking, rub out any remaining dirt spots and rinse the laundry in clean salt water. Then rinse in fresh water to which some fabric softener has been added.

Even when we are cruising where laundromats are convenient, we do not like to feel that we have to put into port just to do the laundry. We do a bucketful of socks, underwear, and shirts about every third day so that we can avoid doing a regular batch of laundry for a month or more. The trick is to keep up with the small stuff. Big items, such as sheets and bath towels, can be kept in the laundry bag until you make the trip to the laundromat ashore.

If you cannot have fresh sheets as often as you would like, spray them each night with one of the antiseptic/disinfectant sprays, such as Lysol. This will extend their usefulness considerably.

Laundries in marinas either cost more than commercial ones, or they hold fewer clothes if the price is the same. If there is a commercial laundromat within a reasonable distance, we always go there rather than use the marina's machines. Marinas usually have only one or two machines, and we don't often do a regular batch of laundry unless we have three or four machineloads.

If you work toward having all washable clothing, your boating life will be easier. We moved aboard while we were still working at "dress-up" shoreside jobs, and we had several items of clothing that could not be washed; they had to be dry cleaned. Now, every stitch we own is washable.

Nowadays there is no need to have an iron if you are careful about what you buy. Most permanent-press fabrics are a mixture of Dacron and cotton. The higher the synthetic content of the fabric, the faster it will dry, with fewer wrinkles, and the hotter it will be to wear. Some people don't seem to mind being in the sun wearing clothes with a high synthetic content, but for many of us, it is like being dressed in a plastic bag — very uncomfortable. Keep this in mind when shopping for clothes.

If you want to have cold-weather clothes that will keep you warm, again stay away from synthetics. Nothing is as warm as natural fibers, especially wool; if left in its natural state, wool is water-repellent. Cool-weather clothing should fit fairly close to the body, without being tight. It is better to dress in several layers than to try keeping warm in only one or two heavy garments. A cotton-knit turtleneck is a good first layer.

Any concentrated liquid laundry detergent is easier to store than the bulky boxes of the granulated type. A liquid also can be used to clean the bilge. Pour it full strength into the bilge. Let it soak for awhile, then pump out the bilge. The sizes of the bilges and the type of muck in them determines how much you need and how long it should soak. We tested a dribble of Joy, Wisk, and a regular bilge cleaner on a spot where some oily sludge had accumulated. The dishwashing and laundry detergents worked just as well as the much more expensive special bilge cleaner.

Joy works better in salt water than any other soap or detergent we have tested. Regular bar soap gave only a fair lather, and the deodorant soaps didn't lather at all. Shampoos were not too satisfactory, but, in a pinch, you can wash your hair with Joy.

One of the easiest places for germs and bacteria to collect — ashore or afloat — is the dishcloth. Unfortunately, the dishcloth is often the same cloth used for wiping off the galley counters, thus spreading the bacteria. The almost perpetual dampness of the cloth is one of the factors that contributes to rapid bacteria growth; another is hot weather.

There isn't much you can do about the weather, but you can do something about the fertile dampness. Use a cloth that will dry out quickly, and use separate cloths for dishes and counters. We use a square of nylon net for the dishwashing and a disposable towel (such as a Handi Wipe) cut in thirds for the counter tops. Handi Wipes dry very quickly, and since they are relatively inexpensive, they can be changed frequently. Nylon net will not work at all for counters, but it is extremely effective for dishwashing.

Laundering will not remove all of the bacteria in a fabric cloth; the water in commercial laundromats is not hot enough. The cloth would have to be boiled to be completely safe. Nylon net costs about 30 cents a yard and lasts a long time. The net construction provides enough friction to loosen cooked-on food and save scouring pads. The net rinses clean with a minimum of water and can be shaken dry.

The same bacteria that thrive in a kitchen cloth also grow in the damp towels in the head. Hang them so they will dry out as much as possible between uses. If you are cruising away from laundry facilities, consider using Handi Wipes as hand towels. You can use regular towels when shoreside facilities are available again. If you prefer to use regular towels and plan to wash them yourself, don't allow them to get too dirty, and use a little bleach in the soaking water.

Bleach can ruin materials such as leather or rubber, but it is handy to have a quart aboard. When you have extremely soiled clothes or items that need to be disinfected, you can pour a little bleach in the soaking water if the fabrics are color-fast.

One of the best uses for bleach when you are cruising in out-of-the-way places is as a water purifier. Add ten drops of bleach to a gallon of questionable water. Let this mixture stand for five minutes before you drink it. When storing the bleach, be sure the container is always upright. Wedge it in somewhere so it cannot fall over and leak if you encounter heavy weather. Whenever bleach is used for laundry, be sure to rinse the items thoroughly with water. Any residue from the bleach in the material could, in time, eat through it.

There are several efficient mildew removers on the market, but they cost about $3 per pint-and-a-half. Read the ingredients on the label of any of these, and you will discover that they contain 4.8 percent calcium hypochlorite and 95.2 percent inert ingredients. The "inert ingredients" are water.

We make our own mildew remover, and it costs only a few cents. Find a chemical company and try to buy a small quantity of calcium hypochlorite. The place we went to would not sell us less than a pound, which was too much for us — so we gave half of it away. The pound cost a dollar. To mix the solution, pour a quart of the inert ingredients — water — into a suitable container. To this add 5½ tablespoons of calcium hypochlorite. Stir lightly. *Caution*: Be sure to put the calcium hypochlorite *into the water*. If you put the powder in first and pour water over it, it will explode. We keep our solution in a plastic bottle with a push-down spray top.

To use this mixture, spray it on any mildewed area. It will take a few seconds for the solution to work, then suddenly the mildew will disappear. Wipe or rinse with fresh water. Test a small, inconspicuous area to be sure discoloration doesn't occur, especially where fabrics are involved. We have used our mixture successfully on painted wood surfaces, plastic-covered items, canvas, and Acrilan. This mixture is not suitable for use on mildewed clothing, but a little bleach in the laundry water removes mildew from most fabrics.

A quick way to remove oil and grease stains from an unoiled or unvarnished teak surface is to cover the stain with acetone. If you want to bleach the teak, use regular household bleach, slightly diluted, followed by a water rinse.

Once we had some oil in the bilge that backed up onto the teak cockpit floorboards during pumping. The oil soaked into the teak because we did not clean it up immediately. Later we poured some full-strength Wisk on the stained parts and let it sit for a couple of hours. When we hosed off the teak, the oil had disappeared completely.

Keep as little glass as possible on board. There will have to be some, since several products you will need or want are not packaged in anything but glass. These containers will have to be stowed so that they cannot slide around and break, no matter how rough the sea.

Since we want our boat to be just as much a sailboat as any weekender's boat, we arrange her so that we can go for a sail whenever the mood strikes us. When we are at dockside, everything below deck is always stowed where it would be stowed if we were under sail. Unless we are taking the engine apart or painting, we can be underway in 15 minutes, no matter how long we have been tied up — and can encounter gale-force winds with nothing falling out of place. It has taken us nearly three years to achieve this state. We don't ever want to be like the live-aboard couple who had been in a marina for over a month and said, "We need a couple of days to get everything stowed, then we will be on our way again."

Shortly after we moved aboard and began cruising, we encountered gale-force winds and found that during long periods of severe heeling in a rough sea, drawers, cabinets, and lockers came open and spilled their contents. After we put into port, we went to the nearest hardware store and purchased 21 ordinary household hooks and eyes in various sizes. We secured them to everything that might, or did, come open. Now we automatically hook most of them when we are underway.

If lightweight items are stored in a locker that has a sturdy catch, the door probably will not come open, since the weight of the items stowed there is not heavy enough to push the door open. But even the sturdiest of catches will open if heavy items slide against the door with any force. These are the lockers that need hooks and eyes. Turn-buttons and barrel bolts can vibrate loose, and we have found them to be much less satisfactory than hooks and eyes.

Sliding doors that run either fore and aft or athwartships may also slide open from the motion of the boat in a seaway. These, too, should be secured with hooks and eyes.

Even if we could have afforded the heavier-duty nautical hooks and eyes sold in marine stores, we would not have used them. Both the hook and the eye are mounted on a square or oval plate that must be screwed in with two or four screws. Even the smallest ones are very obvious wherever they are installed, while the household type screws directly into the wood and has no mounting plates; it is small and unobtrusive. Also, they haven't rusted in over four years in our boat. If they do rust, they will be easy and inexpensive to replace.

In some boats, an open door forms a barricade across another compartment. Properly designed boats will have a means of securing the opened door to keep it in place. Our head door opens out to close off the passageway forward. The head was designed to be used with the door closed, but since it is small and we are tall, we find it more convenient to leave the door open across the passageway when we are using the head.

We thought there was no practical way to hold the head door open until we saw a device on the boat of some live-aboard friends. It might best be described as a wooden spring with a notch cut in it for the door (Fig. 18-1). We drew a cardboard pattern and cut

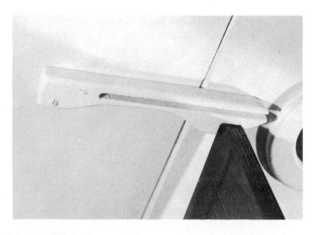

Figure 18-1. Whiffle's door catch on overhead, with head door open. To release door, open ends of catch are pinched together.

it out to test it for size and placement. We then used this pattern to cut the door catch out of mahogany, although any wood that has some spring to it could be used. We were able to screw this into the overhead. In a fiberglass boat, it would have to be glued to the overhead or backed up by a wooden base. Remember that only the unnotched side is fastened to the overhead. The side with the notch must be free to move, so it must be planed down slightly so it will not rub against the overhead. You may or may not have a need for such a device in your boat, but it was a perfect solution for us.

Most live-aboards find that on a boat they cook exactly the same way and eat the same foods they did ashore, so most of the recipes designed especially for boat use aren't worth much. Many "nautical" dishes are planned so that most of the cooking is done at home ashore, and the dish is brought aboard to be warmed up before serving. If you are a live-aboard, you are already home, so you might as well use your favorite recipes and cookbooks just as you did ashore.

If space for cookbooks is a problem, make your own cookbook by cutting out the recipes you use frequently and attaching them to loose-leaf sheets. Several cookbooks can thus be condensed into one smaller one. Most cooks use only a few of the recipes in any one cookbook.

If your boat is outfitted for comfortable living, there will not be many things you cannot cook in your galley. If you make long passages, your cooking and eating habits probably will have to change somewhat, unless you have an elaborate refrigerator/ freezer installation.

Since we have a reputation for getting ashore to the nearest restaurant whenever possible, we are hardly the ones to tell others about cooking and food; but we have had some experiences that might be of interest. Most of us have read about or met long-distance voyagers carrying aboard pounds and pounds of potatoes, some of which were bound to rot before they were used. Why not use instant and/or canned potatoes instead? They take up much less room, there is no danger of spoilage, and they are less expensive than regular potatoes when you consider that you pay for the weight of the skins on regular potatoes. Cooking fresh potatoes from scratch takes about four times longer than the time needed to prepare instant or canned potatoes, so more fuel will be used, and this will have to be included in their cost.

We use canned potatoes for frying or adding to a white sauce, and the instant type for mashed potatoes. There is a great difference in the palatability of certain brands of instant potatoes, so try small amounts of different brands to find one you like. Keep a few fresh potatoes on hand for baking or making french fries.

Bacon is one of our favorite foods, but it emits one of our least favorite odors in the cabin. Even if it is cooked below with all the cabin hatches and ports open, the smell seems to linger. We usually buy two pounds of bacon at a time (only one pound if the weather is hot and we will be away from shore awhile) and cook it all at once, either on deck or on the dock, out of the cabin. The electric skillet is best for this, because it holds so many slices and gets the job over with quickly.

The cooked bacon can be reheated quickly in a small skillet or in an oven. Since we only reheat and don't recook the bacon, we cook it initially to the crispness we want. All the strips should be well drained on paper towels. The cooked strips can be stored in any suitable container, such as a loaf pan, with a paper towel between each layer of bacon and a cover of foil.

Many people like bacon, eggs, toast, and coffee for breakfast or supper, but in many galleys it is difficult to keep all the items hot. Precooking the bacon makes this an easy meal to prepare. If you like bits of bacon crumbled on salads, you are all set. Bacon-and-tomato, or grilled-cheese-and-bacon sandwiches can be made with a minimum of fuss and bother.

No matter where you travel, you will be harassed by insects. The warmer the climate, the more pests there will be. If you have opening ports, every one of them must be screened. The companionway hatch, as well as the other deck hatches, will also need screens. Anything that opens should be screened. There are tiny insects that can get through the screening, and they bite just as viciously as the big insects. Unfortunately, there seems to be no practical way to keep these pests out if you want any fresh air.

Screens on ports should be the permanent kinds that are attached to the frame of the port itself. Many boats are equipped with rigid screens for the companionway hatch, and if stowage is a problem, they should be replaced with a flexible screen that can be rolled and tucked away or folded flat and stored under seat cushions.

We have made a flexible screen for the companionway hatch of every boat we have owned. Velcro makes this an easy job. (Velcro is a versatile product with a two-part closure: you press the parts together to seal them and peel them apart to open them. One part has tiny nylon "hooks," and the other part has dense nylon "fuzz." The "hooks" engage the "fuzz" at the slightest pressure and will stay together until pulled apart.) The screening is flexible fiberglass that can be rolled or folded, without creasing permanently.

Once the screening has been cut to fit the hatch, either part of the Velcro is sewed around the edges of the screen. The other part of the Velcro is glued, nailed, or both, to the inside of the hatch, close to the opening. The screen is pressed in place when needed, amd peeled off and put away when not in use.

Fortunately, our deck hatches were already screened. The screens are mounted in wooden frames that are hinged to fold down for access to the hatch. The screens are held in place by turn-buttons. Stowage is no problem, since the screens are part of the hatch. Some older boats also have this arrangement, but hatch screens of this type could be installed on nearly any hatch.

Flexible screens also can be used on deck hatches by utilizing Velcro the same way we described for the main hatch; sew one part of the Velcro around a piece of screen cut to fit the hatch, and glue the other part around the hatch opening. Velcro is rela-tively expensive, so if you cannot afford to outline the whole opening of each hatch, it is just as effective to use short strips at intervals. Just be sure that the part on the screen lines up with the part on the hatch. We would have needed 13 feet of Velcro to outline the perimeter of our larger-than-normal companionway hatch, but by using short pieces, strategically placed, we were able to get by with only four feet. Velcro can be purchased in fabric and marine stores, and the cost is nearly the same wherever you buy it. It is available in many colors, most commonly white, beige, and black. Velcro comes in many widths, but the easiest to find is the ¾-inch size.

If you have rigid, hard-to-stow hatch screens and are reluctant to give them up, consider making a shallow cabinet or storage shelf for them and suspending it from the overhead, as mentioned in Chapter XI.

When we are tied up to a dock, we depend upon the screens to keep out the normal insects, as well as roaches and rats. Many a boat owner has left an unscreened hatch open, only to find that a rat has used it to get aboard. One family found a stray cat aboard when they returned to their boat. They got rid of him easily, but not before he had helped himself to some of their food. Keep ports and hatches closed off with screens, and don't leave deck and cockpit lockers open if you won't be around to see what's crawling into them.

Should a rat decide to come on board to make your cabin his new home, no screen will stop him if he wants to take the trouble to gnaw through it. Chances are that rats will not go to this ex-treme, so screening does prevent most incidents. If a rat does get aboard, you will probably have the devil's own time getting rid of it. Some of the less intelligent rats can be caught in traps, or you can put some poison out and hope they eat it. All the rats we have dealt with ashore have been smarter than we were, so we are lucky we have never had one in a boat. We have, however, seen their sinister little eyes peering out from under many docks where we have been tied up. It is not a bad idea to use rat guards on your dock lines in some commercial ports.

Roaches also are smarter than people, and they can get into a boat in ways no rat ever imagined. Being small, they can crawl through any tiny opening. They also can fly. One balmy night in North Carolina, a two-inch-long (at least) monster roach flew in through our then-unscreened companionway hatch. That was when we decided that no hatches would ever be left unscreened again.

The more tropical the area, the more roach-infested it is. Those who have cruised in the Caribbean quickly learn never to step barefoot on a dock at night. They also learn to pick over any food they buy before bringing it aboard from the dinghy. If you see no roaches, there will most certainly be roach eggs in the creases of any paper bags or in the labels of canned goods (they like the glue on the labels). The labels must be removed before the cans are brought aboard. Roach eggs can be found in every place you can think of, and in lots of places you would never think of.

We have been lucky, roach-wise, but there have been a few isolated roaches that have made their way aboard. One crawled out of a fold of an acquaintance's clothing while we were sitting below having a chat. It crawled onto the backrest of the settee, where it wandered around for the 45 minutes our friend stayed. As soon as he left, we killed the roach, since it was still on the settee and hadn't had the foresight to crawl into a locker. We doubt that Amy Vanderbilt or Emily Post could have come up with something tactful to say in that situation. Of course, you cannot inspect your friends as they come aboard your boat, but you can keep your eyes open. Some boats are obviously roach-infested, and if their owners are your friends, watch for any crawly visitors they may bring aboard.

Roachiness has nothing to do with cleanliness. Roaches are just as happy in hygienic surroundings as they are in filth. If they cannot find food to eat, they will satisfy themselves with leather, cloth, and paper. One or two roaches cannot cause as much destruction as a hundred roaches can. But if you see a roach and do not kill it instantly, just hope it isn't going to lay eggs anywhere. One or two roaches can become a hundred very quickly. Some people just get used to living with them and don't make much of an effort to get rid of them. One roach, however, is too many for us. If you often find yourself chasing one without getting a good enough swing to swat him, buy an aerosol can of insecticide to keep handy for squirting into confined areas.

It will be worth your while to go out of your way to get some Sla, which is a Reefer and Galler product. It can be purchased in good hardware stores and in the closet shops of department stores.

serve its purpose well, and the dishes really stay in place. If your dishes are slippery, put permanent or removable fiddle rails on the dining table to help keep the dishes on top of the table. But fiddle rails, too, are of little use when heeling considerably.

A blob of florist's clay on the bottom of lightweight items keeps them from slipping around on counter tops. A small piece of this clay keeps a soap dish from sliding into the sink when heeling, as might happen if it were not anchored down.

We became acquainted with Sla when we needed to lic
problem ashore. The label on the can emphasizes tha
killing moths, but on the back of the can, in smaller
product also claims to kill flies, mosquitoes, gnats, wasp
spiders, crickets, ants, bedbugs, roaches, and waterbugs
we have ever used kills these pests quicker than Sla. M
cides do not work fast enough to prevent any memb
order Hymenoptera (bees, wasps, and hornets) from
few good stabs at their tormentors before they die. Sla
a big wasp in midair before it knows what has hit it.
more residual effect, it would be the perfect product. F
this deter you from using it; just spray the needed areas
Sla's vapor kills insects hiding in lockers before they
and run to a more wholesome atmosphere. Also, Sla ca
directly onto clothes. We can't recommend it highly e

If you have several roaches aboard, you might pu
tablet of roach poison in their favorite dining spot.
have never had enough of a roach problem to wan
tablets, a friend claimed he got rid of lots of roa
Harris Famous Roach Tablets. The package is sm
yellow and can be found in supermarkets and ha
We have a box, just in case. Our friend put them in
bins, and shelves where he thought the roaches mi
came across the tablets, dined on them, and died.

If you have a severe infestation of roaches, the
rid of them is by fumigating. Be prepared to do
buy a boat in the tropics, or if the boat has just co

When seat-cushion covers are made of heavy
begin to look worn, you may not need to replace
color wears off or fades before the fabric itself
The color of the duck is usually just as vivid on
the material as it is on the front. If this is so, t
cover, reverse the fabric, and then stitch it up on
lines. You can get new-looking seat-cushion cove
ing a dime.

If a stainless-steel oven gets messy and you hav
use #80 sandpaper to cut through a buildup
When the metal begins to show through, swit
to avoid scratching or scarring the metal. Sa
stains and burned-on foods from stainless-st
aluminum or stainless-steel pots and pans. Do
stainless steel or enameled stoves or ovens.

There are dishes on the market that will no
heels. In theory, this is a good idea, but unt
vented, the dinnerware is useless when a cert
reached. If the angle of heel is not too great,

XIX. TRANSPORTATION

ON LAND AND WATER

Most cruising boats have a dinghy of some sort, and the cruising live-aboard should certainly have some kind of tender. It is diffi-cult to decide what kind and size is best. One perceptive sailor said of all dinghies: "When it is aboard it is too big, and when it is in the water it is too small." Dinghies are available in fiberglass, wood, aluminum, and rubberized materials. They are rigid, fold-ing, or inflatable. The size can range from a tiny cockleshell on up. Some are sailing dinghies, and all can take some kind of out-board motor.

There is not much reason for having a dinghy that will carry more than three people. A large dinghy is only a convenience for any guests you might have and an inconvenience for you. You are the one who has to tow it or stow it, so keep it small — but not too small, because the smaller they are, the harder they are to row. A dinghy needs a little weight to make it manageable.

Of the rigid dinghies, the fiberglass ones are the lightest in weight for their size, until you get to about 10 feet. Then one made of aluminum would be lighter. There are no true dinghies built of aluminum, but there are 10-foot and longer aluminum boats that could be used for dinghies. It's a shame that smaller aluminum boats are not manufactured for use as dinghies, since they are very light in weight. In fact, an aluminum boat is even lighter than an inflatable with wooden floorboards.

Now that we are live-aboards, we have an inflatable; but we had fiberglass dinghies for our previous weekend boats. Of the two types, we prefer the inflatable. Ours is the West Products Sealiner. After comparing it to other more famous inflatables, we are glad we chose the Sealiner. The West dinghy rows better than any other inflatable we have tried. Its wooden floorboard gives it a modified twin keel, instead of the flat type found on other inflatables. A flat-bottomed boat provides no directional stability; it skitters around in any direction the oars happen to push it, no matter how good you are at rowing. We have rowed the Sealiner into a stiff head wind and its accompanying chop with no difficulty; we got where we were going quickly, and we stayed dry in the process.

Now that we have the inflating technique down cold, it takes only 10 or 15 minutes. Sometimes it can be a bother, but it would be more of a bother for us to wrestle with a rigid dinghy.

An inflatable dinghy usually can be stowed somewhere on deck or in a locker when you are trying to make time and don't want to be held up by towing a dinghy. Stowing the dinghy prevents it from being stolen, as it might be if it were tied on astern. Often an inflatable can be deflated only partially for convenient deck stowage. In heavy weather, many dinghies that are towed are lost, or swept off the deck if they are lashed there. These two dangers can be eliminated with an inflatable, which can be brought aboard in heavy weather. If no safe place can be found for it on deck or in a locker, the inflatable can even be brought into the cabin temporarily.

All inflatables have varying numbers of separate flotation chambers, which make them virtually unsinkable. Even if only one of the flotation chambers is intact, there is still something you can hang onto.

If a rigid dinghy is small enough and the boat large enough, the dinghy can be stowed in davits at the stern. If this is done, a cover should be made for the dinghy so it will not fill with rainwater or seawater in rough seas. In high winds, a dinghy stowed in davits will affect your steering somewhat.

If you have a rigid dinghy that cannot be stowed in davits, a place must be found for it on deck, but first it must be manhandled aboard so it can be stowed. This is no easy task with even the lightest and smallest of dinghies. Once it is aboard, the dinghy probably will have to be stowed over a deck hatch or the companionway hatch. On nearly all boats up to 40 feet, dinghy stowage on deck is a compromise. The dinghy will always block out light or air, or it will be in the way when you are walking forward or aft. If it is stowed right-side-up, a cover will be needed, again to keep out rain and seawater.

A motor is a welcome accessory for a dinghy, but always take the oars along just in case. Of course, with a motor you will need gasoline, oil, spare parts, and a place to stow it all. Some sailors do not feel a motor is worth the trouble. The size and type of motor is a matter of personal preference.

Sometimes a sailing dinghy can be useful and fun to have, but room must be found for stowing the mast, boom, and sail. We have the sailing version of the West dinghy, which is the only sailing inflatable. Recently West discontinued the sailing version, even though we have found it very satisfactory.

When towing the dinghy, be on the alert for any signs of chafe on the painter, and replace the line when it shows the first signs of wear. We had a nylon painter for many years, but we replaced it with a polypropylene line with two loops spliced into it. Polypropylene floats, so a loop can be snagged easily with a boathook. We use one of the loops for towing the dinghy well aft of the boat when underway, and we use the other loop for pulling the dinghy up tight against the stern when docking or maneuvering in cramped spaces. For extra security, the loop is slipped over a cleat and the excess line is cleated off on top of the loop in the normal manner.

If you are cruising on a regular basis without the benefit of a permanent home port, bicycles are the least complicated land transport. Several choices are available: the typical small-wheeled boater's bicycle that folds up for easy stowage, the standard bicycle, or the fancy three- to 10-speed models. Unless you have a safe place to store an expensive, many-speed racing bike, it would be best not to have one.

One couple we know has two 10-speed bikes that are taken apart and stowed below in the forward cabin. The bicycles are safe there, but they must be reassembled for every trip. Often it is not worth the time it takes for the trip involved. We know other sailors who lash less expensive standard-size bikes on deck. Some lash them to the shrouds and others favor a position athwartships on the stern. The folding bikes, when folded, measure 18 by 24 by 28 inches, and they are easy to stow in many locations on or below deck. Often they have a zippered plastic case that is relatively waterproof. All of the folding bikes have 20-inch wheels, and most of them are only one-speed, but Sears and Raleigh have three-speed models with telescoping handlebars for about $125.

There is no ideal bike for the live-aboard. The ones that can carry you great distances have no provisions for carrying heavy loads of groceries or bulky laundry bundles. Until recently, our bikes were one-speed models with 20-inch wheels. They did not fold, but they were designed to come apart in the middle. When we first moved aboard, we kept them, dismantled, under the forward vee berths — and we never used them. After a month, we got them out to do some sightseeing and we never put them away again. We found we could stow them, assembled, on deck out of the way. Now that same spot is where we stow our new three-speed folding Raleighs. We use them all the time for even the shortest trips, because they are so convenient.

The Raleighs have a rack on the back and conventional handle-

bars. We have adapted both so we can carry all kinds of packages.
To the rack we have permanently attached two short lengths of
shock cord with clips on each end (Fig. 19-1). To our standard
canvas ice bags we have added two small loops so they can be
hung from the handlebars (Fig. 19-2). One day we carried laundry
on the front and back of Jan's bicycle, groceries in the bag on the
front of Bill's bike, and a pizza for dinner on the back rack.

At the supermarket we do not use the conventional brown
grocery bags, unless the amount of groceries is small. We usually
pack the groceries in the canvas bags at the checkout counter.
By now we have a good idea of how much we can carry, so we
shop accordingly.

Conventional wire bike baskets are not much good on a boat
bike. They do not hold enough, and they present a storage
problem wherever the bike is kept. Our friends with the 10-speed
bikes made themselves backpacks, but the loads they can carry are
quite limited. We have thought about making saddlebags to fit
over the rear wheels, but we haven't worked out the design yet.

We are fairly healthy, middle-aged people, and we can easily
ride several miles if the countryside is flat. Of course, we ride our
bikes at least every other day, so we have developed the muscles
needed for bike riding. Work up to the long distances gradually if
you haven't ridden for awhile.

*Figure 19-1.   Shock-cord tie-downs are useful for securing packages of all
shapes and sizes.*

We have made a small canvas bag that attaches to the underside of a seat. It contains a long chain and padlock, a crescent wrench that can fit the largest nut on the bike, a tire repair kit, extra spokes and a spoke wrench, strap-on leg lights, and a small square of terry cloth. (When we have to leave the bikes outside in the rain, we dry off the seats with the terry cloth before sitting down.) In the bottom of one of the canvas handlebar bags is a good-sized, folded, plastic bag that can be used to cover the groceries or laundry if we get caught in the rain. Equip your bike with reflectors and headlights for night riding, so you can stay out safely after dark if necessary.

If you cannot or will not ride a bicycle, you may rediscover the pleasures of walking — if others will let you. Just after we started cruising, and before we started using the bikes, we were looking forward to walking. We had been caught up in the typical suburban trap of using a car for everything. The first night out, we tried to walk to a nearby restaurant, but a man from the marina insisted on driving us. A couple of days later, we tried to walk to a grocery store, and a well-meaning local sailor drove us to the store and back again. Later we intended to walk to the laundry, which was only two blocks from the marina, and someone else wanted to drive us there. Of course we appreciate rides, and many kind people have gone out of their way to take us where we wanted

Figure 19-2.   Standard canvas ice bag adapted for bicycle handlebars with loop on each side.

to go, but for awhile it looked as if we never were going to be allowed to walk anywhere.

Some live-aboards feel that a motorized conveyance is the only way to get around. Such transportation is the most convenient, but you will not get any beneficial (and sometimes needed) exercise by letting a motor do all the work. The biggest drawback of anything motorized is that it must have a license, usually must pass an annual inspection, and in some states must be insured before a license will be issued. If you cruise from one home port and return there on a fairly regular basis, it is not too difficult to comply with all the rules and regulations. If you do not have a port you call home, the whole business becomes very complicated.

A lightweight motorcycle that can be carried on deck is preferred by some sailors, but even the lightest of these will weigh 80 pounds. We have been in some slips and at some docks where it would have been impossible to get an 80-pound anything from ship to shore. Every person riding a motorcycle must have a safety helmet, and stowage of this item can be a problem.

Many live-aboards have cars; if you can afford it, and have a permanent address, there is no reason not to have one. But if you are moving around, the same complications with licenses, inspections, and insurance will present themselves.

We were in Florida for a time and purchased a car that we planned to sell as soon as we left the state. At the last minute we decided to keep it for awhile, and perhaps shuffle it along with us. The car was due for inspection in May, and we were ready to leave Florida in early April. We had it inspected a month early and told the officials we were going to be traveling out of the state for quite awhile, so had to get it done before we left. This early inspection presented no problem. The new license plates could be obtained by mail and were due in August. Evidently the notices for renewal are sent out but not forwarded, since we did not receive one, though we had filed the proper address change with the post office. We wrote to the Department of Motor Vehicles and explained that we were traveling out of the state for an extended period (true), and that we spent a good part of the year in the Midwest (not quite true), where we have our permanent mailing address; and could they possibly send the new Florida plates to the midwestern address? Luckily, they did. If they hadn't, we would have had expired plates when we came back to get the car, and would have had to go through the whole rigmarole of getting new Florida plates just to transport the car to North Carolina, where we planned to leave it for a few months.

If you reside and own a car in any state, you are required to have that state's license plates. To get the plates, you have to have the vehicle inspected in that state, change the insurance to conform to that state's laws, and in most states have an address other than a post office box or General Delivery.

Each state has different ways of handling vehicle licenses, and never in a thousand years will they understand, or try to understand, the problems of a cruising live-aboard who wants to own a car.   Anything out of the norm is something no local, state, or federal government is capable of handling.   Most of us want to comply with the law, but they make it very difficult for us to do so.

If you have to leave the car for months at a time when you are off cruising, you may have to figure storage expenses into the annual costs of maintaining a car. Since we sold our car, we often rent cars for special trips we have to make or for sightseeing. Most car-rental agencies have special packages for days, weeks, weekends, and months; sometimes it can be quite economical to rent a car rather than take taxis or maintain your own car.

We saw a great solution for motorized transportation recently — "Chicken Power." It is a .85-horsepower motor that fits onto the front wheel of any bicycle with 16-inch to 27-inch wheels. It gets 100 miles to the gallon and propels you at 18 miles per hour, maximum.   This motor costs $100 and can be purchased from Western Auto stores.   The bicycle will have to be licensed according to state laws if the motor is used, but if your license expires, simply take the motor off and pedal the bicycle in the normal manner.

Public transportation still exists in most of the large cities and some of the smaller ones.   Most of the people who live ashore are so car-oriented that if you ask them about getting around on buses, they will not be able to tell you whether you can do it or not.   On a trip down the Mississippi, we stopped at St. Louis, Missouri. We asked the marina attendant if there was any public transportation, and he said there was none.   As it turned out, there was a good bus system, yet a man who had lived there for years did not even know it existed.

The best way to find out about bus schedules is to call the bus company.   Often it will take a few tries to get through, because the larger the city, the busier the line. With a little determination, you can get around on public transportation easily and inexpensively, regardless of what the locals think.

Do not depend on local knowledge for information on how far anything is, or whether you can get to it on foot or by bicycle. Being so car-oriented, they are likely to say you cannot get to lots of places that are, in reality, easily accessible. Once we were told that we could not get to a main post office because it was such a long walk from the bus stop; it turned out to be four blocks away. We have often been told that a given place is too far to ride to on a bicycle, and the place is only a mile or two away.   The fact that we are requesting the information from someone who can see our strange-looking, small-wheeled bikes may have some bearing on the fact that often we are told the place we want is too far to get to on them. We allow for this.

XX. SPECIAL PROBLEMS

OF THE LIVE-ABOARD

The problems of a live-aboard are not problems at all for the individual who lives ashore, because he conforms. The landlubber fits neatly into the niche a land-bound society has made for him. He is a solid citizen firmly anchored down by his job and his mortgages. A person who lives on a boat is almost automatically tagged as someone who leads an unstable, flyaway existence and is not to be trusted. This unfortunate attitude is common with many land people, and it is especially rampant among bankers.

If you are a live-aboard but you work now and then, collect your money, and move on, you may never need to deal with banks, and your life will be a lot simpler. But many live-aboards have a nest egg from which they want to get interest, or they have retirement or social security checks that have to be deposited somewhere. Banks, out of necessity, must enter into their lives.

You will find that your friendly neighborhood banker is only friendly if you live in a dwelling with a solid foundation in his town, and you have an account in his bank. If you also have a steady job, he can be a bundle of cordiality. "Self-employed," "freelance," and "out of town" are words no banker ever wants to hear.

One of the questions most frequently asked of us is, "How do you have money sent to you?" This is usually put to us by new live-aboards who have just been through the traumatic experience of trying to obtain funds, or by potential live-aboards who are perceptive enough to foresee problems in this area.

We had traveled extensively before we moved to a boat, and we knew from our previous experience that personal checks drawn on an out-of-town bank are not accepted for most transactions, and *never* for obtaining cash. We decided to have money sent to us in the form of a certified check or bank draft, made out in both our names. A certified check must be backed up with cash, so we assumed it would be the easiest kind of check to cash. Having it made out in both our names would make it difficult for anyone other than ourselves to cash it if it were stolen.

We were in Florida the first time we tried this method, and we presented the rather sizable check, along with our passports, to the teller who issued traveler's checks in the bank. (We always use passports or driver's licenses for identification, because both have our photographs on them.) We told her we wanted all but $50 of it in traveler's checks. She checked our identification, and in 15 minutes we had our traveler's checks and were on our way, pleased with ourselves for being clever enough to have figured out this easy way to replenish our funds.

The next time we ran out of money was in North Carolina, and we stopped in at the first bank we came to, armed with another sizable certified check and our passports.

"Do you have an account with us?"

"No."

"I'm sorry, we can't cash the check for you, but you can talk with one of the officers. He might okay it."

We had a nice chat with the officer, but he would not okay it. We tried another bank around the corner. We explained our situation to the teller, who said she could not cash the check unless we had an account with the bank. We told her we would be glad to pay for a phone call to the bank on which the check was drawn, so they could verify it. The teller was sympathetic. We gave her our telephone credit card number, and she placed the call. Just as the proper person came on the line, a bank officer appeared and gruffly told the teller to hang up, which she did, without a word of explanation to the party on the other end. The officer grabbed the check out of her hand and shoved it back at us, saying they would not cash it. He offered no explanation for his actions or attitude, so we left him and his bad manners and tried another bank, and another, and another.

At the fifth and last bank in town, we decided to question an officer about why we could not cash the check. We also wanted to pick his brain so we would not have this problem in the future. First, he told us, the check was too large. If a bank cashed it, they would, in effect, be lending you the money without getting any interest on it until the check cleared. Banks, contrary to their ads and television commercials, are not friendly and helpful to you unless you can make some money for them. Cashing a check for a nondepositor is not going to put any money in their pocket, so they do not want to do it, no matter how much you smile and say, "Please."

Having the check made out in both our names didn't help, because the bank really doesn't care that much whether you are who you say you are. They are only concerned that the check is not forged. A telephone call to the issuing bank to verify the check is not satisfactory either, because a forger can have one good check, with a number on it that can be verified, then proceed to make forgeries, with the same number, for the same amount of money as the one good check. And it will be verified every time, until the original, or one of the forgeries, finally gets back to the bank it was drawn on.

That informative officer said his bank would have cashed the check if our bank had called them in advance and told them they were sending a check to us for a certain amount. It seemed strange that a bank officer who was so careful in so many ways would even suggest something like that. Even to our noncriminal minds, it was immediately obvious that, in these days of direct dialing, we could go right outside the bank to the phone booth there, dial the bank's number and say, "This is Elmer Stodgy of Unilateral Fiduciary and Fidelity. We are sending a check to Mr. and Mrs. Moeller in the amount of $500, and we would like you to cash it for them." We were tempted to try it, but we didn't.

We also were toying with the idea of opening an account and keeping it long enough for the check to clear, then withdrawing the full amount and closing the account. There wasn't any bank that would not have handled the check if we had had an account with them. *We* thought of opening the account for the express purpose of cashing the check. It is amazing that the banks didn't think that someone might do just that. It would cost a bank more money to open an account than to cash a check of any reasonable amount.

The officer told us that a postal money order, as far as banks are concerned, is almost worthless. So many of these are stolen and cashed by the wrong people that banks will not touch them, no matter what the amount. He said that Western Union money orders probably were the best way to have money sent. These money orders usually can be cashed by the Western Union office, or Western Union will have an arrangement with a local bank that will honor them if the amount is sizable. Western Union money orders are costly, but they are the fastest and, we found out later, one of the surest ways of receiving money.

After all the illuminating conversation with the unyielding officer, we were still walking around with our uncashed check and wondering what to do. We finally called the owner of the marina where we were staying. Luckily, he was a personal friend. He told us to take the check to his bank, which was a neighborhood branch of one of the downtown banks, and he gave us the name of the officer to see. This officer reluctantly cashed it, but not without checking with the marina owner first.

Since we could not afford Western Union money orders all the time, a few months later we followed the other advice given to us and had several certified checks sent to us in the amount of $100 each. We easily cashed one in a small town in Virginia, and they even gave us a ballpoint pen. We were on our way to Washington, D. C., and when we arrived there, we were down to a few dollars and planning to cash another $100 check there. That was when we found out about the hostility and nastiness of the big-city banks. Banks in large cities have more problems with crooks and con artists; so the larger the city, the more difficult it is to cash anything. You can safely assume that any banks in a city with a population of more than a quarter-million will not do anything for you unless you have an account with them. In cities like New York and Washington, your answer is a rude, unembellished, "no," with the officer looking at you as if to ask, "How dare you waste my time by asking for such a ridiculous thing?"

We tried to cash our $100 check at four Washington banks before giving it up as hopeless. We finally telephoned for a Western Union money order, and we had the cash we needed within hours.

We still don't know why we had no problem with the first Florida bank. It may have been that the person handling the transaction was new on the job, or she just forgot to be as cautious and careful as she should have been. If you have good luck in one instance, as we did, accept it as just that — good luck. Be prepared for trouble sooner or later. We thought the Florida bank may have cashed our check because we wanted to put most of it into traveler's checks, on which the bank makes a commission. But we tried that ploy in North Carolina at some of the banks, even though we really didn't want traveler's checks, and it didn't work.

If you have a checking account, you can have money transferred from your checking account at your regular bank to a bank in the place where you have run out of money. By mail, it takes about a week. Telegrams and phone calls can speed up the process.

We used small certified checks for a year or so and encountered only a little difficulty, but they were nonetheless a nuisance. We decided there must be a better way. We eventually hit upon three better ways. One was to use our Master Charge card and/or Bankamericard to get cash. Each card allows you to obtain a certain amount of cash, depending on how good your credit rating is. There is no charge for this, as long as you pay the bill promptly when you receive it. If you don't pay in time, there is a small interest charge added to the next bill. This monthly interest is

much smaller than the charge for a Western Union money order,
as long as you do not let it go on for several months.

Another, and better, way is to have cash sent to you, but only
by *registered mail*.   First-class mail cannot be insured, but a
registered letter can be insured for any amount up to $10,000,
and it is under lock and key constantly. The cost (in 1976) is $3.50
plus postage for a registered letter with a $1,000 valuation. It is a
bit expensive, but it is still much cheaper than a Western Union
money order for the same amount.

Even though banks will not cash postal money orders, post
offices will. Money orders can be purchased in any amount up to
$300. When you pick up your mail at the post office, open the
envelope containing the money order and simply hand it back to
the clerk for cashing. The only problem you might encounter
with postal money orders is cashing them in a very small post
office early in the morning, since the post office might not have
enough cash on hand at that time.

If you do have to deal with a bank, there are a few things to
remember. Don't go into a bank looking like a hippie or a boat
bum and expect to do business. And, unless you cannot avoid it,
don't tell them you live on a boat. Just say you are traveling
through the area.   The banker will probably assume you are
traveling by car, and he will not mentally put you in the drifter/
vagabond/gypsy/hippie/undesirable category in which they classify
boat people. Don't be hostile. Control your temper. Try a little
humor. Even though bankers are a rather humorless lot, when
you want something out of the ordinary, humor might work.

Once, in Michigan, we wanted to get $100 by using our Master
Charge card. We presented the card to the teller and she telephoned
for the okay and got it. The Master Charge card was issued from a
bank in Maryland. When the teller asked for identification, Bill
showed her his driver's license, which was from North Carolina.
The teller gave him an icy look. She was becoming balky about
giving us the money and decided to check with her supervisor.
After she told her boss the story, he was suspicious. He wanted
to know why we had a card from a Maryland bank and a North
Carolina driver's license. Bill told him the truth: "I travel a lot,
and my driver's license expired when I was on an extended stay
in North Carolina — so I got one there." Then he laughingly said,
"That's nothing — the billing address for my Master Charge is in
the Midwest."

Both the teller and the supervisor chuckled in that dry way
they have when they don't know whether something is funny or
not, but they did give him the money. Just keep smiling, and try
not to lose your temper, as bankers keep asking you the questions
whose answers they will never understand.

You may find it to your advantage to have several bank accounts in several states, as we do. Once you begin cruising regularly, you probably will find that there are certain areas in which you will stay for weeks or months at a time, and you will find it convenient to establish banking connections in some of them.

We always thought that traveler's checks were the safest way to carry money. They are, in a sense, but it is too costly for us to do it that way. Now we have smaller amounts sent to us more often, or we get a little cash with our credit cards and never have much cash on hand.

We have had trouble cashing traveler's checks in some places. Clerks in some stores have refused to take them unless they were okayed by a supervisor. On occasion, we have had trouble getting the supervisor's okay if they were not American Express traveler's checks. In many areas, people do not seem to be familiar with the traveler's checks issued by the First National City Bank of New York or the Bank of America.

If you need to carry a large amount of money with you and want to make some money on it at the same time, carry it in the form of Series E savings bonds. You can buy them at banks and savings and loan institutions in denominations of $18.75, $37.50, $56.25, $75, $150, $375, and $750. The bonds begin to draw interest six months after the issue date, at the rate of 4.5 percent the first year. The interest increases gradually, so the final yield, if they are held to maturity, is six percent. They can be cashed in at most banks and other financial institutions any time after two months from the issue date. If the bonds are lost, stolen, or damaged, they can be replaced, so they are as good as traveler's checks in this respect.

All things considered, getting mail is much easier than getting money. You do not have to deal with a bunch of tight-lipped bankers with rigid rules. Postal employees generally are friendly and understanding. However, receiving mail on a regular basis is well-nigh impossible if you are cruising on a regular basis. Anyone who has cruised at all knows that you can never say definitely when you will arrive at a given point. Weather and breakdowns always must be taken into account.

We have all our first-class mail sent to General Delivery when we are cruising. We have parcel post and lesser classes of mail sent only when we will be in a town long enough for them to arrive. General Delivery is an easy address for people to remember — all they need is the town, state, and zip code.

General Delivery mail is held for 10 days. If you do not get to the post office in time to pick up your mail, all first-class mail will be returned to the sender. Or you can notify the post office and they will hold it for 30 days or forward it to another post office.

For example: if you are having mail sent to Annapolis, Maryland, and you have an engine breakdown at Cape May, New Jersey, that will delay you for some time, let the Annapolis post office know, and they will forward all first-class mail to whatever address you give them.

The official way to have your mail forwarded is to fill out a change-of-address card (Form PS 3575) and mail it to the post office that is holding your mail. (Keep a few of these forms with you on the boat.) Sometimes a letter to the postmaster will suffice. If you are dealing with a small, friendly post office, you might be able to telephone the postmaster and give him your forwarding information.

If your mail is addressed: Bill and Jan Moeller, Yacht "Whiffle," General Delivery, Main Post Office, Town, State, Zip, it will indicate you are on a boat. Some postmasters along the waterways might hold mail for a little longer than normal, even without notification, because they know boats do not always arrive when they are supposed to. Most will always hold mail for you beyond the time allotted if you telephone them and confirm your arrival.

Unless you are familiar with the town where your mail is being sent, have it addressed to the main post office, just in case there are two or more branches. If one of the branches is more convenient for you to reach, have the mail addressed with the zip code for that branch. Annapolis, for example, is a small town, but there are two post offices, each with a different zip code.

It is best to avoid having mail sent to very large cities unless you are sure where it will end up. In St. Louis, Missouri, the main downtown post office is within easy walking distance of the marina, but General Delivery mail is never sent there. It goes to another branch that is not in the downtown area.

If possible, try to plan to pick up your mail in small towns rather than cities, because the smaller the town, the closer the post office is to the harbor. Also, there is less chance of thievery by the postal employees or outsiders, and things are not as likely to get lost or misplaced in a post office that handles a small amount of mail.

We always try to get a regular road map of states and cities where we will be. These show where the post office is located, or, if not the post office, the location of City Hall, and the post office usually is nearby. Also, you can use the maps to get an idea of the physical size of cities and towns, so you will know if you can get to the post office easily on foot or by bicycle.

Never use General Delivery for something that is to be delivered by the United Parcel Service. They will not deliver it to a post office, and even if they did, the post office would not accept the package, because it is not mail.

Handling business affairs can be the biggest problem for the full-time, cruising live-aboard. Unless you spend quite a bit of time in the same place and can handle your business yourself, you will need some reliable person who stays put to do it for you. It is almost impossible to simplify your life, in this complex society, so that you will receive no mail, you will have no bills to pay, and you will have no money to deposit in and take out of banks. It will be to your advantage, however, to simplify business as much as you possibly can.

Before we became live-aboards, we were caught up in the maelstrom of credit cards, charge accounts, utility bills, magazine subscriptions, and association, club, and society memberships. We canceled all the charge accounts. We kept our Master Charge card and our Bankamericard, because we can get cash with them. We found that one major gasoline credit card comes in handy now and then, but several of the cards are a nuisance.

We keep American Express and Carte Blanche cards, although we don't use them often, since we do not stay in the hotels or eat in the fancy places where these cards usually are accepted. But they can be used for charging airline fares and renting cars, and once we even bought an old rattletrap of a car with one. If you have a gold American Express card, you can present it at any American Express office and get $50 in cash and $450 in traveler's checks. If you have the standard green American Express card, you can write a personal check for $500 and receive the money as above — $50 in cash and the balance in traveler's checks. If you want a gold card, you will have to fill out a special application for it.

A Carte Blanche card is good for $500 cash when it is presented at any office of Avco Financial Services in the United States or Canada. The card only establishes your credit rating. In receiving money, you are borrowing it from Avco. You must agree to repay it with their schedule of payments and their interest rates.

Certain useful medical and insurance benefits can be obtained by card holders, so it is worth paying the annual fee to have at least one of these cards.

Sometimes a telephone credit card is useful. If you have one, you won't need a pocketful of change to make a long-distance call. Perhaps you can have your land-based mail-forwarder apply for a telephone credit card for his phone, and you can use his credit card number for your calls when necessary. Make some arrangement for paying for your own calls.

We canceled all magazine subscriptions, as well as all our memberships in everything except our yacht club. Unless you are able to handle all your own business, it is not fair to burden someone else with all the junk mail that you receive when you have credit cards, magazine subscriptions, or when you "belong" to anything. If you want to keep up your magazine subscriptions because you think it is cheaper that way, think again. If they are sent to the person handling your mail and then forwarded to you at a later date, the forwarding postage, plus the subscription price, make the magazine cost more than if you purchased it at a newsstand.

Even though we have several credit cards, we avoid charging purchases whenever possible. It makes less work for our "book-keeper." Also, every time you use any credit card, there is the possibility of a billing error; sometimes they charge you too much and other times they don't charge you enough. Either way, it takes reams of correspondence and months of waiting to straighten things out, and we don't want to foist this unpleasant and all-too-frequent chore on anyone.

Sometimes, being a live-aboard can work to your advantage. Often, when we need medical or dental attention, we explain that we are traveling through town and cannot get to our regular doctor or dentist. This often results in an appointment that others might have had to arrange for weeks in advance.

There are many places to keep your boat: resortlike marinas, ordinary boatyards, private docks, moorings, and anchorages. But when you are actually *living aboard* that same boat, the selection of places to keep it narrows considerably. There are many localities where living aboard is prohibited — period. Some places have laws prohibiting live-aboards, but the laws are not enforced.

Most municipalities don't want live-aboards, although nobody seems to be able to explain why. We are given vague answers that skirt around the issue, if indeed there is an issue. One person told us that the other townspeople resented us because we did not pay real estate taxes, but apartment dwellers don't pay real estate taxes either. Pollution is hinted at, often in the towns that are dumping all their untreated sewage into the water that live-aboards are accused of polluting.

Some members of one community were offended by the laundry hung out to dry on live-aboard boats, so they passed a law for-bidding living aboard in their town. They didn't want live-aboards there, and that is why they didn't simply pass a law banning the hanging out of laundry. With their law, they got rid of everything that was offensive to them: the live-aboards and the laundry.

If you want to live aboard your boat, don't ever give anyone cause to complain about anything. Conduct yourself like an honest, upstanding citizen. Keep your boat well maintained, and maybe you will be permitted to stay without being harassed.

One move that is sure to upset the locals is enrollment of your children in a shoreside school for a semester or two. In this situ-ation, people always feel that your children are getting a free ride on the school taxes they are paying. They again forget that the parents of children who live in apartments aren't paying school taxes either.   Their taxes come out of the rent they pay to the landlord, and he pays the taxes, just as the marina owner pays your share of the taxes out of the rent you pay him.

Animosity toward you as a live-aboard will be just about doubled if you are living aboard a multihull. A large majority of land and water people alike seem to be infected with the peculiar attitude that anyone living on a catamaran or trimaran is undesirable. These narrowminded people think: "Multihulls are built by amateurs who didn't have enough money to buy a 'real' boat, and if they didn't have any money then, they certainly don't have any now, so we don't want them bumming anything from us or our town, and we would prefer that they leave."

Some multihull live-aboards have no money and are freeloaders and ripoff artists, but so are some monohull live-aboards. It is unfair for anyone to make such sweeping generalizations, but unfair or not, the attitude exists, and we know of no way to overcome it. A multihull boat-home is always considered to be "on the wrong side of the tracks."

As long as we are on the subject of undesirables, we might as well tell you that to some people, anybody on any kind of a sailboat is an undesirable — live-aboard or not. Many marinas will not allow sailboats to stay overnight; they feel we do not buy enough fuel to pay for the services we use, even though we pay the same amount per foot for dockage as powerboats. While we do not condone the practice, we can see how it started. Many cruising and/or live-aboard sailors pull up to the gas dock and buy a few dollars worth of fuel, or, once in awhile, no fuel at all. They fill their water tanks, maybe wash down the decks, dispose of a large amount of trash, perhaps take a shower if they can get away with it, then cast off their lines and anchor out overnight, often in the same basin in which the marina is located.

As one marina owner put it, "Just because the wind is free, that doesn't mean everything else is."   There is one marina in the Chesapeake that has a large sign posted with their rates for everything on it: filling water tanks — $2.50; dumping trash — .50; showers — $1.50; parking at gas dock — $1.50 an hour. These extra charges did not apply if you stayed overnight, and they were only instigated to foil the take-everything-give-nothing sailors. Sailors who don't pay their way are found everywhere, and they have given all of us a bad reputation. All sailors, by their behavior, should try to help improve the sailor's status in the boating world.

Before you decide to settle down in a community, whether for a week or a year, find out their regulations concerning live-aboards. Florida and California have the most restrictions, but each municipality sets up its own laws about whether or not you can live in a boat.

Even though you may escape real estate taxes by living on a boat, you may have to pay personal property taxes on your boat sooner or later. Different states and towns have different rules about this, and it should be investigated. One town's law is that any boat docked within the town's boundaries on January 31 is liable for the personal property tax. The way the law is written, a poor unfortunate who sails into the town's harbor on January 30 to stay only overnight, and is forced by bad weather to stay over, is liable for the taxes — if they catch him. The townspeople skirt this crazy law in reverse: they remove their boats from the city limits on January 31, then bring them back the next day.

If you keep a car, no matter how or where it is licensed, you may have to pay a personal property tax on it.

Income taxes have to be paid in the normal manner. If you will be off cruising in faraway places when they are due, either file early, before you leave, or apply for an extension.

As we mentioned in the preceding chapter, cars must be licensed in the state where they are kept. You are also required by law to have a driver's license for that state, if you are planning to reside there for a specified length of time. Different states have different time limits. But no one will know whether you have it or not, unless you are stopped for a traffic violation. Let your conscience be your guide. If we had complied strictly with the various states' laws regarding driver's licenses, a short time ago we would have had to have had three different driver's licenses in a period of nine months.

Wherever you live with your boat, you will attract attention and have many visitors, unless you are living at a mooring or at anchor. Even then, you still will attract a lot of attention, and you will not be able to avoid the visitors completely. Unfortunately, many of these callers do not seem to care that your boat is your home and that you should be entitled to as much privacy there as they have in their homes ashore.

Most live-aboards know how to conduct themselves around other boat-homes. It is the curious weekend or day sailor who will deal you fits. They will clamber onto your boat without any warning. You hear a heart-stopping thump and feel the lurch of the boat when they come aboard, and you have no way of knowing whether they are friend or foe. Some of them will barge right down the companionway if you can't get there in time to stop them. Along with those rude boarders, you will be plagued to some degree by hull-thumpers and porthole-peepers. It is part of the price you will have to pay if you want to live on a boat. Happily, these annoying incidents don't happen too often.

On the other hand, there are many interesting visitors who stop by — often land people who plan to become live-aboards soon or sometime in the future. They want to see how you "do" it. There always are other live-aboards who also will be curious about how you are managing, and you, no doubt, will be curious about them. Even some of the hull-thumpers and port-peepers turn out to be nice people and interesting to talk to.

We don't mind occasional uninvited visitors, as long as they show some common sense about how they attract our attention and how long they stay if they see they are interrupting our work. But we can do without the thoughtless clods. There is always some way to get our attention either by calling or knocking, instead of just jumping aboard. Nautical etiquette, even interpreted loosely, requires that the question, "May I come aboard?" be asked before anyone's boat is boarded.

If you invite guests to cruise with you, make your plans well in advance and make it understood that you might not get to the rendezvous spot exactly on the day agreed upon. Be sure there is a way you can communicate if you, or they, are held up. We have seen instances where the guests have arrived at the appointed time and place, only to sit on the dock with all their seagoing gear and wait and wait and wait, with no way of knowing for sure when their "ship" will be coming in.

Before you invite anyone to cruise with you, remember this: crews are bad news. Your best friends can turn into psychopathic weirdos in a cruising environment. Being at sea in close quarters during calm or storm affects people in unpredictable ways, whether they have been sailing for years or have never been to sea before. The most stable person can be reduced to a quaking mass of useless flesh, and the meek can turn into defensive tyrants. Some lapse into near-catatonia until they are taken back to land.

We *never* cruise with anyone. We feel our boat is only comfortable for two, and we want to avoid any personality problems. So, then, how do we know that guests often turn a pleasure cruise into something so unpleasant? We have been told countless stories by friends and acquaintances who have found themselves in impossible situations when cruising with their friends, who are sometimes not their friends anymore when the cruise is over. More times than not, your kindness and generosity in inviting friends to cruise with you will be repaid with animosity. They will think that everything that happened to their personalities was *your* fault. If you want to cruise with others, "try them out" on short jaunts before committing yourself to two weeks or a month with them.

Lest we end on too discouraging a note, let us say that if your boat is large enough, and you find some people who really enjoy cruising with you, by all means, take them along as often as you can.   A relationship such as this is all too rare, and it is worth savoring and enjoying.

Although anyone who chooses to live on a boat will be faced with the many peculiar problems that go with this lifestyle, the live-aboard's existence will be rewarding and gratifying in many ways.   You will have chosen the way you want to live and will not have been pushed into a way of life you dislike.   You are relatively free to come and go.   And, perhaps most important, the people you meet on and along the water are, on the whole, the nicest, friendliest people in the world.

Living aboard a boat is a great way to live, and we prefer our boating existence over any other we have ever had.

INDEX

alcohol, 114-15, 118; kerosene, 114-18; safety with, 115-16; propane, 116-17; comparison of types, 117; electric, 117-18; solid fuel, 117, 145; diesel, 117, 149; costs of, 118; ovens, 118; heating, 144. *See also* Heaters

Stowage: clothing, 79, 165-67; sails, 79, 177-78; chart, 80, 94, 169-72; galley, 111-12; shelf, 112, 165, 167-68; hook, 112, 160, 166, 168, 173-74, 271-72; head, 160, 172-73; hanging locker, 165-66; book, 165, 167-68; drawer, 167; bin, 167-68, 172; overhead, 171-72; refrigerator, 172; food, 172, 174, 176; cockpit locker, 173; electric cable, 173; line, 173; transom, 174-75; plastic box, 174, 234; lumber, 175; forepeak, 175, 177; canned goods, 176; paint, 176; lubricants, 176-77; bilge, 176-77, 180; log book, 177; PVC pipe, 178; waterproof, 233; tools, 233-34

Subscriptions, 3, 294-95

Survey, 33-34

Swimming ladder, 257

Switch: pressure-water foot, 121; master battery, 130; battery selector, 134

Tabernacle, 77

Tables: dinette, 90; permanent, 91; folding, 91, 93; gimballed, 93; chart, 93-94; stowage of, 172

Tahiti ketch 30, 59

Tanks: water, 124

Tape players, 133, 194

Taxes, 296-97

Telephone: 2; credit card, 294

Television: 188, 190; weather, 189; antennas, 189-94; color, 194; 12-volt, 194

Telltales, 202

Tester: outlet circuit, 139

Theft, 154, 244, 261-64

Tide, 200, 204-205, 237, 239-40, 250, 252, 254

Tiller, 75-76, 219-21

Time: W.W.V., W.W.V.H., 188, 204; chronometer, 203; watch, 203-204

Toaster: oven, 117-19, 137

Tools: 260-61; nonmagnetic, 25; cost of, 25, 80, 233-35; 12-volt, 132; stowage of, 233-35

Topping lift, 210-12

Topsides, 224

Towing, 255-57

Towline, 255-57

Transportation, public, 285-86

Trimaran, 3, 37-38, 64-65

Trunk cabin, 75, 81, 90-91, 98

Upholstery, 87, 269

Vacuum cleaner, 265-67

Varnish, 223

Velcro, 103, 274

Ventilation: 79, 94; berths, 81; hatches, 81, 100-101, 103-104; skylight, 98; ports, 99-100, 104; wind scoop, 102-103; companionway, 103-104; when cooking and heating, 104-105, 147-49; fans for, 105; locker, 105; ceilings, 105-106; battery, 130; generators, 140; dodger window, 216

Ventilators: Dorade box, 81, 103-104, 148; mushroom, 103; dome type, 104; turbines, 105

Voltage: 12 volt, 129-30, 32-34, 160-61; 115 volt, 129, 132, 134-36, 139, 142, 160

Voltage regulator, 134

Voltmeter: 115 volt, 137; VOM (volt-ohm-milliammeter), 235

Water: pressure, 120; hand pump, 120-21; foot switch, 121; foot pump, 121-22; tank, 123-24; drinking, 123-24; consumption, 124; jug, 124; purifier, 124, 270

Weather cloths, 213-14

Weather helm, 76

Westsail 32, 61

Wheel steering, 75-76, 219-21

Whiffle, 41, 75, 84, 90, 124, 129, 152, 155, 224, 236

Winch: reefing, 207; halyard, 208; sheet, 209; downhaul, 210; lazyjacks, 211; use with bosun's chair, 260

Wind direction indicators, 202

Windlass: anchor, 218, 255

Wind scoop, 102-103

Wind vane, 75, 219-21

Woolsey Vinelast, 224-25

Worms, 65, 222, 225

W.W.V., W.W.V.H. radio stations, 188, 204

Yacht brokers, 26-27

Yankee, 77

Yawl, 72